KEEPER OF THE RULES

Congressman Howard W. Smith of Virginia

Frontispiece: Chairman Smith and the House Rules Committee,
ca. 1959 or 1960. (Courtesy of the Office of Photography, U.S.
House of Representatives)

KEEPER
OF THE
RULES

Congressman
Howard W. Smith
of Virginia

Bruce J. Dierenfield

University Press of Virginia

Charlottesville

To my parents
Richard Bruce Dierenfield
and
Yvonne Fahlgren Dierenfield

THE UNIVERSITY PRESS OF VIRGINIA
Copyright © 1987 by the Rector and Visitors
of the University of Virginia
First published 1987

Library of Congress Cataloging-in-Publication Data

Dierenfield, Bruce J., 1951–
  Keeper of the rules.

  Bibliography: p.
  Includes index.
  1. Smith, Howard Worth, 1883–1976. 2 Legislators—
United States—Biography. 3. United States. Congress.
House—Biography. I. Title.
E748.S664D54   1986   328.73'092'4   [B]   86–19026
ISBN 0–8139–1068–4

Printed in the United States of America

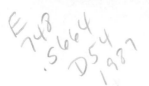

CONTENTS

ILLUSTRATIONS

FOREWORD

In 1935 second-term congressman Howard Worth Smith became a member of the House Committee on Rules. It is hardly an exaggeration to say that for the next thirty-two years he was the most powerful single influence in Congress against the surge of progressive legislation that began in the early days of the Great Depression. *Keeper of the Rules: Congressman Howard W. Smith,* by Bruce J. Dierenfield, is an excellent, well-researched treatise on the Smith career. I am honored by the invitation of the author to write this foreword.

By birth and by choice Judge Smith, as we knew him around the Capitol, was an unreconstructed nineteenth-century Virginian. He spent his entire legislative life trying to ward off federal encroachments into the world in which he was born. He had all of the attributes, including all of the prejudices, of his native state. He distrusted all influences outside of his own area. He was brought up believing that Yankees, carpetbaggers, Republicans, and foreigners were enemies of his people and of the way of life they enjoyed. He was a white supremacist who fought racial integration to the bitter end. He opposed nearly all federal social reforms, including health, education, and welfare bills. He believed in the Constitution "as written." He was a strict constructionist and a states' righter. He was a Tenth Amendment congressman.

The influence of Congressman Howard W. Smith did not spring from his beliefs. Many other congressmen shared his views. It was his rare talents and the way he used them that set him apart. He was one of the brightest, shrewdest, most determined human beings I ever knew. Yet he was a study in contrasts. He was low-key, kind, genteel. This was a veneer, however, under which there were ribs and guts of iron. He spoke softly, but he carried a dagger.

Howard W. Smith, from the day he was assigned to the Committee on Rules, put his extraordinary talents to work making

himself a power center in the House. He became a master parliamentarian and a legislative expert. He never let his committee or
the House catch him unprepared. He seemed to have a unique
talent for anticipation. He saw the "bad bills" coming; he was
ready for them when they arrived. He created alliances in the
Committee on Rules and in the House itself. He was the un-
crowned king of his committee long before he was made its chairman. He became the leader of the southern conservatives and of
the conservative coalition in the House.

He opposed most of the New Deal and Fair Deal domestic
programs sent to Congress by Roosevelt and Truman. Even with
his few attempts to sponsor and promote positive law, such as the
Alien Registration Act and the Smith-Connally Act, he was taking aim at the social and liberal thrust of the times.

Judge Smith fought with every weapon at hand. He went for
the kill head-on when he could, but he always guarded his flanks.
He would delay, amend, or use any other tactic that might help
defeat a bill, weaken it, or slow down its passage. He may not
have stopped the flow of federal involvement in human affairs in
his day and generation, but he certainly slowed it down.

During the Eighty-eighth and Eighty-ninth Congresses the
House passed its "packing" and "twenty-one day" rules, giving it
at least partial control over a committee that had almost become
an independent legislative body. These actions were essential to
the passage of the New Frontier–Great Society bills that revolu-
tionized America. These were the rules with which John Mc-
Cormack and I had to deal after Sam Rayburn's death. They were
of course very helpful, but basically they were little more than
cosmetic, band-aid remedies. We never knew whether we had
eight votes or seven on the Committee on Rules. What was required was institutional reform of the committee. That did not
come until 1973.

Carl Albert

[Howard W. Smith] was attempting to perpetuate the philosophy that prevailed in this country from the time of the Declaration of Independence and the Constitution, which was consistently . . . eroded. . . . He was a strong believer that government was created by the people and that the people were to serve the government and the government wasn't just designed to take care of everybody. That old saying that they brought him kicking and squealing into the twentieth century doesn't exactly apply to him, but he didn't come into it willingly.

Thomas G. Abernethy (1984)

PREFACE

For thirty-six years after the Great Depression began, Representative Howard W. Smith was one of the most powerful figures in Congress. He wrote or helped write major laws against government subversion and labor activism. More importantly, he skillfully used his chairmanship of the House Rules Committee to strike down or to weaken legislation that called for the federal government to address long-standing social problems, including civil rights, education, and public housing. His penchant for keeping a low profile belied the fact that many observers of the late 1950s regarded Smith as one of the three most important politicians in Washington, surpassed only by President Eisenhower and House Speaker Sam Rayburn.

Smith's career as a congressman provides an opportunity for better understanding political maneuverings in Congress and the conservative perspective on American society, as well as certain influential laws, all of which have shaped our nation's history from 1930 to the present. The portrait that follows attempts to delineate Smith's substantial impact on legislation and to show how he reflected the prevailing attitudes of many white southerners.

This study concentrates on Smith's congressional career, for Smith left few glimpses of his private life. What materials are available reveal a man preoccupied with his work to the exclusion of nearly all other interests. In discussing Howard W. Smith and his career, I have primarily addressed these questions: What was the ideology of Smith and like-minded southern Democrats? Given his minority position, how was Smith able to exercise substantial influence over legislation? What means did he employ to kill undesirable bills supported by liberal Democrats? And finally, why did the liberal reaction to Smith ultimately prevail?

Political terminology is always troublesome and controversial. Some readers may prefer other terms or definitions than the ones I have chosen. What is most important is clear and consistent

usage. Hence, in this study I have used the definitions offered by
Woodrow Wilson, a native Virginian and a onetime political science professor. To him, a "conservative" was someone who would
not adapt fully to social and economic changes, whereas a "reactionary" was a person who refused to accept any change at all.
According to this definition, Smith can easily be classified as a
"reactionary." He opposed change as a matter of principle, arguing that the Constitution was not an organic document. In addition, Smith's opponents repeatedly used this word to describe
him. In fact, Smith himself accepted the label because he believed it implied adherence to the system of government created
by the founding fathers, including another Virginia Democrat he
revered, Thomas Jefferson.

I am indebted to many individuals and institutions whose assistance and encouragement made the writing of this book possible. At the University of Virginia, the late Edward E. Younger
suggested this subject; and Carl M. Brauer and William H. Harbaugh offered early guidance in completing it. Kathleen Murphy
Dierenfield, more than any other individual, eased the manuscript through its several passages. An incisive historian in her
own right, she contributed much-needed research, judicious editorial skill, and unflagging encouragement, usually at the expense
of her own scholarship. Maarten Ultee, Philip L. Cantelon, Martha H. Swain, Philip Vandermeer, Watkins M. Abbitt, Richard
D. Bolling, Carl Albert, and Virginia Mitchell also provided valuable editorial criticism.

As I went to far-flung libraries to conduct research, I found the
archivists and reference librarians to be courteous and knowl-
edgeable. In particular, I wish to thank the manuscript staffs of
Alderman Library and the Arthur J. Morris Law Library, especially Marsha Rogers, at the University of Virginia; the Lloyd
House in Alexandria, Virginia, where Allan Robbins was so cooperative; the Virginia State Library in Richmond; the Earl Gregg
Swem Library of the College of William and Mary in Williamsburg, Virginia; the William D. McCain Graduate Library of the
University of Southern Mississippi; the Franklin D. Roosevelt
Library; the Harry S Truman Library; the Sam Rayburn Library
in Bonham, Texas; the Dwight D. Eisenhower Library; the John
F. Kennedy Library; and the Lyndon B. Johnson Library.

A manuscript on a contemporary figure lends itself to interviews of those who knew him well, and my work sometimes relies extensively on such interviews. I wish to express my appreciation to Watkins M. Abbitt, Thomas G. Abernethy, Carl Albert, Richard D. Bolling, Armistead L. Boothe, the late Albert V. Bryan, Sr., Harry F. Byrd, Jr., Leslie D. Campbell, Jr., the late T. M. Carruthers, Samuel B. Chilton, the late Luther H. Dudley, Mrs. James M. Dyer, Carl Elliott, Sr., Lewis P. Fickett, Jr., Ed Gossett, Francis B. Gouldman, the late Charles A. Halleck, H. Ryland Heflin, A. Sydney Herlong, Jr., Henry E. Howell, Jr., Hanno W. Kirk, Gordon Lewis, Virginia and the late Landon Mitchell, Roger Mudd, Paul Muse, David M. Olson, John Painter, W. R. Poage, Kenneth W. Rapp, George C. Rawlings, Jr., William L. Scott, the late Howard W. Smith, Sr., Howard W. Smith, Jr., Lewis A. Stearman, Violett Smith Tonahill, the late William M. Tuck, Kenneth T. Whitescarver, and John W. Williams.

With pleasure, I also acknowledge permission to reprint copyrighted material. The *Magazine of Albemarle County History*, the *Virginia Magazine of History and Biography*, and the *Northern Virginia Heritage* have graciously given permission to revise and include portions of articles of mine that appeared in 1979–80, April 1980, and February 1982, respectively.

I would be remiss if I did not thank my dear parents for their support, occasional financial assistance, and editorial help. With the dedication of this work, I am at last able to repay part of the large debt I owe them. My uncle James W. Fahlgren and my former roommate Hans G. Jellen offered timely advice and thought-provoking interpretations of evidence I unearthed.

While I have accepted the advice and assistance of many individuals and institutions, they are not culpable for the errors of fact and interpretation that remain. That responsibility is mine alone.

KEEPER OF THE RULES

Congressman Howard W. Smith of Virginia

CHAPTER 1

Growing Up at Cedar Hill

Our family was fortunate that their home was not burned as so many of the Confederate homes were during the war. While we suffered from a lack of many material things, we still had the roof over our heads, a fertile farm, a beautiful well-constructed house, and strong hands and backs to work the soil.

Howard W. Smith (1976)

The Civil War and its aftermath devastated Virginia. One Englishman recalled that the Shenandoah Valley in the west "was almost a desert. There were no fences. . . . Barns were all burned; a great many of the private dwellings were burned; chimney standing without houses, and houses standing without roof, a door, or window; a most desolate state of affairs." But the physical damage was only the most apparent cost. Blaming their troubles on spendthrift carpetbaggers and their black allies, white Virginians soon adopted laws designed to preserve social stratification, to remove blacks from the political arena, and to keep government spending to a minimum. As a result, Virginia in the late nineteenth century was a stagnant, rural society, plagued by Negrophobia and inadequate government support for schools and roads. More than most states, the Old Dominion fostered a world-view that inhibited change.[1]

The preeminent characteristic of Virginia at this time was its rural nature. In 1880 urban areas of at least 2,500 people accounted for less than 13 percent of the state's total population. The largest cities were in the Tidewater region or on the fall line between the state's eastern and western areas. Only the old Confederate capital of Richmond was truly a big city; it ranked as the country's twenty-fifth largest city. Nevertheless, its total of 63,000 residents was far below that of the major northern cities, and it lagged even more in growth.[2]

The state's poorly developed transportation and communication network isolated Virginians still further. Only the James, Rappahannock, and Appomattox rivers provided adequate passage for commercial vessels within the state. Most waterways were small and shallow, choking off travel to the hinterland. These creeks, or runs, provided enough moisture for raising crops but could carry no boats. The state's roads seldom offered a better means of transport. One account in 1892 described the country roads as "ditches and a series of mudholes running around every man's cornfield, leading everywhere and nowhere in particular." Another observer, Edward A. Pollard of Richmond, was struck by "the distressing uniform want of practicable roads." He concluded that "the method of building roads in Virginia is the old-time one which belonged to the exigencies of our early backwoods life."[3]

To some degree the railroad boom of the Gilded Age remedied the inadequacies of water and road transportation. Compared to the decade after the Civil War, railroad mileage increased nearly fivefold in the 1880s. By 1899 railroads in Virginia laid 3,721 miles of new track, which doubled the 1880 total. The track connected the Southside, the Shenandoah Valley, and the Eastern Shore with the Tidewater and Piedmont. In 1876 the Norfolk and Western Railway ran from the port of Norfolk to the coalfields near Bristol. Six years later, this same railroad bought the Shenandoah line, which ran from Hagerstown, Maryland, to Roanoke at the southern end. Also during the 1880s, the New York, Philadelphia, and Norfolk Railroad extended its tracks on the Eastern Shore below Maryland to Cape Charles. Finally, in 1893 the Southern Railway consolidated many of Virginia's lines, linking them to a regional and even national railroad network. At the same time, railroads constructed smaller lines to reach formerly remote places. Despite this railroad boom, however, poor communication persisted. Outside of cities and the Tidewater, few Virginians had either electricity or its offspring, the telephone. Mail service bridged part of the communication gap, but letters

arrived just twice weekly. Inevitably, these factors hindered business and social contacts.[4]

Virginians, therefore, remained isolated from each other. In
1874 a planter admitted to his brother, "I stay closely at home &
know but little of what transpires beyond the home circle." Virginia novelist Thomas Nelson Page painted a tranquil picture
when he recalled his early life in Hanover County near Richmond. He pointed out that his experience in the Gilded Age was
common elsewhere in the state:

> Set back among the forest, far from the currents of modern life,
> and divided from the outside world by the little streams which for
> long distances flowed only a few miles apart; accessible only by
> roads which during a considerable part of the year were well-nigh
> impassable, the life was as quiet as though it had been caught in
> an eddy, and old habits of thought and old customs of speech and
> of life survived for generations, almost without change.[5]

Thus, for the average Virginian, long-standing social connections rather than current employment determined one's identity.
One student of this period has described this web as "a set of
interlocking institutions and groups," the most important of
which were, in descending order, race, class, and family. This
was especially true because Virginia society still was rigidly hierarchical and because business matters usually were discussed in
person.[6]

From colonial times Virginians accepted without question the
primacy of the white race. This belief seldom wavered even after
the Civil War dissolved black slavery. At the turn of the century,
the Old Dominion, like the rest of the South, enacted segregation
statutes known as Jim Crow laws. Its white government also took
steps after Reconstruction to prevent blacks from ever exercising
political clout in proportion to their numbers. In 1901–2 a state
constitutional convention ratified a poll tax, ostensibly to fund
Virginia's public school system. But as Congressman Carter Glass
asserted, the real purpose was to disfranchise blacks and poor
whites: "Discrimination! Why, that is precisely what we propose;
that, exactly, is what this convention was elected for." The poll
tax had to be paid during the planting season, months before the
election; and failure to pay the required tax increased the amount

for the next time. When racist ordinances and taxes did not function as planned, some white Virginians resorted to lynching recalcitrant blacks.[7]

In most southern states, white skin alone assured superiority over blacks. But in Virginia skin color by itself did not guarantee one's status; class was nearly as important as race. Early English ancestry, family name, and wealth assigned crucially important qualities to their owners. At the 1901 constitutional convention, white politicians excluded lower-class whites, the "poor white trash," from the political arena in the same way that blacks were removed.[8]

Beyond class and race, Virginians placed great emphasis on family ties, perhaps to ease the pain of isolation. Often households went beyond the nuclear unit, incorporating aunts, uncles, and grandparents. A traveler to the state observed, "One thing in Virginia households struck me as very remarkable: that is, the way in which members of a family of various generations live together, year after year, in peace and harmony." Even when families were dispersed, they surmounted difficulties in travel and communication to maintain contact. There were occasional reunions across county and state lines, and letters frequently changed hands. As a result, close family ties led to considerable socioeconomic and political influence.[9]

One other institution afforded rural whites the opportunity for camaraderie and influence—the county courthouse. Usually located near the center of the county, the courthouse served officials wielding local authority. These officers included the county treasurer, commissioner of revenue, commonwealth's attorney, sheriff, and clerk of court, who managed county finances, collected taxes, prosecuted wrongdoers, kept local order, and maintained official records. These officeholders frequently replaced their fathers and grandfathers and held their positions until they assumed a loftier post, retired, or died.[10]

But the courthouse itself, rather than these officials, served a more crucial function for most rural Virginians. Once a month when the circuit judge convened court, residents gathered at the county seat almost like "a religious duty." On these "court days," farmers swapped gossip, news, and animals. While in town, residents also listened to the judge decide local disputes before their ritual visit to a nearby tavern. Court days thus offered an occasion to renew old acquaintances and to preserve the informal but hierarchical system.[11]

Shortly after Reconstruction passed, state Democratic leaders developed an organization that dominated county courthouse politics for three-quarters of a century. Led by railroad magnate John S. Barbour, conservative Democrats for philosophical and self-interested reasons objected to a proposal delaying payment of the state's pre–Civil War debts. This suggestion—known as Readjustment—was championed successfully for a time by the eccentric former Confederate general William Mahone, who by his own admission relied heavily on newly freed black voters. The machine then vowed never again to let fiscal liberals and blacks gain sway over the state's affairs. Under Barbour's successor, Thomas Staples Martin, a railroad attorney turned senator, Virginia Democrats instituted the poll tax at the turn of the century to reduce sharply voter participation, especially of blacks. The machine also tightened its grip on local officials, not only by approving their selection but by fixing their salaries.[12]

This was the world into which Howard Worth Smith was born on February 2, 1883, at Broad Run near Warrenton. The Old Dominion at that time was largely rural and isolated. Most Virginians farmed, attended Baptist services, paid low taxes, and mingled with family members and close friends. In this ordered, backwoods environment, country life was, in Thomas Nelson Page's words, "so sequestered, so self-contained" that Virginians were "indifferent to public opinion—at least, of all public opinion outside of Virginia itself."[13]

Smith's background both reflected and diverged from this society. Like most Virginians, his father, William Worth Smith (1851–1924), was a farmer. He grew corn, raised pigs, milked cows, and sold horses. His mother, Lucinda Lewis Smith (1848–1937), was a homemaker who bore four children, of whom Howard was the third child and first son. The family was close-knit, and from time to time the Smiths traveled twenty-five miles over rough, muddy roads in a servant-driven English coach to visit relatives in neighboring Culpeper County. In addition, Howard Smith accompanied his maternal grandmother to the Hard-Shell Baptist church that abutted their farm.[14]

As a boy, Smith rode his father's horses, hunted rabbits with his Irish setter Rixey, and picked wild strawberries and raspberries, chestnuts, walnuts, and hazelnuts. To be sure, he had chores. He tended dairy cows, chickens, and turkeys and in winter collected ice chunks from nearby streams for the family icehouse. But his father hired farmhands to do the heavier work. In July they threshed wheat, oats, and barley by "crude and laborious methods," and when fall came, they slaughtered up to fifteen hogs for hams, spareribs, sausage, bacon, pigfoot jelly, and chitterlings. After the chores, meals provided welcome relief. Smith recalled devouring cantaloupe, corn muffins and honey, sweet potatoes, pork chops, and homemade strawberry ice cream.[15]

The Smith farm, known as Cedar Hill for its many trees, was near the sleepy hamlet of Broad Run in Fauquier County. The village received its name "from the bold stream of water nearby" that ran through Cedar Hill. The community was largely self-sufficient, supporting a creamery, a merchant mill, a country store, and neighboring schools and churches. Will Smith and other dairy farmers cleared thirty dollars annually on each cow's milk sold to the creamery.[16]

Fauquier County, in the northern Piedmont, was entirely rural. By the end of the nineteenth century, the county had just three incorporated towns, and only one of these had a population exceeding one thousand. Warrenton, the county seat, had 1,464 residents in 1893. Of the county's population of 16,595 in 1890, only 1,977, or 11.9 percent, were black. By contrast, blacks constituted 38.3 percent of the state's population. The county's chief economic activity was animal grazing. Blessed with abundant rainfall, the gently rolling terrain primarily fed cattle. A farmer with eight hundred acres of land made as much as $8,000 a year from cattle raising. Other farmers bred horses and mules and raised sheep, hogs, and chickens. Moreover, the land yielded bountiful harvests of corn, wheat, hay, apples, peaches, and vegetables. Most of the produce ended up thirty-five miles away in Washington, D.C., a city growing by seven to ten thousand people annually.[17]

Fauquier residents held conservative social and political values. According to the Warrenton newspaper, the *Virginian*, the local populace resisted such threats to its worldview as untrammeled immigration, black equality, and northern political hegemony. As the United States accepted millions of Jews, Italians, Russians, Poles, and other Slavs from the 1880s onward, the *Vir-*

ginian reacted sharply. The editor, W. C. Marshall, blamed these ethnically diverse people for leading northern radical groups, especially unions. He wondered when the nation's lawmakers would stop making the country "a dumping ground for the balance of the world's refuse." "We do not," he added, "want the anarchists, the tramps, the bomb throwers, the strikers, the fire bugs, and the murderers," all of which he believed formed the bulk of the immigrant tide. In his view, these "undesirable" non-Anglo-Saxon immigrants would "surely drag us down" since they were unable to sustain America's democratic government.[18]

Even more than immigrants, the *Virginian* castigated blacks. The newspaper argued that the very nature and behavior of blacks justified racism. In the first place, the editor believed blacks mentally incapable of self-government. As proof, he quoted Mississippi governor James K. Vardaman, one of the country's most virulent racists: "The absolute domination by the white race means race purity. It means order, good government, progress and general prosperity, both for the negro and the white man. But when the negro is taken into partnership in the government of the country, demoralization, retrogression and decay ensure—just as surely as the night follows the day." The editor also asserted that blacks could never improve their intellectual capacity. He pointed out that since the Civil War $250 million had been spent "in a foolish endeavor to make more of the negro than God Almighty ever intended." He then contended that blacks were uninterested in the political process; instead, they pursued criminal activity. The president of North Carolina Agricultural College had stated that blacks were "three times as criminal" as whites and that literate blacks committed more crimes than those who were illiterate. The worst aspect of black behavior, editor Marshall claimed, was their threat to "the chastity of white women," the most "heinous" of crimes, demanding immediate lynching. At stake, the *Virginian* contended, was the "purity of Anglo-Saxon blood."[19]

Old Dominion editors believed the best way to preserve this rural white society was adherence to the Democratic party. As the *True Index* of Warrenton insisted, southerners in general and Virginians in particular were logically Democrats by reason of "inheritance, patriotism, and race creed": Virginians belonged to the Democratic party because they had traditionally belonged, because the party's southern wing had supported secession, and because whites held sway over the party. The *True Index* declared, "All that the South is today she owes to the Democratic party."[20]

The Warrenton papers found the Republican party anathema. Their editors accused the northern-based party of intending during Reconstruction "to deprive the South of all political power and even to efface her civilization." The *Index* offered a catalog of horrors perpetrated by the Republicans on the South since 1865.

> The bitterest and most relentless foe that the South ever had is the Republican party. All of the political evils that the South has suffered since the Republican party came into existence and power sprang from that party. The Republican party deprived Southern States of their individuality, put criminals in authority, turned thieves into the State Treasuries and their Legislatures and held them there at the point of the bayonet. It incited the recently freed slaves to deeds of violence, and made liberty a farce. The people of the South have not forgotten, and will not forget the reconstruction period and the Republican party's part in that black page of American history.[21]

These ideas printed in the local press were undoubtedly absorbed by young Howard Smith. He learned that immigrants were troublemaking radicals who disturbed hitherto tranquil labor relations. He embraced the view that blacks occupied a lower mental and social order than most whites and that they were likely to be criminals. His teenaged brother, Worth, wrote from Alexandria to his mother in 1902 that "the Italians went on a strike down here last weekend. The police got after them. They ought to be put out of this countrie or drownd. They are worse than the nigers, (negros) [sic]." Smith probably shared in the common belief that the South had been oppressed by the Republican-dominated federal government. He accordingly trusted the Democratic party to preserve his race, caste, and local autonomy.[22]

If Smith was a typical Virginian in his social attitudes and in his agrarian origin, he was exceptional, too. He came from a distinguished and well-to-do family. His father was descended from a long line of prominent Englishmen. One of them became governor of the East India Company and was knighted by James I. In Virginia another ancestor built an estate near Warrenton which was one of the area's wealthiest and most important plantations before the Civil War. The Smiths' red-roofed brick home was built by slaves in 1797 and had been passed down through Mrs. Smith's family. Compared to the average Virginia farm of 150 acres in 1890, Cedar Hill had 500 acres. Despite raids by Yankee soldiers for food and valuables, the mansion itself went untouched by the Civil War's ravages.[23]

Smith's father, Will, a stern-faced redhead with large ears, thick eyebrows, and a long forehead, was also an exceptional figure. By the end of the nineteenth century, he had expanded the family's holdings to seven farms and a large tract in Hampshire County, West Virginia. Besides operating his own farms profitably, Will Smith supervised the federal government's experimental farm in Arlington starting in 1901. To work there, he caught the Monday morning train to Alexandria and remained away until Saturday afternoon. This hectic schedule meant his family, including his teenaged sons, saw little of him. A shrewd businessman, he also shipped beef cattle, hogs, and grain to Baltimore and sold highly prized Percheron breeding stallions to neighboring farmers. Howard Smith's cousin Gordon Lewis recalled that "his father was a great trader. He'd trade you out of your pants. That was no lie." Indeed, young Gordon actually lost his own clothes once in a deal with his Uncle Will. According to Lewis, Howard Smith was "brought up" as "a sharp trader."[24]

Howard Smith caught his first glimpse of political life from his mother, Lucinda Lewis Smith, a woman with light wavy hair, thin lips, a prominent nose, and recessed eyes. Mrs. Smith, nicknamed "Lutie" or "Tee," supplemented the family income in the 1880s by turning her thirteen-room home into a retreat for politicians and well-to-do businessmen anxious to escape Washington's summer heat and humidity. At a time when most southern women shunned politics, Tee Smith not only fed her influential guests but swapped stories and entertained them with her piano playing. Gordon Lewis recalled: "[Howard's] mother was a great politician. She used to really . . . mix with these people who were in politics who came up from Washington for one reason or another." She also took her children to every presidential inauguration from Grover Cleveland's second term in 1893. Three of her four children entered politics, including her daughter Lucy Smith Price, one of the first women legislators in West Virginia.[25]

Besides his unusual parents, Smith observed other able relatives. While most Virginians struggled at farming, several of Smith's relatives entered the professions. His uncle P. Alex L. Smith practiced law in Danville. Two cousins taught at Bethel Military Academy near Warrenton, and one of these was a licensed physician. On his mother's side, cousin John F. Rixey, who owned two thousand acres in northern Virginia, also entered law, after graduating from the University of Virginia, and served for twelve years as Culpeper's commonwealth's attorney. In 1897, when Smith was fourteen, Rixey won election as congressman of the Eighth District. With Virginia still suffering from the panic of 1893, Rixey rode the emotional issues of free silver and monetary inflation to victory. Rixey's well-to-do older brother, Rear Admiral Presley M. Rixey, won acclaim as surgeon general of the United States Navy and served as the personal physician of Republican presidents William McKinley and Theodore Roosevelt. Rixey's friendship with McKinley was probably instrumental in the appointment of his Democratic cousin-in-law Will Smith to the federal government's farm in Alexandria.[26]

At home, Howard Smith enjoyed a higher standard of living than most of his peers. While farmhands did the heavy chores, Smith accompanied his family on periodic excursions to visit relatives, especially the Rixeys. His two older sisters organized neighborhood parties and dances and prepared fancy cakes with chocolate or lemon icing. For the guests, a three-member black band played waltzes, the Virginia reel, and square dances. Other times, Smith amused himself by jousting with local boys for the hand of the neighborhood's prettiest girl. The participants donned their finest clothes for the ball afterward.[27]

Much of the time, however, Smith insulated himself from social contact. Other young boys climbed trees, competing to see who could go higher. But Smith declined their invitations to join in the fun. Instead, he usually hunched over a book inside his home. His cousin remembered his own father saying that Howard "would just spend his time reading. He was always a studious type of person." Hence, when school was in session, Howard Smith had an enormous advantage over other pupils. He never forgot the virtue of exceedingly careful preparation throughout his life.[28]

Smith's education also offers a clear indication of his family's living standard. Most Virginia farmers depended heavily on their children to help plant and harvest crops. One farmboy remembered that there was always work to be done: "From the time each of the boys would become old enough to do any kind . . . of work, we had to help do anything that we could to aid in the farm duties. One who was reared on a farm in those days can recall that work of some type could always be found to employ the time and labor of even small children." In 1890 farm demands proved so heavy that 62 percent of white children in Virginia did not attend school regularly.[29]

For the average white pupil before 1900, Virginia's new public school system hardly looked inviting. A typical rural school was housed in an "unsightly" frame building with little light or ventilation. The schools also lacked adequate equipment. One teacher lamented that her schoolhouse had "neither tables, chairs, black board, chart register, water bucket or axe. There are but two windows and . . . small light in all so that the business of the school can with difficulty be carried on in bad weather." The teachers tended to be both poorly educated and woefully paid. In the 1880s Virginia, as did other states, encouraged single women to become schoolteachers, for which they were paid at least 20 percent less than male instructors. In 1885 only 6 percent of Virginia teachers had earned a college degree. Even when school was in session, it met for just six months.[30]

Smith's father found the sorry state of public education deplorable. He wrote to his wife not to spare any expense in educating their children, even if that meant going into debt: "If anything happens to me . . . I want you to Give [them] a first class education no matter how hard it may be." As a result, their two sons attended private academies and graduated from law school, while at least one daughter received a finishing school education. Smith grasped the rudiments of learning at a private one-room red schoolhouse near his home. During these early years, he was taught by his cousin Sally Conway, who "nearly slap[ped his] head off" every time he wrote left-handed. In 1896 Smith entered Bethel Military Academy for boys, seven miles from Warrenton. The school was founded in 1869 by his cousin Major A. G. Smith, who had joined Pickett's celebrated charge at Gettysburg. Not only did two of Howard Smith's cousins teach science, preparatory medicine, mathematics, and Latin at the school, but his cousin John Rixey had graduated from the academy.[31]

Of the 118 public schools in the county and five private institutions near Warrenton, Bethel was evidently the best. The academy also claimed that its $100 charge for tuition, room, and board was half that of competitors. In addition, the school, which was patterned after West Point, drilled its cadets into fitness and instilled moral values. The catalog announced that a primary aim at Bethel was the "entire removal from all contaminating agencies," including alcohol and "city influence." By all criteria, Bethel Academy exceeded the average single-room school's performance. The nine-member, all-male staff included former professors from Randolph-Macon College, two medical doctors, and a clergyman. They taught a wide variety of difficult courses, ranging from the liberal arts, including ancient and romance languages, to preliminary professional and military training. The school also boasted of science laboratories. Its local advertisements declared that the curriculum "prepares boys and young men for business or Universities and for the Government Academies."[32]

Smith, the youngest and smallest cadet, excelled at Bethel. In his junior year in 1900, he captured the Payne Medal awarded annually to the best student. To win the gold medallion, he earned the highest marks in intermediate Latin, advanced German, and advanced English. These courses required him to translate Virgil and Cicero, read Goethe, Schiller, and Lessing, and study Shakespeare and English history. The next year Smith once again was the academy's top scholar. This time, he won "certificates of special excellence" in political science, analytical geometry, integral calculus, and organic and inorganic chemistry. At graduation, Smith was class valedictorian. Though offered a place at West Point, probably with the help of his cousin Congressman Rixey, he declined.[33]

While shining academically, Smith remained a loner at school. For most, if not all, of his days at Bethel, Smith did not board with the other cadets. At first, he stayed off grounds with his cousin Thomas Smith, who taught medicine and science. Later, he lived at home, riding his horse several miles to school. As a day student, he also did not wear the requisite military uniform because he disliked "military order." At the close of his life, he recalled incidents at Bethel in which he sought attention in the hope of becoming "somebody."[34]

After graduation, Smith decided on a law career. His interest in that profession came quite naturally. The family already had two successful attorneys, and his mother "was determined he was going to be a lawyer," too. For years she had been saving up her "egg money" to pay for his legal education. She also realized that law was the first step into politics. In the South, as one Alabama congressman declared, "you were raised to be a politician or reach a prestigious position, and you dedicated your life from your early days to achieve it." Smith remembered that his farmer father "hit the ceiling," but Howard's mind was made up.[35]

For years, Smith had been captivated by the court days in Warrenton when circuit judges arrived for the spring term. Farmers quaffed their thirsts in noisy saloons, and nearly always, the town's sergeant and his deputies had to arrest disorderly patrons for public drunkenness and for carrying concealed weapons. Competing for public favor, local Democratic politicians plied crowds with handshakes, promises, and bourbon. On the court lawn, horse-breeders like Smith's father paraded their prize Thoroughbreds. But for Smith, the most memorable moments occurred inside the courthouse. There he heard disgruntled neighbors resolve their disputes before a circuit-riding judge according to prescribed rules. One case in particular lodged in his memory. A certain successful but pompous lawyer had the irritating habit of referring constantly to his copy of the common law, *Bacon's Abridgement*, to influence the jury. To break this practice, another attorney concocted a "fiendish plot" and substituted a wrapped package of bacon. When the pompous lawyer next reached in his green bag for the book, he was understandably dumbfounded.[36]

Smith's fascination with courtroom proceedings led him in 1901 to the University of Virginia, which had the state's leading law school. Founded by Thomas Jefferson, the university had already trained many prominent state and local politicians. The university's legal program had made giant strides during the fifty-year tenure of one of the nation's most influential legal scholars, John B. Minor. In the last half of the nineteenth century, Minor—known as "the Virginia Blackstone" for his *Institutes*—set forth some unorthodox ideas for training lawyers that dominated the school for years afterward. In his view, the Socratic technique of question-and-answer was less efficient than lectures, and he also rejected the case study approach that had gained sway at

Harvard University under Christopher C. Langdell. Few students, Minor believed, could master a rigorous program; so he withheld diplomas from 85 percent of those who attended. Above all, he stressed education before firsthand experience and preparation over the "Gift of the Gab."[37]

After Minor's reign ended in 1895, the law school moved into a transitional period until William Minor Lile became dean in 1904. During this time, the school was plagued with a number of festering problems that hurt its national reputation. To begin with, the school's admissions standards did not require any college work, a prerequisite that more prominent law schools had adopted. The teacher-student ratio was also too high at Virginia. With only three professors for two hundred students, the instructors faced heavier than average teaching and examination loads. Finally, the law library lacked the resources to expand its collection. As a result, the school was denied membership for a time in the Association of American Law Schools.[38]

Virginia's law program then lasted two years and covered twelve courses. In the first year, the professors taught personal property, wills, and administration; contracts; criminal law; mercantile law; courts, bailments, and carriers; and theory of government, constitutional law, and international law. In the following year, they presented classes in equity jurisprudence and procedure and bankruptcy; pleading and practice in civil cases; real property law; corporation law; evidence; and conflicts of laws. Each student listened to nine lectures a week, each lasting ninety minutes. By the end of the program, the faculty expected its graduates to have developed "a complete mastery of [the] elementary principles" and to have the ability to think for themselves, even if their conclusions were "at variance with the decisions of the court."[39]

The law school's outstanding instructor was Charles A. Graves, recently arrived from Washington and Lee University to teach contract law. John W. Davis, later Woodrow Wilson's solicitor general, and law professor T. Munford Boyd lauded "Old Charley" as their greatest teacher. Graves had a style of teaching and thinking that Smith adopted in law practice and in politics. Graves's method, another student remembered, was "strictly socratic," combining "pungent and searching questions" with "a fine thread of subtle humor," which became Smith's trademark. Although never dramatic and always restrained, the distinguished-looking Graves was a master at holding his classes' attention, often employing hypnotic mannerisms. Like Smith, too, Graves labored far into the evening—a fact his students knew from the ever-burning light in his office—memorizing the intricacies of the law. Newton D. Baker, another student and Wilson's secretary of war, recalled: "To Mr. Graves, legal principles had biographies. He knew their parentage, their dates of birth, the history of their development to maturity and, with regard to some of them, he could accurately diagnose symptoms of senility and decay." Similarly, Smith would be unexcelled in his knowledge of the origins and content of congressional bills.[40]

While Graves's manner and methodology in the law exerted a pronounced influence, Howard Smith was affected most by constitutional law. Minor's mild-mannered son, Raleigh C. Minor, whose works on tax titles in Virginia and conflicts of laws had already given him his own national reputation, taught this course. Discussing the Constitution, Minor accepted the document literally, which to him meant the primacy of state over federal rights.

> Since, in the belief of the States Rights school, the States retain their sovereignty and all powers and rights not clearly delegated to the United States or prohibited to the States, the disciple of that school will . . . favor a strict construction of the Constitution and the holding of the federal government closely to its delegated powers, because he believes that any other course would be a usurpation of power by the federal government, harmful alike, in the end, to the Union and to the States; and because he believes in local self-government, and in the principle that the further removed the rules are from the people they are to govern the less likely is their action to be wise and just.[41]

So extreme was Minor's support of states' rights that in his treatise *Notes on the Science of Government and the Relations of the States to the United States*, he argued at length that neither the failure of the Articles of Confederation nor nullification and secession had stripped away state sovereignty. Referring to Madison's and Jefferson's Virginia and Kentucky Resolutions and to the *Federalist Papers*, Minor concluded that the states had not surrendered their supremacy in creating a federal system with a central government. In the Virginia Resolution, for example, Madison maintained that the federal government's powers resulted "from the compact to which the States are parties" and are "no further valid than they are authorized by the grants enumerated in that compact." Minor also borrowed from South Carolina's John C. Calhoun, who agreed with the founding fathers from Virginia that the federal government was "excluded from an interference with the reserved powers" of the states collectively. Unlike these early nineteenth-century political theorists, however, Minor avoided any discussion of the purpose of the states' rights school. He did not contend that protection of states' rights would preserve individual freedom, protect private property, guarantee democratic government, or assist the agrarian economy. Rather, he interpreted states' rights as an abstract principle permanently enshrined in the Constitution. This concept had the practical effect of elevating power over principle and allowing an adherent, such as Smith, to fend off any action by the federal government that he found undesirable.[42]

The problem, as Minor saw it, was that states' rights had in practice been shorn "by construction." The federal judicial, legislative, and executive branches had relied on the excuses of "convenience" and the inefficiency of states to expand the national government at the expense of the states. Minor denounced this "insidious" trend as a "canker that is slowly but surely eating away the reserved rights of the States and sapping their powers." He recognized that changing circumstances might require the federal government to assume some state responsibilities, but this transfer of power should be accomplished exclusively by a constitutional amendment. Unless such care were taken, Minor worried, there would be "many dark days" ahead in "preserving immaculate and untarnished the reserved powers of the States."[43]

To supplement his own rigid constitutional views, Minor assigned his law classes Thomas M. Cooley's *The General Principles of Constitutional Law in the United States* (1891). Cooley had been a member of the Michigan State Supreme Court and the Interstate Commerce Commission. When Cooley died in 1898, Virginia law professor William Minor Lile ranked him as the nation's "foremost legal mind." Cooley's influence spread considerably beyond his legal decisions. According to a sympathetic obituary in the *Virginia Law Register*, "It was Judge Cooley who taught the generations of the present day how to think correctly on constitutional questions, and his teachings have been obeyed far and wide, as if spoken by an inspired oracle."[44]

Like Minor, Cooley was a strict constructionist and an advocate of states' rights. He argued that the founding fathers framed the Constitution, not to weaken or destroy the individual states, but to "perpetuate" and to strengthen them. With respect to limited government, Cooley relied on the Ninth and Tenth Amendments, which specifically delegated some powers to the federal government. To prevent the central government from exceeding its narrow bounds, the justice offered a test: "To ascertain whether any power assumed by the government of the United States is rightfully assumed, the Constitution is to be examined in order to see whether expressly or by fair implication the power has been granted, and if the grant does not appear, the assumption must be held unwarranted." Needless to say, Cooley found few actions by the federal government permissible.[45]

Minor's lectures and Cooley's text inbued Smith with a reverence for the states' rights doctrine. As he recalled nearly sixty-five years later:

> I never saw a law book until I was eighteen years old and got through cutting a crop of corn on the farm and arrived at the University of Virginia a couple of weeks late, and started to study law. And I got my views about constitutional law there, under very able professors with national reputations. And other people did too in those days. I just haven't changed my views about what the Constitution says. If it says that, as it does in the tenth amendment, that the federal government shall have no power to do anything unless it's contained in that Constitution and the authority is given them, I think that's what it means.

He never wavered from this position throughout his political career. At the height of his congressional power in the 1950s, he fended off possible charges of being "extravagant and reactionary" in unraveling the Constitution, reminding Virginia's current law dean that "I learned my constitutional law at the University at the feet of that great triumvirate Raleigh Minor, Charles Graves, and William Minor Lile." A Richmond reporter gave a more colorful picture of Smith's constitutional views: "His position with respect to a strict interpretation of the Constitution, was as basic and hidebound as that of a Hard-Shelled Baptist preacher's ever was to the literal interpretation of Holy Writ."[46]

At the same time that Smith adopted strict constructionism in law school, a broad social and political reform movement known as progressivism swept the land. The movement spawned a number of institutional changes that Smith eventually tried to reverse. Theodore Roosevelt and other like-minded reformers greatly enlarged the federal government in order to tackle problems beyond the states' interest or ability. The emerging industrial order had exploited labor, adulterated foods, and gouged farmers and consumers. Roosevelt responded by freely interpreting the interstate commerce clause, by mediating labor disputes for the first time, and by setting up new government bureaus that issued far-reaching edicts.[47]

Despite his sympathy with the professors who were giving him the principles to oppose this growth of the federal government, Smith, like his fellow students, found the studying rigorous. Writing to his grandmother in October 1902, he called Virginia "a hard old school. They work us all week & give us an extra allowance on Sunday." A few months later, he confided to his mother that he was "right busy" preparing for an upcoming equity examination. "As usual I'm getting right badly scared up about it. I would hate so to fail on anything." He studied so much that he had few friends besides those made at his cousin Henry Marrs Lewis's boardinghouse. The school yearbook reveals that Smith was in the small minority of law students not belonging to any academic or social club. About his only activities were a thrice-weekly exercise class in the school's gymnasium and periodic walks toward Jefferson's mountaintop home, Monticello. Part of his social isolation stemmed from the ridicule his peers heaped on him for being a farmboy. He complained bitterly to his mother in 1902 about the school's social snobbery:

> I've been "quizzing" Conflicts of Laws, with Reardon this evening. He is a farmer's son also and we exchanged opinions on U. Va. college customs society etc. very freely. I think if some of the college sports or rather "bums" could have heard themselves discussed their self esteem would have received quite a shock. But it does seem rather ridiculous, not to say unhealthy state of affairs

when men . . . who I would care to see at Cedar Hill dont care to know me because my trousers haven't lately been acquainted with a tailor's goose.[48]

Lonely much of the time, Smith relied on his family for emotional support. Too often for his taste, his parents let him down. He was especially disappointed by his peripatetic father. He told his mother, "I've got to write to papa tonight. It's awful hard to write to him because he never answers my letters and I feel like he don't take any interest in what I have to say." Smith's mother sometimes grew so despondent at her husband's lengthy absences at the federal government's farm that she wrote only infrequent and "doleful" letters to her son. At the start of his second year, Smith pleaded with his grandmother "to get [him] the news from the neighborhood."[49]

Smith completed his Bachelor of Laws in 1903, and his proud mother, who "rarely left Cedar Hill for any distance," attended the commencement address delivered by President Roosevelt. Smith then discovered that he was too young to take the state bar examination. Worried about forgetting his training, he sought a legislative remedy from his General Assembly delegate, M. M. Green of Warrenton. When Green proved inept at drafting general laws, Smith took matters into his own hands. At the age of twenty, he prepared his first bill, persuading the legislature to give any Virginian over nineteen years old the right to take the bar exam, though not to practice until twenty-one. Able to sit for the test at last, he passed it and then returned to Cedar Hill until he could legally start his law career in Alexandria, where his father worked, his cousin the congressman lived, and his younger brother attended school.[50]

CHAPTER 2

Law and Politics in Alexandria

I know the people of this district, remembering the glorious political traditions of the past, intend to elect their representative upon his record of public service, and honest personal endeavor; that they intend to select him for energetic public work and assiduous attention to public matters. On this basis I respectfully submit my qualifications for your studious consideration, appealing to your sense of fairness, your love of clean government, but not to your passions or your prejudice.

Howard W. Smith seeking support for the Democratic nomination

to Congress (1930)

Smith moved to Alexandria in May 1904. At that time, the city of fifteen thousand was still suffering from economic and demographic stagnation; in particular, it had lost much of its coal trade to Baltimore, and new residents in the area were choosing to settle in the District of Columbia across the river. Nevertheless, Alexandria's economic foundation enabled it to expand commercially when conditions improved in the early twentieth century. Once a major shipping depot, it boasted six railroads, five steamship lines, and enormous freight yards. Alexandria was also a center for groceries, leather, mill and lumber work, cigars, drugs, agricultural implements, lime, and fertilizers. Its factories produced a wide variety of goods, including bottles, steam pumps, and finished lumber. Indicative of the improving local economy, the value of city products doubled between 1904 and 1909, from $2.2 million to $4.4 million.[1]

Alexandria was an attractive city. Its avenues were laid out in a gridiron, and many of the original brick sidewalks and sandstone curbings remained. Most of the town's residents lived in century-old Georgian or early Federal style houses of brick, gray stucco, or white clapboards. Behind their homes, Alexandrians cultivated mimosas, boxwoods, and magnolias. Even the decaying water-front on the Potomac disclosed signs of Alexandria's former prominence, although some of the wooden wharves, fish markets, and taverns had fallen into disuse.[2]

Smith saw Alexandria, the largest city near his home, as the most suitable place to pursue his ambitions. He soon set about making influential friends, joining prominent civic organizations, and entering highly visible business ventures—all of which would help him climb the rungs of the city's political ladder. Smith's native intelligence and skill as an attorney contributed mightily to his advancement in politics. But these attributes, by themselves, were only preconditions to a political career in early twentieth-century Alexandria, or Virginia as a whole, for that matter. Three other qualities were necessary for a successful political aspirant. First, he usually had to have a law degree, preferably from the University of Virginia, the best-connected school in the state. Most of Alexandria's top attorneys and judges had graduated from Mr. Jefferson's university. Second, he had to be sponsored by the city's leading lawyers and politicians. Finally, once in office, a young politician had to demonstrate political fitness, customarily defined as preserving the status quo and controlling expenditures.[3]

Smith's schooling at Virginia had established him as a political contender, and newfound friendships would add immeasurably to his quest. He also had the powerful advantage of being the incumbent congressman's cousin in a small city whose political offices and economic operations were controlled by a few families. Though never gregarious, Smith now deliberately overcame his natural diffidence to acquire influential companions. During his first years of law practice, he ate lunch at the Hotel Fleischmann with other lawyers from the downtown area. He also joined the downtown Elks Club, a local "political force." A close friend of Smith's, Luther Dudley, recalled that club membership was "preparation for political office, especially commonwealth's attorney." In the club, Smith became friendly with prominent citizens, such as Louis C. Barley, judge of Alexandria's corporation court. By 1908 the young lawyer had attained the position of esteemed loyal knight, the club's third-ranking office. He also participated in the Masons and Odd Fellows. Smith even shed his Baptist upbringing to attend the more socially prominent Christ Episcopal Church with its wine-glass pulpit and old box pews that George Washington had attended.[4]

Smith found that even the theft of his horse could be put to political advantage. One summer shortly after Smith moved to Alexandria, a thief had stolen eight horses from neighboring Fairfax County farmers. Smith ignored the uproar until his own horse disappeared; then he organized area farmers into the Fairfax Horse Protective Association. The younger men patrolled the country roads at night and soon caught the rustler red-handed. The return of their stolen horses brought Smith to the attention of the farmers.[5]

As a new lawyer in town, Smith scrambled for clients. His unprepossessing appearance was of no help. Slightly built and boyish-looking, Smith often seemed dour, if not stern. His most prominent features were those of his father—large, low-set ears, coallike eyes, a tall forehead, and bushy eyebrows. Unlike his redheaded father, however, the younger Smith had black hair. Astutely, he located his law office on North Fairfax Street, almost directly opposite city hall and the clerk of court's office. To bring in additional customers, Smith qualified as a notary public. But he still found law practice difficult at first. Half a year after setting up his office, he complained to his mother: "I've been pretty busy lately but not making much money. Guess I'm doing about as well as the rest of the young lawyers though, but that's not saying much." Within a few years, however, Smith was processing deeds and handling other legal work for some of the most important figures in town, including the Democratic power broker and city attorney, Gardner L. Boothe.[6]

Smith's legal and civic work had given him an enviable reputation. Yet, to move into the political arena, he needed the blessing of Alexandria's Democratic Club, whose members included Boothe, Judge Barley, Mayor Fred J. Paff, Commonwealth's Attorney Samuel G. Brent, police court judge James R. Caton, and all of the city councilmen. These leaders dominated the city, making their support essential to a political bid. This was particularly the case because Smith's cousin, Congressman Rixey, had died in office in February 1907 from tuberculosis and incompetent surgery. In 1908 the club loyally endorsed the twenty-six-year-old Smith for city council. The move was not altogether surprising, given Smith's friendship with Alexandria attorney Charles C. Carlin, who had filled Rixey's seat in Congress by forging close ties with Governor Claude A. Swanson and building his own local organization.[7]

As part of the political inner circle, Smith ran unopposed from the second ward, which encompassed important city and professional offices. Indeed, none of the candidates for the sixteen-member lower, or common, council faced opposition, such was the control exercised by the local Democratic organization. The city newspaper claimed that Alexandrians did not need contested elections because Smith and the rest of the Democratic slate promised to maintain the status quo.[8]

On the council, Smith worked on mundane local projects. While the state machine politics of U.S. Senator Thomas S. Martin dealt with small and balanced budgets, appropriations for dilapidated roads, and Prohibition, Alexandrian councilmen decided which streets to pave, which areas to illuminate with electricity, and which special petitions to grant. Smith distinguished himself in his duties, especially on the general laws committee, and in 1910 the other councilmen installed him as vice-president. He managed to consolidate his position with the aid of powerful political patrons like Albert Bryan, who headed the local Democratic Club. In 1912 Bryan returned to the lower council in time to help make Smith president.[9]

By then Smith had raised his political star even higher by acquiring part of the *Alexandria Gazette*, the nation's oldest continuously published daily newspaper. Apparently a fellow Elk named Robert South Barrett, who had once published a Mexican newspaper, convinced Smith to secure a loan in 1911 to buy the paper, which had fallen on hard times. Smith, according to his daughter, was normally "so cautious with money" but reluctantly invested in the paper anyway, "without even knowing anything about it." The loan, Smith recalled, "haunted my footsteps night and day as I wondered just when the whole thing was going to blow up." The *Gazette*, first under Barrett's direction and later under Smith's when Barrett left again for Central America, adopted a conventional, conservative attitude toward local politics and local politicians. With his name prominently listed in large letters on the editorial page, Smith had discovered a convenient way to keep himself and his ideas in the public eye. Eventually, however, his growing legal practice and successful land investments led him to sell the paper in 1921 to his old crony and patron Charles Carlin, whose editorials would remain friendly to Smith and the Democratic machine.[10]

Smith had one major preoccupation throughout this period besides politics—real estate. As part owner of the *Gazette*, Smith had early access to bank and real estate reports. He examined his newspaper's financial section to find out where the best deals were available. Then, sometimes he bid—from $2,400 to $6,500— upon the properties being put up for auction for overdue mortgage payments. Other times, he purchased homes from recently widowed women who were willing to sell for no more, and possibly less, than the full market price. From all accounts Smith won recognition as a shrewd investor, who "wouldn't dream of buying a piece of property without walking over every inch of it."[11]

At first, Smith bought small parcels in Alexandria's residential section. He quickly sold these lots "to build up working capital" for larger, more lucrative transactions. His cousin Gordon Lewis recalled that Smith had a theory about real estate investment: "He didn't keep anything any longer if he could make a profit on it. He sold it; he didn't try to keep it for any length of time." In January 1912, for example, he bought six houses at $2,000 each in the town's west end. He sold half of his investment within three months and the remainder before the year ran out. These small sales permitted him to hold on to other property until a more profitable sum could be realized. By the end of 1912, Smith had purchased thirteen desirable lots with houses—all within walking distance of city hall.[12]

By 1930 Smith had bought and sold about sixty plots around Alexandria. He wisely purchased many plots at depressed prices. Real estate had been hurt by the closing of the city's shipyard. But as land prices soon recovered, Smith profited substantially. He sold one seventy-two-acre plot between Alexandria and Washington for the substantial sum of at least $20,000 in 1931. Smith also helped set up the Arlington Development Corporation to shelter additional property in the names of relatives. In one instance, he held on to an undeveloped thirteen-acre tract near Washington while its value climbed to $1 million by the 1970s, according to Smith's former business associate, real estate assessor Luther Dudley.[13]

As time went on, Smith invested in more affluent areas. He began buying up property in the fashionable Rosemont section where he had moved. While houses in central Alexandria sold for about $3,000, empty lots in Rosemont went for nearly double that sum. With the city's population moving westward toward the suburbs, a land investor stood to profit handsomely. Rosemont lots—probably in line with local ordinances—carried two provisos, requiring that buildings erected on them be worth a specified amount and stipulating that the property could never be "sold, leased, rented, or in any way conveyed to anyone not of the Caucasian race." Both covenants helped ensure high values for Smith's investments.[14]

Besides enriching him financially, Smith's land deals were lucrative in other ways. When he bought and sold property, he met prospective clients for his law business, which was tied to land sales. More importantly, he solidified his relations with the city's legal, financial, and political elite. He sometimes purchased land with Commonwealth's Attorney Brent; police court judge Caton; and former congressman Carlin. He also had his deeds notarized by the sons of prominent Alexandrians. In this way, he renewed and strengthened his ties with the town's most influential men.[15]

With his career in perfect order, Smith decided at age thirty to settle down and start a family. On November 4, 1913, he married a "charming" twenty-two-year-old, Lillian Violett Proctor of Alexandria. This match did not elevate Smith's social and political position, for his bride came from a lower middle-class background. Her father had been a paperhanger before rising to a clerical job, a typical move as the state became more industrial and bureaucratic. Her sister was a stenographer. But for a reserved man consumed by his work, Smith's marriage to Miss Proctor was a natural step because she had notarized some of his legal work for at least two years. His marriage to a notary public ensured a mate familiar with, if not sympathetic to, his demanding profession.[16]

After exchanging vows in the town's Second Presbyterian Church, the couple left for an extended wedding trip to the North. When they returned, the newlyweds made their home away from downtown, in what would be the first of three moves to progressively more affluent neighborhoods in Alexandria. Less than eleven months later, Violett delivered a baby boy, named Howard Worth Smith, Jr. Four years later she gave Smith his second and last child, Violett Adelaide Smith.[17]

During these years, Smith's political career matured. He demonstrated adroit, conservative leadership on several sensitive subjects, including Prohibition and crime. One damaging problem to hit Alexandria in the fall of 1914 was the loss of hundreds of glass bottle–making jobs while the state debated the manufacture and sale of alcoholic beverages. Finding the alcohol issue needlessly inflammatory, Smith used his editorial page to brand the Prohibition question as an "unnecessary battle"; he expressed hope that the moral reformers would simply worry about themselves.[18]

Alexandria's present difficulty, Smith believed, had economic, not moral, roots, and he took two steps in 1916 to solve the problem. To create additional jobs, he strongly supported a council resolution to secure an armor plant. He also came to the aid of local merchants. When rumors about scarlet fever kept buyers from downtown retail stores, Smith's *Gazette* minimized the danger by reporting only a few mild cases of rash.[19]

Smith then tied together the questions of public health and crime. In 1918 he lashed out at the city's poor sanitary conditions. He urged the police to arrest those who dumped refuse on the streets, allowed putrid water to run in alleys, or failed to join the sewer system. By the fall, he had obtained an ordinance that defined and set penalties for health violations. His actions were irreproachable, as well as politically beneficial, for no one could oppose improved public health.[20]

With respect to race relations, Smith accepted the prevailing belief in white supremacy. Having grown up with a paternalistic view, Smith thought blacks incapable of helping themselves without white assistance. A story later recounted by Smith illustrates his racial attitude, one that did not change appreciably during his political life. During his council years, Smith returned on weekends to his parent's farm, where he occasionally helped troubled black farmhands. One of them wanted his child to attend the local all-black school but seemed at a loss to obtain transportation. Interceding on the farmhand's behalf, Smith prodded the superintendent to make one trial run past the farm to see whether a bus stop was justified. On the appointed day, a surprisingly large number of well-dressed black children met the bus, which thereafter continued to take that route. Smith believed that the local black children had been given the chance to improve themselves only by a white man's intercession. [21]

As a prominent conservative local politician and real estate attorney with powerful friends, Smith soon became Alexandria's commonwealth's attorney. Shortly before the new city council convened in September 1918, the incumbent commonwealth's attorney, Samuel G. Brent, resigned to become judge of Virginia's sixteenth judicial circuit. A deal was cut in which Smith handpicked his successor as council president, then resigned, and waited to be named to his new post. Soon his old friend and judge of the corporation court, Louis C. Barley, appointed him the city's new attorney. Throughout his four years as commonwealth's attorney, Smith pursued his duties with vigor, much of the time dealing with misdemeanor cases of selling alcohol or with violent crimes. [22]

One reason for Smith's devotion to his public responsibilities was the sudden loss of his twenty-nine-year-old wife, who died in the worldwide flu epidemic of 1919. So stunned was Smith that he never again referred to her, and he gave the nickname "Monk" to his five-month-old daughter, Violett, who had been named for his wife. His parents agreed to take his son and daughter to Cedar Hill until he remarried, a move designed to give the children more attention than a busy widower could provide. [23]

Smith used public law as an outlet for his grief and politics to fulfill his growing ambitions. In the summer of 1920 he took the train to San Francisco, where he attended the Democratic national convention. This was a remarkable journey for Smith because he disliked long-distance travel and had not gone to a national political gathering since his childhood. In July he vividly described the convention to his children's governess as "a great

sight, with its parades and banners, and the moving picture machines reeling it off from every side." He was most amused by the
novelty of "lady politicians"—the proposed Nineteenth Amendment would soon give women the vote—especially when some
of them wrestled with each other over a campaign banner. He did
not mention his view of the progressive Democratic presidential
candidate, Ohio governor James M. Cox. After the proceedings
ended, Smith allowed himself some leisure time for a change,
sightseeing through the majestic Rocky Mountains that were so
different from the smaller Blue Ridge near his home.[24]

After returning to Alexandria, Smith laid the groundwork for
higher office. This time he sought a judgeship, which required
the backing of state Democratic leaders. His opportunity to curry
favor with the party organization came in 1921 when two Democrats sought a U.S. Senate seat. The front-runner was the incumbent and head of the state party, Claude A. Swanson, who
boasted of improvements in Virginia school facilities, rural mail
delivery, and free diagnostic health tests while he had served as
governor. Smith had known Swanson for at least fourteen years,
when Swanson was the state's chief executive. In late August 1921
Smith reassured Swanson, who was ill in Washington, D.C., that
he was "doing all that I possibly can to aid your re-nomination.
In fact, I have been for sometime working quietly in conjunction
with your other friends here," especially former congressman Carlin, who had resigned in the fall of 1918, and his son, Keith.
Smith estimated that the campaign in Alexandria was in "pretty
fair shape." In the face of a united organization, Swanson's mav-
erick challenger, Governor Westmoreland Davis, lost by the
greatest primary margin in Virginia history. Alexandria cast three
votes in every four for Swanson, who awaited the election result
at Carlin's home. Thus, Smith's first recorded foray into state
politics proved extremely successful.[25]

When a corporation court vacancy soon appeared, Smith was
the party's logical choice. In late 1922 Judge Robinson Moncure
resigned to resume his more financially rewarding private law
practice. Since Moncure had been disloyal in supporting Davis
for Senate, the Democratic machine wanted a reliable replace-
ment. Smith had never wavered in backing organization candidates or in upholding the principles of limited government and
fiscal conservatism. Accordingly, the local bar association, led by

former corporation court judge Charles E. Nicol, nominated Smith to fill Moncure's position. Virginia governor E. Lee Trinkle, who owed his election in the previous year to Swanson and to Democratic party leader Harry F. Byrd, Sr., of Winchester, approved Smith's selection. Smith wasted no time in drawing the legal circle behind him, for one of his first acts as judge was to name his taciturn law partner, William P. Woolls, a specialist in land titles, to follow him as commonwealth's attorney.[26]

"A very serious-minded" judge, Smith presided over a variety of cases, sometimes misdemeanors (violations carrying penalties of up to a year in jail), but more frequently felonies (violations carrying a penalty of more than a year in jail). His case load ranged from routine matters such as adoptions, gun permits, guardianships for the feebleminded, alimony default, and financial claims to those involving violent crimes. He also heard bootlegging cases, which convinced him to abstain from alcohol lest he appear hypocritical. Fellow jurist Albert V. Bryan, Sr., son of Smith's early ally and an occasional practitioner in Smith's court, gave him a high grade for possessing "a very keen and quick mind" and for being well-read in legal matters. Bryan also praised Smith for avoiding lengthy discussions until he charged the jury. In short, he let the lawyers try the case. He was, Bryan concluded, "like a well-tuned cymbal," speaking only when absolutely necessary—a trait the University of Virginia law school had inculcated. When the proceedings adjourned, however, Smith exhibited "a delicate sense of humor" that led him to mimic courtroom participants.[27]

As corporation court judge, Smith also wielded important patronage powers that contributed to his political advancement. By naming many local officers, Smith solidified his hold over the city's political affairs. He was responsible, for example, for the membership of the school and public welfare boards. He also helped to maintain the Democratic organization's control over the local election machinery by appointing the electoral judges.[28]

In 1923, after four years of widowhood, Judge Smith, as he always preferred to be addressed, remarried, this time to Ann Corcoran of Washington, D.C., the young woman who had cared for his children after his first wife's death. Smith had become attached to "Annie," as he called her, because she had been good for his children and promised to be a supportive wife. His judgments were not hastily arrived at, for Annie had lived in the Smith household for more than a decade after she lost her parents. In 1909 Howard's father had brought eight-year-old Annie from a Washington, D.C., orphanage to provide his lonely wife with a companion while he was away supervising the federal government's farm. At the age of forty, Howard Smith married twenty-two-year-old Annie in a small ceremony witnessed by family members, including his seventy-two-year-old father, who had less than a year to live. Once more, this private man wed a woman close at hand. As in his first marriage, Smith traveled northward for his honeymoon. This union, while childless, proved splendidly suitable to the "Victorian" Smith because his wife devoted herself to his political and personal needs. Annie's stepdaughter later recalled: "My father was the king in our house. My mother absolutely worshipped the ground he walked on. I mean her whole life was tied up around him."[29]

Five years later when Judge Brent of the circuit court died in the spring of 1928, Smith's friends vigorously pressed his candidacy, first choosing him as president of the circuit bar association and then endorsing him to replace Brent. As usual, Smith had avoided making a public and unseemly play for political gain. This time, Harry Byrd, was the governor who selected him for the judicial post, marking the start of a half-century political relationship that would directly affect state and national fortunes. Once again Smith orchestrated his former partner Woolls's appointment to his old post.[30]

Smith had gained the circuit court appointment at its earliest vacancy, an indication that he was considered politically reliable, not to mention a fine jurist. Legal and popular opinion of Judge Smith remained highly favorable as he handled divorce and felony cases. Bar association members, particularly in Fairfax, lauded his elimination of case backlog and saw him as a judge with "ability, fairness, energy and dignity."[31]

Complementing his new judicial post, Smith "inherited" the presidency of the Alexandria National Bank in 1928. According to bank officer and future president Luther Dudley, this bank, like the other city banks, searched for "the most prestigious man it could find to head it up." Because a judge was widely known, Smith served as "window dressing," lending credibility to the bank in the days before deposits were guaranteed by the federal government. As a bonus, Judge Smith possessed "hard financial sense" and encouraged a wide circle of acquaintances to patronize the bank. Smith took his banking duties seriously, attending the weekly board meetings until 1958, when he cited health reasons for his retirement.[32]

To this point in his career, Smith had operated within the unwritten code for ambitious political figures. He dutifully waited his turn for office, never challenged an incumbent, and compiled a conservative record once in a post. Suddenly in 1930 he had an opportunity to run for the House of Representatives when Eighth District congressman R. Walton Moore, a widely popular figure, resigned.[33]

Smith had long admired his cousin, John F. Rixey, who had served as a free silverite and antitariff congressman at the turn of the century. He had even stayed with Rixey in Alexandria while beginning his law practice. For almost twenty years Smith had been biding his time, waiting for a challenging post such as this one. Except for the General Assembly, he had already filled nearly every prominent local office, including city councilman, commonwealth's attorney, and judge of the corporation and circuit courts. Timing was also crucial. At forty-seven, Smith might not have another chance to run for Congress, for whoever won this time was likely to stay in office until retirement or death.[34]

To run for this post, Smith had to consider the complexion of the entire Eighth District. Heretofore, he had represented Alexandria, the northern district's only city with more than 2,500 people. The rest of the district was overwhelmingly rural and was experiencing slow growth. Of the ten counties, seven had populations of at least 50 percent farmers. A third of the populations of two other counties were employed by the federal government. The remaining occupations of importance included the building and retail trades. Alexandria alone was notable for its unions, which numbered sixteen in 1936, mostly connected with railroads. Most of the district's 184,000 inhabitants were of British or German descent; just 1 percent of the district was foreign-born. Blacks constituted almost one-fourth of the population but were largely nonvoting farmers.[35]

Smith was able to take advantage of the district's character in several ways. Most significantly, he controlled Alexandria—the district's financial, legal, and political nerve center. He was president of the Alexandria National Bank, former owner of Alexandria's only daily newspaper, a wealthy real estate magnate, a highly respected judge, and the leading politician. In addition, he had the support of other local luminaries. At an organizational meeting in an Elks hall in March, 150 prominent Alexandrians endorsed his candidacy, including former congressman Carlin, Eighth District Democratic chairman and bank president Gardner L. Boothe, and Judge Moncure. Thus, Smith enjoyed the backing of the district's most politically powerful men upon entering the campaign.[36]

Smith could also claim identification with most district residents. Like them, he had come from a long line of English ancestors. He also had a farming background. Although he had been a city lawyer and politician for twenty-five years, he dubbed himself a "dirt farmer." This appellation was far from the truth but enabled him to appeal to the district's largest voting bloc. In fact, he was more of a gentleman farmer, overseeing his mother's dairy farm on weekends and occasional visits during the corn and grain harvest. As an absentee farmer, Smith protected his investment by compelling his manager to buy a half interest in the milk cows, on the theory that no one would neglect an animal he partly owned.[37]

The district's poor roads and inadequate communication system worked in Smith's favor, too. In this isolated society, the political world operated by word of mouth, newspapers, and the courthouse crowd. With Alexandria safely in his corner, Smith went after the outlying areas. He was aided considerably by having been circuit court judge of Arlington, Fairfax, and Prince William counties, as well as of Alexandria. His legal duties introduced him to local politicians, and newspapers put his name on the front page when the court decided local cases. In addition, he was able to control the *Alexandria Gazette*, of which he had remained a large stockholder even after having sold it. Since the *Gazette* was the district's most important daily paper, the weeklies often reprinted its news items and editorials. More directly, Smith had close and unequaled associations with several counties. He was reared in Fauquier and visited his family's farm there frequently. In Culpeper, his cousin had been commonwealth's attorney. Smith had also long been in touch with Arlington officials when he consummated county land deals. Down in Louisa, his brother Worth had served in the state senate since 1924.[38]

Despite Smith's apparently unbeatable lead, the open congressional seat lured four other men. State senator Frank L. Ball of Arlington posed the most serious threat. He represented the most populous county and had compiled a record of reform in road building, schools, taxation, and farming. Two other candidates were largely frivolous. Crandall Mackey had been commonwealth's attorney of Arlington more than a decade earlier and had gained acclaim only as a foe of bootleggers. Since that time, Mackey had built his own law practice and owned two muckraking county newspapers, the *Commonwealth Monitor* and the *Clarendon Chronicle*. E. H. DeJarnette, Jr., a lawyer in sparsely populated Orange County, was the least known candidate. Smith's final challenger came from Fairfax. At the last minute, attorney Thomas R. Keith entered the race. Although he had served on many commissions, he had never been elected to public office. A pleasant, handsome man with large features, Keith was known in the campaign as an able lawyer who happened to be the incumbent congressman's brother-in-law and former law partner.[39]

But Smith held the upper hand, and he knew it. As a party loyalist, he had the support of the state Democratic machine headed by Governor Byrd. The cherubic-faced Byrd, whose principal accomplishment had been building state roads without indebtedness, wanted an organization regular to succeed the independent-minded Moore, who had been at odds with the organization, particularly senators Martin and Swanson. The *Fredericksburg Free Lance-Star* described how the machine worked its will: "The Virginia Political Machine picks the candidate it thinks will win and usually puts him across. This time it has picked Judge Smith. It is not improbable that the certain number of machine votes which the Judge will get at each precinct throughout the district, will be sufficient to elect him. The organization thinks he will be." Seemingly assured of victory in his first competitive race, Smith made no joint campaign appearances with the other four candidates. Instead, he quietly contacted organization supporters throughout the district, "hustling . . . night and day, trying to line up all the voters I could." He delivered only one speech, shortly before the election, thereby offering no platform for his foes to shoot at. On a few occasions he paid news-papers to print a large photograph of himself looking like a droopy-faced Saint Bernard wearing an old-fashioned batwing collar.[40]

To narrow the Judge's lead, one of his opponents indulged in a mudslinging barrage. Crandall Mackey accused Smith of unfair, if not illegal, campaign practices in accounts reprinted in district papers. Some of the charges contained at least kernels of truth. The first allegation claimed Smith had intimidated Representa-tive Moore into retirement. Moore, who had been ill, made an oblique announcement in October 1929 that he might retire be-cause of poor health. Smith waited until January to enter the race, but his declaration preceded Moore's definitive withdrawal by several days. Mackey criticized Smith's "arrogance and conceit": "It was being said by Candidate Smith to friends of Mr. Moore, that he knew would tell Mr. Moore, that he, Smith would run whether Mr. Moore ran or not." DeJarnette may have come closer to the truth than Mackey. "Moore, like the blushing school girl who wants to be kissed, but says 'no' over played his hand when he said he did not intend to run again, secretly hoping to be persuaded to do so, but was taken at his word . . . by H. W. Smith." In any event, most newspapers had long since believed Moore was retiring when Smith declared his candidacy.[41]

Mackey's second charge was more serious. He alleged that Smith's chief backer, former congressman Carlin, had tried to bribe state senator Ball to abandon the primary campaign. Ac-cording to Mackey, "the offer was that Ball shall agree not to run for congress in exchange for the Carlin-Smith support to land Ball in the judgeship" then held by Smith. Ball reportedly nixed the proposal by informing Carlin that the constitution prevented a state officeholder from being named a judge. Whether this charge had merit cannot be determined. But Smith's camp did not feel compelled to publish a refutation, and the story vanished quickly.[42]

The most damning indictment against Smith came less than a month before the August primary. Smith was accused of financial impropriety in the 1911 sale of an Alexandria bank building owned by the defunct Virginia Safe Deposit and Trust Corpora-tion, which he had served as its attorney. At the time of the sale, the court had appointed him to manage the bank's affairs, as well as to serve as one of six commissioners to sell the empty building at auction. Robert S. Barrett, president of the newly formed Alexandria Gazette Corporation, offered the highest bid. Smith sat as secretary-treasurer of this new corporation, and he combined his assets with Barrett's to secure an $8,000 loan to buy the property. This sum fell far below the building's actual value, which Alexandria's commissioner of revenue, Charles H. Callahan, set at $34,000. Naturally, some suggested that Smith had manipulated the sale to his advantage.[43]

For the first time, Smith's supporters responded to a campaign allegation, defending his conduct as a commissioner of sale. His campaign chairman, Gardner Boothe, presented a rebuttal on the front page of district newspapers. Boothe claimed that the charge was politically motivated because no one had brought it up during the twenty years before the campaign began. He also pointed out that the auction was public and that Smith's associate, Barrett, simply had made the highest bid. In addition, Boothe claimed the other commissioners were men of unimpeachable character. Finally, he concluded, if Smith had been guilty of wrongdoing, he would not have thenceforth been chosen for Alexandria's most responsible positions.[44]

But Boothe's refutation contained holes. The building was clearly worth much more than the purchase price, as revealed by that year's tax assessment. City homes far from downtown, where the bank was, sold for up to $4,000, and the bank was many times more valuable. Moreover, the transaction went previously unexamined because the auction was run by Smith's associates and because Smith had had only one contested election before 1930. As for the other commissioners, they were his patrons, clients, or business partners. Apparently having no designs on the building themselves, the commissioners allowed Smith to profit substantially. In subsequent years, Smith advanced in political and legal circles partly because the same men involved in the sale were promoting him. Beyond question, Smith had used his position and connections to secure the building at a price considerably below its worth.[45]

These charges nonetheless struck many newspaper editors as unfair attacks on Smith. The *Fauquier Democrat* was particularly chagrined, insisting that Smith was being slandered.

> We are utterly amazed and astonished at the methods used in the present Congressional campaign by supporters of some of the can-

didates. . . . Four against one! Fair play and from our own Virginia people! Can you beat this! Attacking Judge Smith in every
conceivable way—questioning his honesty, his word, his integrity,
taking reports and statements not supported by fact and from unscrupulous individuals and spreading this filth throughout the district to weaken his candidacy.

The *Fairfax Herald* observed that Smith was able to ignore "the
rather childish and groundless attacks" made on him because of
his lead. The paper compared Smith's position in the campaign
to that of a winning pitcher in the ninth inning: "He can afford
to smile genially at the yowping of the coaches who are trying to
rattle him."[46]

Amidst the flurry of charges against Smith, the candidates expressed contrasting views on the only important issue, Prohibition. In 1916 Virginia had limited individual purchases of
alcoholic beverages to a quart each month, and the country had
banned alcohol completely in 1920 with the ratification of the
Eighteenth Amendment. Since then, popular support for Prohibition had slipped, though how far was unclear.[47]

As a result, Prohibition was a slippery but potentially winning
issue. On one side stood Ball, who claimed to be bone dry, "publicly and privately, personally and politically." Of the five candidates, only Ball received the Anti-Saloon League's stamp of
approval, a move that surprised political observers. Many district
newspaper editors had believed that the heretofore powerful
league would "overlook" Smith's fence straddling on Prohibition.
On the other side, Mackey and DeJarnette posed as "damp" candidates. Arguing that Prohibition had not worked, Mackey called
for a dispensary system of light wines and beer patterned after that
of Sweden. He reminded voters that as commonwealth's attorney,
he had "rid Arlington County of Bar Rooms and Gambling
Dens." DeJarnette called only for a return to Virginia's quart-a-
month law. As for Keith, he moved to the middle. He believed
the Eighteenth Amendment had usurped states' rights and urged
its repeal. At the same time, he was "unalterably opposed to the
reestablishment of the saloon, or any institution that savors
of it."[48]

Desperate to drag Smith into the fray, the other candidates publicly challenged him. Keith demanded he "answer categorically

the question whether the present prohibition policy has his approval." At a Drainesville campaign forum in July, DeJarnette noted Smith was again the only candidate absent and suggested that "those who voted for Smith would buy a pig in the bag as nobody knew what Smith stood for except for office." Ball painted Smith as "a wet heart disguising himself as a dry to get dry votes." Mackey, on the other hand, made light of Smith's equivocation:

> Voter: Do you intend to inform the people of your district of your views on prohibition?
> Smith: Ask C. C. Carlin. He must dictate that for me.
> Voter: Are you wet or dry?
> Smith: I am.
> Voter: Am I to vote for you without knowing your opinions on any public political question?
> Smith: Ask C. C. Carlin. He says: "Dear Howard, don't talk."[49]

After consulting with another organization stalwart, Senator Swanson, Smith let his opponents debate among themselves. Swanson admitted that he had once faced a similar dilemma, telling his constituents: "There have been only four men in our history who could sit on the fence, and be shot at, and never falter. They were George Washington, Robert E. Lee, Stonewall Jackson and Claude Swanson." Smith followed Swanson's lead in drawing on the memories of famous Virginians and later informed the senator, "Add Howard W. Smith to your list of immortals."[50]

At the end of July, a week before the primary, Smith finally responded to his opponents in an address broadcast by a Washington radio station. The late date prevented the opposition from replying. To begin, he explained why he refused to campaign openly. "I was . . . actuated," he said, "by the conviction that joint debates and public discussions in Democratic primaries lead to party discord and bitterness, resulting in mud-slinging and personalities." He accused his opponents and their supporters—he called them "enemies"—of resorting to the lowest tactics, including "abuse, villification, slander and libel," to beat him.[51]

Smith then spelled out his platform and attacked his nearest competitor. Because farmers were the district's largest uncommitted voting bloc, Smith appealed first to them. He reminded them

William Worth Smith, Sr., and Lucinda Lewis Smith. (From Lucy Price, *The Sydney-Smith and Clagett-Price Genealogy* [Strasburg, Va.: Shenandoah Publishing House, 1927])

Cedar Hill. (From Price, *Sydney-Smith and Clagett-Price Genealogy*)

William Worth Smith, Jr., and Howard Worth Smith. (Tonahill Collection)

Judge Howard W. Smith in the late 1920s. (Tonahill Collecti

William E. Dodd, Jr., during the 1938 Eighth District
Democratic primary in Virginia. (From the *Washington Star*,
July 25, 1938)

that he came from a Fauquier County farm, which he still maintained. He sympathized with their "deplorable situation": "When
the farmer is prosperous, the country is prosperous, but he can
not be made to prosper with kind words or futile promises." As he
saw it, farmers suffered because of overproduction, grain speculation, and the Republican Hawley-Smoot tariff "designed in the
interest of the great manufacturers and combinations of wealth,
and with utter indifference to the welfare of agriculture." His
views reflected the traditional agrarian outlook of southern Democrats, including those of his cousin, former representative Rixey.
If elected to Congress, Smith pledged to push for a law ending
grain speculation, but he stopped short of urging tariff reform.[52]

To draw farm votes from state senator Ball, Smith criticized
him by name. He chided Ball's vote for the federal child labor

amendment that gave "the United States Government absolute police power to control and prevent labor by all persons under 18." As a result a struggling farmer's teenaged sons "could not work in the field, milk the cows, or cut the wood without the consent of a United States Bureau in Washington." Just as bad, black teenagers without work would be "a burden and a menace to society." But the amendment had a still more pernicious possibility. Smith blamed Ball for having "opened the door to other invasions that would eventually deprive the states of all powers of self-government and centralize police regulations of local affairs under federal control." No charge in Virginia could have been more severe.[53]

Having acknowledged farmers' problems, Smith next discussed immigration. This was an ideal target because the district contained few first- or second-generation immigrants. Moreover, immigration to the United States had slowed markedly since 1924, when Congress shut off the southern and eastern European influx. Smith called for "selective" as well as restrictive immigration, that is, admitting immigrants who could fill specific jobs. He also wanted a law that "throws them out" because, as he was reared to believe, foreigners committed crimes and espoused anarchy. Smith then proposed a modified indentured servant scheme in which some immigrants would have to work for several years on labor-poor farms in order to remain in the country. This suggestion appealed both to nativists and to farmers.[54]

Smith rapidly disposed of two other issues. With respect to native labor, he admitted that workers produced "the wealth of the country." But he made a minimum pledge to "give careful study and sympathetic consideration to all [labor] measures coming before the Congress." As for Prohibition, Smith once more sidestepped the question, even though he was, his son recalled, personally "horrified by bootlegger alcohol." He would, of course, uphold the nation's laws, including the Eighteenth Amendment. But a "permanent and satisfactory" answer to alcohol consumption demanded an "open mind and free hand." Blasting his opponents, Smith insisted Prohibition would "never be settled as long as candidates for office choose to use it as a footstool for every office." In short, Smith hinted he was taking the political high road on the controversial problem. Not coincidentally, his position permitted him to avoid antagonizing voters on both sides.[55]

On election day, August 5, 1930, Eighth District voters gave Smith a smashing victory. He received almost 49 percent of the votes, more than twice as many as his nearest rival, state senator Ball. He carried nine of the district's eleven electoral units, including Fairfax County, Keith's political base. His only losses occurred in the home counties of Ball and DeJarnette. As expected, Smith reaped the richest rewards in Alexandria, where nearly three votes in four went his way. Almost 30 percent of his total votes came from that city, which had the district's highest turnout. Once the election results were revealed, his friends in Alexandria staged a colorful parade in his honor.[56]

Smith captured the congressional primary for several reasons. First, Alexandria's political machine backed him enthusiastically. He had served as an organization stalwart since he moved to the city twenty-five years earlier. In part, Smith won merely because the organization backed one of its own. In a postelection analysis, an anti-Smith paper offered this assessment: "Smith was the organization candidate. He was the first to announce. He had financial means and backing to prosecute his campaign. Senator Swanson's choice was Smith. Former Congressman C. C. Carlin was one of Smith's chief advisers. These factors, not prohibition, are held to account for his victory." This kind of support was crucial in a district in which less than one-fourth of the quarter million residents voted. Yet, Smith was also easily the most familiar name in the primary. In more than half the district, he was known directly as circuit judge, gentleman farmer, entrepreneur, or relative. His opponents were weak favorite sons, who divided the rest of the votes between them. Moreover, he won plaudits from newspaper editors, and presumably voters, for his dignified campaign style. Virginians had long valued style, as well as substance, in their politicians. In Alexandria, for example, one well-known supporter commended Smith for "not being of the back slapping, handshaking school of politicians but rather of the intelligent and energetic type."[57]

In his first major congressional race, Smith learned certain truths of political life in the Eighth District. Active campaigning was not necessary to win. Local organization support, supplemented by newspaper endorsement, sufficed. Smith also deliberately ignored his opponents' tar brush, correctly thinking that some voters would find his conduct alone worthy of support. If he defeated a weak Republican challenger in the general election, Smith might well remain in office indefinitely, thanks to Virginia's tradition of retaining its politicians. All he had to do was to act circumspectly and seek reelection in the same way.[58]

After the primary, rumors of election fraud momentarily marred Smith's victory. In Stafford County, E. E. Harley charged William A. Woodward, a prominent farmer, with illegally distributing marked ballots for Smith just outside polling booths. Before a grand jury, Harley testified that Woodward approached him to vote for Smith. When Harley claimed not to know Smith, Woodward allegedly replied, "Well, go ahead and vote for Smith anyway, and I will see that you get paid" twenty-five dollars. The two men then walked down an alley between stores, where Woodward handed Harley a marked ballot, which Harley promptly turned over to the county clerk's office. With two dissenting votes, the jury composed of seven current and former local Democratic officeholders dismissed the charge. According to newspaper accounts, the county remained "agog" at this incident and several others for some time. But one prominent Republican claimed that "the Democrats have been indulging in such practices in Stafford for years and no one has ever done anything about it or protested it." Indeed, none of Smith's primary foes asked for an investigation.[59]

Smith appealed to all Democrats to unite behind his candidacy in the general election. The fraud charge against him died down quickly, and the fall campaign proved anticlimactic. There was little attention to issues, and the voters forsook their support of the Republicans in 1928 to return to the Democratic party. Smith won every district subdivision, including Fairfax County, which had not supported a Democratic congressional candidate since 1926, and Arlington County, which had often voted Republican in previous years. In fact, Smith received almost four times the combined vote of his opponents—Frank M. Brooks, a Fairfax Republican, and John M. Daniel, a Stafford County prohibitionist.[60]

After his smashing victory, Smith prepared to cross the Potomac to Capitol Hill as one of Virginia's nine-member delegation. In line with his conception of the office, he had not made any "extravagant" promises to assist any special group. He had only pledged to do his best as representative. But as the economy slipped into depression, the country was on the verge of a liberal revolution—a New Deal—that no one could have foreseen. With an antiquated vision of society, Smith was more attuned to the laissez-faire politics of Calvin Coolidge and Herbert Hoover than to the spate of unorthodox proposals of the new era. For the first time, he would find his constitutional and political ideas, and indirectly his own socioeconomic station, under severe attack.

CHAPTER 3

An Anti–New Dealer

*Theorists, jingoists, and demagogues in our country
are taking advantage of the present abnormal conditions of distress of their fellow citizens to promote idi-
otic and impractical schemes of government utterly
subversive of our constitutional form of government.*
Howard W. Smith (1935)

When the forty-seven-year-old Smith left Alexandria for Capitol
Hill, he left behind his status as the leading local politician to
become one among many faceless freshmen representatives. The
House Ways and Means Committee assigned him seats on the
minor committees of the District of Columbia, which was responsible for the city of Washington; Public Buildings and
Grounds, which looked after Washington's buildings and parks;
Civil Service, which handled government employment, especially large in Washington; and Elections, which passed judgment
on contested House elections. Because some of Smith's constituents worked for the federal government in Washington, his
membership on the District and Civil Service committees were
important to him. But these lesser committees afforded Smith
little opportunity to propose major legislation in 1931. Instead,
he introduced private bills to assist a handful of constituents and
quietly voted with his Virginia colleagues as he learned the ropes
of parliamentary maneuvering.[1]

Like the rest of the state delegation, Smith supported the few
measures that President Hoover brought forward to revive the
faltering economy. After his first attempts to maintain the nation's

banks and large businesses proved inadequate, Hoover submitted new legislation. He wanted to reestablish the War Finance Corporation, renamed the Reconstruction Finance Corporation, in order to loan up to $1.5 billion to banks, insurance companies, and railroads. Faced with growing unemployment and even starvation in urban areas, the exhaustion of private charities, and a dearth of capital in lending institutions, Congress approved the measure in January 1932. While some southern Democrats opposed the bill for giving "too much political and financial power" to the handful of men in charge of the corporation, Smith sided with the majority, among whom was North Carolina Democrat Frank Hancock, who declared that the financial crisis demanded prompt legislative action "so that the country may at least enjoy a brief if not permanent breathing spell against the turmoil, excitement, and cruel destruction of values and wreckage of homes."[2]

This belated measure aside, most Virginians eventually concluded that their support for Hoover and his Republican administration had been dreadfully misplaced. In the fall presidential election, the Old Dominion returned to the Democratic fold, casting its ballots for Franklin D. Roosevelt, as well as for Smith and all other Byrd Democrats. According to leading state newspapers, most Virginians had tired of the Republican-backed class legislation that had been passed in the 1920s. Seeing the Democratic victory as more than the rejection of an individual, the *Richmond News Leader* singled out such unsound Republican practices as wasting public funds, the consequent increase in taxation, the "scandalous" schedules of the Hawley-Smoot tariff, and laws favoring large contributions to the party campaign chest. The newspaper lauded Roosevelt's conservative approach to federal spending and pinned its hopes for economic recovery not on government programs but on "the slow cycle of depression and revival."[3]

In 1933 as Franklin D. Roosevelt began the first of his four terms, Howard W. Smith unexpectedly secured a seat on the mighty House Rules Committee. This committee assignment was actually a consolation prize to the Democratic congressional faction led by John W. McCormack of Massachusetts and Sam Rayburn of Texas. These men lost control of the House leadership when Texan John ("Cactus Jack") Garner, an often "vindictive" Speaker, was elected as Roosevelt's vice-president. McCormack and Rayburn therefore sought to regain influence through strategic committee appointments, including placing a little-known Virginia Democrat on Rules. According to Smith, his new post came without warning. During a walk from the Capitol to the House Office Building, William B. Bankhead of Alabama, the ranking Democrat, casually told Smith, "I would like to have you on the Rules Committee." Because of his lack of seniority, Smith quickly searched for additional support. He urged other Virginia congressmen to speak on his behalf to the Ways and Means Committee, which assigned committee seats. The courtly Virginia gentleman then prodded his friend on that committee, Fred Vinson of Kentucky, to push his nomination, which came in early March. After a mere two years in the House, Judge Smith thus joined its most powerful committee.[4]

The Rules Committee had changed significantly since its creation in 1789. For nearly a century, Rules had remained a select committee, with the largely inconsequential task of recommending that the new session adopt the old procedural rules. Then, at the end of the nineteenth century, the Republican leadership gave it new powers to counter special interests on revenue and tariff bills. Under the czarlike sway of Speakers Thomas B. Reed and Joseph G. Cannon, Rules became one of the most influential and sought-after committees because it could bring specific measures to the floor more easily. During the Wilson and Coolidge administrations, Rules functioned as an integral arm of the party in power, whether that meant supporting Wilson's expansive programs or suppressing embarrassing investigations of the Harding administration. Shortly before Smith ascended to Rules, the outgoing Republican chairman, Bertrand H. Snell of New York, defined the committee's role as acting "as far as possible, for the protection of the administration and the administration programs." The committee had always had the potential ability to obstruct legislation, given its power to strangle pending bills. Only when given a rule could any measure reach the full House for consideration. But up to this time Rules had consistently acted as a "traffic cop," flashing a green light to all major administration-backed bills to reach the House floor while at the same time stopping antiadministration bills.[5]

Initially, the committee cooperated closely with Roosevelt and his New Deal recovery program. Its Democratic leadership—

Bankhead of Alabama and Edward W. Pou of North Carolina—
viewed the committee as a tool by which the president could
expedite the essential parts of his emergency proposals. With the
exceptions of the Glass-Steagall banking bill and the economy
bill, both of which did not require Rules action, every other major
New Deal measure in this early period received the committee's
complete cooperation. In fact, during Roosevelt's first hundred
days, from March to June, the Rules Committee shielded more
bills from crippling floor amendments than it had in any previous
session.[6]

At first Smith, the Virginia delegation, and the rest of the
southern Democrats as a group backed the administration's anti-
depression measures. As long as Judge Smith and his southern
colleagues believed that they were being asked to support proposals essential to the nation's and to their region's recovery, they did
so. Like Virginia's Clifton A. Woodrum, a member of the Appropriations Committee, these representatives viewed the 1933 and
1934 sessions as "a testing time for us Democrats as to whether or
not we are going to back up the President in a crisis." In these first
two years, Smith backed such fundamental New Deal measures
as the emergency banking bill, which briefly closed down the
nation's banks to verify their financial soundness; the Glass-
Steagall bill, which guaranteed small deposit accounts; the Home
Owners Loan Corporation bill, which made more than a million
loans to homeowners facing foreclosure; and the securities exchange bill, which established a commission to oversee stock
markets. On important regional issues like farm relief, Smith
joined the nearly 96 percent of all southern Democrats who supported the Agricultural Adjustment Administration bill. To secure this badly needed farm aid for his district, Smith either set
aside his constitutional scruples or failed to recognize the act's far-
reaching provision to regulate local production by the interstate
commerce clause.[7]

But during the New Deal's first Hundred Days, Smith's attention to national politics was often diverted to the southern part of
his home district for personal reasons. Here, his "brighter and
more efficient" younger brother, W. Worth Smith, Jr., needed
help to mount a strong primary campaign as he sought the Democratic nomination for governor. Despite being state senator from
Louisa County, he lacked local support. For several years, the

county newspaper, the *Central Virginian*, had sharply criticized
him as unrepresentative of his constituency. While most residents
were "dirt farmers," Worth Smith was a successful attorney, no-
torious as the local debt collector. This was hardly an attractive
former career in the midst of the depression. Worse yet, he lived
outside the senatorial district and was president of a million-dollar
bank in Richmond. The newspaper concluded that "all sensible
people know that he can not have the time to mix and mingle
with the people of this District, ascertaining their wants and needs
regarding legislation for their betterment."[8]

Howard Smith shared many of his brother's "defects," but he
developed the attributes to overcome them. Both Smiths were
successful attorneys with driving political ambitions. And both
were wealthy bank presidents who polished distorted images as
typical farmers. Yet, the congressman, in contrast to his brother,
established himself in his district's preeminent city, where he carefully cultivated Democratic organization endorsement. Cautiously advancing his career, the elder Smith never moved faster
than the organization could carry him. In fact, his support for
Worth's gubernatorial campaign marked his only open defiance
of the state machine during nearly sixty years in politics.

Because Worth Smith was unable to garner the state Democratic machine's approval, he resorted to an unorthodox slate of
ideas that appeared opportunistic to critics. Smith raised a reform-
ist banner in the faint hope of appealing to voters who had just
supported President Roosevelt. In sharp contrast to his brother
and many other party leaders, Worth Smith endorsed repeal of
state Prohibition, lower automobile license taxes, reduced electric power rates, continuation of the state welfare program, the
end of expensive school textbook changes, and the abolition of
the poll tax. But as a candidate for the General Assembly, he had
petitioned and obtained the support of the Reverend David Hep-
burn, superintendent of the Virginia Anti-Saloon League. As
state senator, he had voted for the present automobile license tax
and for every bill increasing police patrol forces. Moreover, the
tax reductions he advocated threatened the newly constructed
state road system.[9]

The Louisa newspaper criticized Worth Smith's inconsistent
record, particularly his "fleeting interest" in education. To save
money, Smith had assailed frequent and unnecessary changes in

textbooks; when his opposition dried up, "his purported excite-ment . . . immediately subsided." Given the state senator's "sud-den and spectacular conversion" on these matters, the Louisa editor asked what the candidate really believed: "If his political and governmental thinking in the past is any guide of future per-formance, then the voters need to be told what assurance they have that his present position is the real one and the past record just a mistake; or whether the present attitude is a bid for votes, and the written record an indication of where his political think-ing really lies."[10]

Worth Smith's chief opponent was George C. Peery of Taze-well, former Ninth District congressman and member of the pow-erful State Corporation Commission. Peery attracted Byrd organization support when he heralded the Old Dominion as one state where "there has been no increase in State taxes, a balanced budget has been maintained and there has been no increase in the State's bonded indebtedness." He pledged to "continue this policy of sound government finance" during the depression. Party regulars, who opposed public debt as an article of faith, also ap-plauded Peery's promise to maintain the road system constructed during former governor Byrd's term on "the pay-as-you-go plan." With Byrd's blessing, Peery adopted a moderate wet position on Prohibition repeal when public opinion shifted to that view. In reversing his stand in order "to eliminate bootleggers," Peery robbed Worth Smith and Joseph T. Deal of Norfolk, the other antiorganization candidate, of their most telling issue.[11]

The organization also rallied around Peery to protect itself. Early in the campaign a Byrd supporter named F. McCall Frazier of Richmond wrote Senator Carter Glass that he thought Peery would win handsomely, but Worth Smith's "very active" chal-lenge to Peery constituted a serious threat to Byrd's carefully nur-tured leadership. "We feel that it is absolutely necessary to crush Smith and his corhots [sic]. If we should win by a small majority or even normal majority, we can expect more trouble next year and if our vote is not qualified, a double burden will fall upon Senator Byrd in 1934" when he would run for reelection.[12]

Although he remained a Byrd organization member, Howard Smith quietly supported his brother for governor. He campaigned in his usual manner, telephoning and writing a few influential officeholders in his own congressional district. In a circular to a

Fauquier County precinct captain, Smith praised his brother's "sound and progressive" platform. But the only plank the Judge specifically endorsed was the elimination of frequent textbook changes, which he called "a source of heavy expense." Aware of his delicate position in stepping outside the machine, Smith took care to commend his brother's opponents for their "excellent qualities." He nevertheless hoped the Fauquier Democrat could "see your way clear to support him in the coming primary."[13]

Smith's letter-writing campaign stunned the organization, which expected total loyalty. Harry Byrd was particularly taken aback. Writing to Glass a month before the primary, the senator confessed, "I was very much astonished to see, a day or so ago, that Congressman Howard Smith is sending out, on government stationery as per copy enclosed, literature advocating his brother for Governor." Byrd did not, however, seek retaliation. Years later, Smith recalled that "Harry was a little miffed for a time, but he got over it."[14]

Senator Byrd had little reason for alarm. Smith never again explicitly broke from the organization, though he often operated independently from it. Of more immediate interest to the Democratic machine, Peery gained an overwhelming victory in the August 2 primary. He carried every district in the state except the Eighth, where the popular Smith had marshaled sufficient support for his brother. Worth Smith finished third, capturing just 17.1 percent of the vote.[15]

Back in Congress, Howard Smith began to defy the national Democratic chieftains as well. The first sign that he would oppose the New Deal came in May 1933 when he voted to recommit to committee the national industrial recovery bill. By 1933 American industry produced only half the value of goods manufactured in 1929. To cut costs, businesses trimmed their work force, which in turn reduced the number of workers who could afford their finished products. Daily, the industrial slowdown became more evident. In association with the U.S. Chamber of Commerce, the administration proposed creating an agency which would encourage business and labor to sit down, industry by industry, in order to prepare codes setting production goals, fair prices for products, and minimum wages and maximum hours for employees. These codes were to be exempt from antitrust prosecution. At the insistence of Labor Secretary Frances Perkins, the bill explicitly stated labor's right to organize and to engage in collective bargaining. The bill also called for an appropriation of several billion dollars for a Public Works Administration (PWA) that the White House hoped would increase the purchasing power of workers faced with higher prices prescribed under the codes.[16]

A minority of southern Democrats, with Smith among them, opposed the industrial recovery measure because the bill conflicted with their interpretation of the Constitution and, not incidentally, their region's interests. Speaking for this group of twenty, Georgia Democrat E. Eugene Cox conceded that unemployment relief was imperative, but he condemned the public works bill for surrendering individual freedom and states' rights to federal control. The Constitution, he declared, specifically forbade Congress from delegating to the president powers it did not have, including the regulation of local commerce, production, and workers' hours and wages. As a second-term congressman, Smith refrained from speaking publicly at this time. Much later, he explained why he opposed New Deal recovery measures. Congress, he argued, warped the Constitution to control business activity through a misreading of certain provisions, especially the interstate commerce clause. Congress then simply abdicated its lawmaking responsibility to the president, who set up agencies that issued regulations with the force of law. "Through this process," he concluded, "the myriad of bureaucratic agencies, with their long tentacles of power and their hordes of subordinate federal officials, extend to every State, county, town and hamlet throughout the country."[17]

These disgruntled southern Democrats believed that the bill threatened southern industrial growth. Writing months after its passage, Virginia's senior senator, Carter Glass, characterized the measure as "unconstitutional, and tyrannical and literally brutal" because its provisions for hours and wages harmed individual initiative and the small industries of the South. Only the congressional delegations from Virginia and Florida had a majority voting for recommittal, and the Old Dominion supplied more than one-third of the southern Democratic votes for returning the bill to committee.[18]

Economic and social conditions in Virginia permitted its representatives to hold steadfast to the principles of a balanced budget and low government spending. Historian Ronald Heinemann has concluded that "Virginia was relatively better off than most other states during the depression." Its agriculture survived because the diversity of crops—perishables, cotton, and peanuts in the Tidewater, orchards, dairying, and wheat in the Piedmont, and tobacco in the Southside—kept farming afloat when the price of one crop sank. Moreover, many Virginia farms produced enough to feed their owners. In industry, Virginia had a substantially smaller proportion of its population than the rest of the states employed in factories, and many of its products were consumer goods indispensable even to destitute people—food, clothing, and cigarettes. Financially, too, the Old Dominion handled the emergency well, losing few banks and commercial institutions. The "mildness" of the state's depression prevented long breadlines, mob action against judges and sheriffs, or milk spilled by angry farmers. The poor and the blacks who suffered most had no political voice due in large measure to the continuing machinations of the Byrd regime, and the state lacked a powerful middle class pushing for relief. As a result, politicians such as Smith could take strong stands against the New Deal.[19]

In late January 1935 Smith broke openly with the Roosevelt administration for the first time. Although the president was under attack from the conservative Liberty League to abandon what it regarded as his unconstitutional, spendthrift, and prolabor policies, he paid more attention to the liberal critics led by Huey Long of Louisiana. Buoyed by his party's tremendous victory in the 1934 election, Roosevelt launched a second New Deal, pledging that the federal government would assume direct responsibility for the economic well-being of all Americans. The key proposal of the president's new plan was the $4.8 billion work-relief program contained in the emergency relief appropriation bill. Roosevelt wanted to give jobs to 3.5 million unemployed laborers, who would be paid more than those on relief but less than the average wage of workers in private industry. After the Appropriations Committee cleared the bill, the administration sought to have the Rules Committee assign a gag rule, so that on the House floor no representative could amend the measure, alter the dollar amount, or specify the purpose of the funds.[20]

In his first major address on the New Deal, Howard Smith, ever the Virginia gentleman and politician, paused to voice his general support of the popular president before attacking the appropriation bill. Conceding that he had endorsed gag rules in the past, he censured this particular limitation on the deliberative process as clearly unconstitutional. Blaming his colleagues, Smith scorned the bill as "a clear and complete abdication by the Congress of the United States of its functions to the President." He then reminded the House of the recent "hot oil" case (*Panama Refining Co. v. Ryan*), in which the Supreme Court had invalidated the petroleum code of the National Recovery Administration (NRA) on the ground of excessive delegation of legislative power to the executive. Smith asserted that the Court had prohibited Congress from delegating "into any other person or body its constitutional duty to lay down the legislative policies of the Government in specific terms." He later explained that the work-relief proposal was decisive in alerting conservatives that the president believed economic conditions were so poor that "desperate," and often illegal, innovations would be pursued.[21]

Smith's stance against the emergency bill signaled his willingness to adopt a minority position when labor legislation was under consideration. Ninety percent of the southern Democrats, including a majority from Virginia, supported the bill. Leading Virginia newspapers also backed the measure. The *Richmond News Leader* concluded that, although the economy in the past year was "undeniably" improving, additional relief monies might be necessary anyway. After signing the act, Roosevelt created the Works Progress Administration (WPA), which provided needed jobs for unskilled and skilled workers and professionals.[22]

Although Judge Smith resisted the WPA, he did support a few of the president's new proposals, including social security. As the nation moved from an agricultural to an industrial economy, the traditional ways of aiding poor and unfortunate individuals proved inadequate. Instead of crowding them into institutional buildings as in the past, state and federal governments gradually assisted needy people through cash relief, workmen's compensation, military service pensions, and, in some cases, retirement benefits. But the United States lagged behind other industrial countries in helping the destitute. The public still believed that individuals had the ability and responsibility to care for themselves. Skilled workers did not press for broad government protection because they had been bought off in the 1920s by relatively high wages and new job benefits. In addition, the influential private insurance industry lobbied against further government involvement. [23]

When the depression struck, American attitudes toward a federal government social insurance program changed dramatically. With one-fourth of Americans unemployed and one-sixth subsisting on direct relief or work relief, the public demanded emergency legislation. A number of panaceas received widespread popular support, especially the one offered by Dr. Francis E. Townsend, who wanted to fuel the economy by giving every senior citizen $200 a month. [24]

The popularity of Townsend's proposal spurred Roosevelt to tackle the problems of old-age dependency and unemployment compensation. In the spring of 1935 the president proposed a more modest plan that established a contributory old-age and survivors' insurance fund and a federal-state plan of distributing payments to the unemployed. The federal government would make quarterly payments equal to half the amount spent by the state, up to $30, to persons at least sixty-five years old and to the blind. Unemployment benefits would be paid from a federal payroll tax on employers with at least eight workers, beginning at 1 percent of annual wages in 1936 and rising to 3 percent. In presenting the bill, Roosevelt explained its limited nature: "We can never insure 100 per cent of the population against 100 per cent of the hazards and vicissitudes of life, but we have tried to frame a law which will give some measure of protection to the average citizen and to his family against the loss of a job and against poverty-ridden old age." [25]

Neither Smith nor any of the other Virginia congressmen spoke during the floor debate. But some insight into Smith's reasons for favoring social security can be gained from conservative Robert L. Doughton of North Carolina, one of the few southerners who participated at length in the deliberations. He pointed out that the bill did not overturn the American free enterprise system: "While it is designed to enhance very greatly the security of the American worker and to provide a larger measure of social justice, it does so within the scope of our existing economic order. In no way does it . . . upset our established economic and political institutions." Doughton also observed that the social security program did not interfere with the state governments' "primary responsibility" in caring for dependents. In fact, the federal program would be administered through the states. Smith may also have been attracted to the bill because it set forth how the funds were to be spent; excluded farm laborers, which helped his district's farmers, including himself; and confined public assistance to the small number of truly indigent. When Smith voted for the bill, which passed overwhelmingly, he was in the mainstream of southern Democratic thought, though four of his Virginia colleagues dissented.[26]

In contrast to Smith, the Virginia state legislature dragged its feet on social security. Under the national law, states had to establish their own old-age assistance programs to qualify for matching federal funds. The Old Dominion's General Assembly studied the question for two years and finally determined that almost $3 million annually would be needed to pay the state's share. The retiring governor, George C. Peery, left the knotty financial problem to his successor, James H. Price. Price, a New Dealer, pushed the state's companion social security program through the legislature by means of budgetary juggling. But the governor could only wrangle a modest program from the tight-fisted Assembly, which funded just one-third of the $30 a month that the federal government allowed. In March 1938 Virginia became the last state to secure federal support for old-age assistance.[27]

The conservative-minded Smith went as far as he could go ideologically in supporting social security. When Roosevelt next moved to assist organized labor in June, the Judge could not contain his ire. In the wake of the Supreme Court's decision of May 1935 to strike down the NRA, the president responded by embracing the Wagner-Connery labor disputes bill. Also known as the national labor relations bill, this measure strengthened the right of workers to bargain collectively, outlawed certain unfair practices of employers, created machinery to insure fair treatment of unions, and allowed workers to compel their employers to negotiate with freely chosen representatives. To Smith, these rights to be extended to labor transcended the limits of the Constitution. As a self-proclaimed guardian of that sacred document, he announced without hesitation: "Mr. Chairman, I am opposed to this bill because it is obviously unconstitutional; because it forbids the courts of the land to consider the controversies arising under it under the usual rules of evidence and procedure pertaining to other litigations; because it abrogates the right to contract; and because I believe it holds out false hopes that cannot be realized under the present Constitution, and which will lead to strife rather than peace."[28]

Smith could speak boldly because he thought the Wagner bill would no more survive judicial scrutiny than its predecessor, the National Industrial Recovery Act. Both proposals, in his mind, illegally relied on an overly broad definition of the interstate commerce clause to control labor disputes. He reasoned that only through a constitutional amendment could Congress acquire authority over national labor problems. Pointing to Virginia's coal industry, Smith observed that the labor disputes bill would affect only the coal mine operators who might restrain interstate coal trade but not the striking miners who might cause the same result. Here, as elsewhere in the New Deal years, Smith relied on his strict and unchanging view of the Constitution to support his own socioeconomic notions, which were oriented toward business.[29]

Smith's pronouncements did not go unchallenged. Liberal Ohio Democrat Charles V. Truax, for example, denounced the bill's opponents as "assassins of labor, exploiters of labor's toil and despoilers of the meager benefits that might accrue to labor." He argued, in effect, that Smith and others opposed the bill for its intention to aid the producers, not the consumers, of wealth. In the end, the House passed the Wagner bill by a voice vote, and the president signed it. In 1937 the Supreme Court, disagreeing with Smith's logic, ruled that the act was indeed constitutional.[30]

Despite this setback, the determined Smith searched for new ways to attack organized labor's newfound power. Unexpectedly, his chance came in mid-1935 when Congress considered abuses by utility companies. After an intensive investigation, the Federal Trade Commission demonstrated pervasive manipulation and fraud by large investors in gas, light, and power companies. These investors had set up dummy corporations to control and extract profits from operating utilities, forcing consumers to pay higher rates. The administration attempted to stop these excesses by presenting a bill which provided federal supervision and a "death-sentence" clause which would dissolve holding companies without an economic justification. By June 1935 Montana senator Burton K. Wheeler had steered the bill through the Senate. In the House, Texas Democrat Sam Rayburn held extensive hearings but could not prevent conservative frustrations with the New

Deal from erupting. The House then attached an amendment deleting the controversial death-sentence provision.[31]

To reinstate the provision, the administration sought a roll-call vote putting representatives on record as supporting or defying the still-popular president. This tactic required a special rule from the House Rules Committee. Here was the opportunity the Virginia representative awaited. Howard Smith and his hot-tempered colleague Gene Cox of Georgia teamed with the new conservative Rules chairman, Tammany Democrat John J. O'Connor, in refusing the administration's request. Rules had begun to abandon its traditional role as party agent; it was embarking instead on a thirty-year period as an agent of opposition.[32]

The warfare over the death-sentence clause brought dozens of utility lobbyists and millions of utility-inspired letters to Washington. The Rules Committee reported in February 1936 that "the campaign to influence utility holding company legislation was probably as comprehensive, as well managed, as persistent and as well financed, as any in the history of the country." This pressure fortified conservative resolve against the measure and sparked the first successful defiance of the New Deal. More than half of all Democrats and 60 percent of the southern Democrats fled party ranks. These rebels eventually forced a compromise on the utility bill that excluded the controversial death-sentence section. The president nevertheless signed the measure. According to historian James T. Patterson, this episode was the first evidence that a durable conservative coalition had formed in the House.[33]

By the spring of 1936, Smith had decided to use the lobbying drive as a means of reducing the political clout of labor. He introduced a bill requiring the registration of all Washington lobbyists seeking to influence legislation or the outcome of an election. Under the bill's terms, lobbyists had to disclose their employers, how much they were paid, and how their funds were spent. In March, Smith insisted the proposal did not stop a lobbyist from seeing legislators. Declaring that only a "dishonest person" could object to his bill, he pointed out that the measure was patterned after legislation already enacted—the Corrupt Practices Act— which required congressional candidates to file a financial statement on their campaigns.[34]

Superficially, the bill dealt with aggressive lobbying of all kinds. But Smith was unconcerned with business lobbying, which he believed could evade the measure's strictures. For years the Judge himself had worked closely with the lobbyists of the National Association of Manufacturers and similar business groups. In 1936 his principal target was the newly created Committee for Industrial Organization (CIO), headed by John L. Lewis, who wanted to match industry strength with industrywide unions. Moreover, Smith had an active labor constituency in the northern part of his district, and he wanted to prevent well-financed labor candidates from running against him.[35]

Most House members supported the bill's apparent intent. But its vague language aroused a long discussion and a series of amendments to clarify its purpose. Some representatives feared that disclosure would unfairly burden poorly funded labor unions, while privileged interests could hire "clever specialists" to write evasive legal reports. The House, however, was eager to establish any form of control over lobbying, and it passed the bill at the end of the month. But when the conference report appeared to exempt utility and not labor lobbyists, the House rejected the "infamous" Smith bill just six weeks later. For the next few years, the Judge reintroduced his antilobbying bill only to have it stall in the Judiciary Committee. Finally, in 1940, the House set up a committee to investigate lobbying abuses, which produced no lasting change.[36]

As Congressman Smith carried on his lobbying fight, an embarrassing investigation of a construction firm in his home district forced him into battles on two fronts. In 1930 the Kanawha Power Company of West Virginia, a Union Carbide–owned utility, paid the Charlottesville firm of Rinehart and Dennis $4.2 million to divert water from the New River in West Virginia to its generating plant located thirty miles southwest of Charleston. The most difficult task required the firm to blast a tunnel through Gauley Mountain. When the Federal Power Commission pursued allegations of contractual collusion involving several state power companies, the Kanawha utility ordered Rinehart and Dennis to finish the two-year project before the federal government stepped in.[37]

As directed, the Charlottesville firm sped up drilling, but it disregarded human safety. The largely black labor force recruited from the South faced shameless exploitation. Rinehart and Dennis ignored the contract provision calling for the wet-drilling method of cutting through pure silica ore, even though this well-known procedure reduced the incidence of silicosis, an incurable lung disease caused by silica dust particles. The company also refused to buy masks "for all the niggers on the job," citing the protective device's expense. Rinehart and Dennis realized that unprotected workers would succumb to the disease, but it thought the disease would take ten to twenty years to develop, long after the job was finished and the company was out of range of West Virginia courts. The only concession given to the workers' health was a fan blowing air through a tube running to the outside of the mountain. But rocks had ruptured the twenty-four-inch canvas tubing repeatedly, rendering it useless. As a result, the dust-laden air went unventilated. One worker recalled that visibility was so hampered "you had to *bump* a man before you'd know where he was at." According to company records, the dust drove away one-fifth of the three thousand workers who worked inside the mountain within a week, and one-half of them left in two months.[38]

For their trouble, the workers received as little as twenty-five cents an hour, nearly all of which went back to the company in payment for housing, heat, and food. Crews who complained to the company doctor of chest pains or shortness of breath received placebos—bitter-tasting soda tablets called "little black devils." Many of the workers paid the company with their lives. By 1936 nearly five hundred laborers had died from silicosis, and fifteen hundred more suffered from its debilitating effects. Independently conducted autopsies revealed gritty lungs with silica content five times greater than the percentage usually found in the average adult male. Many of the bodies were dumped in a single trench with cornstalks as their grave markers. When the story reached Capitol Hill, New York's Sicilian gadfly, Vito Marcantonio of the House Labor Committee, charged the Charlottesville company with committing "the greatest industrial tragedy of the Twentieth Century." He promised a full-scale investigation by the Committee on Labor.[39]

Rinehart and Dennis launched an all-out campaign to save itself. The company's president, P. H. Faulconer, denied all allegations: "We did everything within our power to make the working conditions of our employes free from hazard, and we saw to it that any one who died while in our employ received a decent burial, with every grave marked and recorded for future identification." Faulconer insisted that only forty-eight workers had died from lung-related diseases, "unusually low for projects of this character." To avoid legal penalties, the company tampered with juries and bribed three hundred complainants with just $130,000 of the $4 million sought; and half of the out-of-court settlement went to lawyers. Fearful of future prosecution by silicosis victims, Rinehart and Dennis also lobbied successfully for a West Virginia compensation law for lung-damaged victims. Even the law represented a cruel joke to the victims because it stipulated that compensation was due only to those who had worked two years in the same job, but no man worked on the tunnel for more than eighteen months. Throughout the uproar, the company maintained that the alleged victims were bilking the firm with false claims. The linchpin in the company's defense came when its executives convinced their congressman, Howard W. Smith, to use the Rules Committee to stop the Labor subcommittee's preliminary investigation. In the spring the Rules Committee obliged, sidetracking the authorizing resolution. As a result, the Charlottesville firm emerged unscathed from the sordid affair.[40]

With the silicosis issue silenced, the Judge resumed his efforts on the national scene, the arena he always preferred. He tackled the problem of dangerous immigrants. Though immigration had fallen sharply since the onset of the depression, Smith was concerned about the German Jews and Italians still arriving in 1936. To him, they posed threats as union organizers, potential subversives, and violent criminals. Smith was not alone in his views. After the Committee on Immigration had completed an investigation of aliens engaging in unlawful political activities, Chairman Samuel Dickstein of New York declared of "foreign visitors" that "almost all of them are here more or less in the role of foreign spies to spread un-American propaganda." He presented a bill authorizing the secretary of labor to expel any alien who disseminated anti-American statements.[41]

In mid-June, Smith insisted the bill did not go far enough. Borrowing liberally from another immigration measure proposed by North Carolina Democrat John Kerr, he recommended deporting any alien found guilty of possessing narcotics or dangerous weapons, of assisting the illegal entry of another alien, or of moral turpitude. Smith decried the practice of House members who habitually agreed with him that aliens were undesirable but would not vote for alien exclusion or deportation. His appeal to the Immigration Committee's "good faith" went for naught because Dickstein was interested in saving his own antiradical bill. Dickstein contended that Smith's amendment, dealing primarily with criminal aliens, was not germane. Smith's effort to show how his amendment was pertinent died when the speaker pro tempore ruled that it "relates to entirely different classes than the class covered by the pending bill." When Judge Smith appealed the chair's decision, the House sustained the ruling.[42]

Other representatives indicated only weak support for the Virginian's amendment and objected to the intent of Dickstein's bill. New York Democrat Emanuel Celler worried that the bill struck at fundamental guarantees embodied in the Bill of Rights. He also warned that the bill's enactment might lead to a fascist government in America. Ultimately, the bill lay over to the next congressional session, when Smith reintroduced it. While a handful of anti-immigrant laws passed Congress in 1937, Smith's measure remained bottled in the Immigration Committee.[43]

Though Howard Smith's legislative endeavors repeatedly caused headaches at the White House, the Virginia congressman showed no qualms about capitalizing on President Roosevelt's popularity in the 1936 election. At the annual Jackson Day dinner in Charlottesville in January, Smith prophesied that history would rank Jefferson, Jackson, and Roosevelt "as the great defenders of human rights." He deplored the Supreme Court's recent decision overturning the New Deal's Agricultural Adjustment Administration and praised the Home Owners Loan Corporation for saving more than eleven thousand Virginia homes. Smith's efforts to latch on to the president's coattails even extended to his widowed eighty-seven-year-old mother, who remained fiercely anti-Roosevelt just months before her death. When the Judge held a summer rally at his farm for two hundred campaign workers, he warned her to be silent, especially since the president was to visit Jefferson's home, Monticello, at his behest on Independence Day. Smith's daughter remembered the slightly embarrassing outcome: "My grandmother couldn't wait for them to get there. She loved to talk politics, and she loved men. She'd sit out on the front porch with Daddy, and he'd say don't say anything, don't talk about Roosevelt. She promised him she wouldn't. And the next thing, she'd have all these men standing around, and she'd be saying, 'That man in the White House . . . if he doesn't mind his business. . . .' She'd just be giving him hell." Because Roosevelt's public appeal outweighed the animosity Tee Smith felt toward him, candidate Smith continued rebutting Republican charges that the president had neglected promises dating to 1932. At an October rally in Fluvanna County, Smith remarked that the primary complaint of his Republican opponent, John Locke Green of Arlington, was that the president's policies "have been carried out and made law."[44]

Because the contest was, at bottom, a test of party loyalty and not a fight over local issues, Smith, the organization's choice, had little trouble winning reelection in the heavily Democratic district. He captured better than three votes out of every four. Smith and Roosevelt received much the same number of votes in each locality in 1936, indicating that the voters had not turned against the president or their local Democratic tradition.[45]

With another election behind him, Smith joined growing congressional resentment over organized labor's drive for power in the spring of 1937. By April the CIO had shut down U.S. Steel and General Motors by using the new, paralyzing tactic of the sitdown strike, in which employees occupied their factories. This method of securing union recognition and economic benefits horrified conservative Democratic representatives. Martin Dies, Jr., of Texas, blamed aliens and unionists for the unrest and demanded an investigation. Like many other southerners, he did not believe that labor should organize on equal terms with large corporations. The proposed investigation, which the unpopular Dies claimed would not affect unions, cleared the Rules Committee in an effort to embarrass President Roosevelt. But the revolt was quickly beaten back; the House soon defeated the Dies resolution convincingly.[46]

This setback did not deter Smith. Within days, he pushed for Judiciary Committee approval of his February bill to preserve state control of labor relations. He took advantage of what he believed was the Supreme Court's willingness to permit either the federal government or the states to set minimum wage levels. In particular, he pointed to the decision of *Kentucky Whip & Collar Co. v. Illinois Central Railroad Co.* (January 4, 1937), in which the Court ruled that any state could prohibit the introduction of convict-made goods from other states. Smith interpreted that opinion as barring goods made under any conditions, including minimum wage laws, that a state found objectionable. Hence, in his view, a state could enact laws "to protect itself against any goods or practices [of] which it disapproves." By passing local laws, backed by federal enforcement, states could maintain their independence of the national government. Smith did not mention the possibility that a multitude of different regulations could arise, creating havoc for interstate commerce. Nevertheless, his appeals were unavailing, and his bill went nowhere.[47]

Other events in 1937 dramatically undercut the New Deal and strengthened the position of those who had already broken with the White House. Early in the Seventy-fifth Congress, prospects seemed excellent for a broadly written bill to shorten the workday and to establish minimum wages. The president and his party had just scored an overwhelming triumph at the polls, partly on the pledge to better the lives of workers. Roosevelt had intended to introduce his wage-hour measure early in the new session, but he suddenly changed his mind and submitted a court-enlargement plan to bend the Supreme Court to his economic recovery program. Over the preceding months, the justices had sent New Dealers reeling with decisions that severely restricted federal control over manufacturing, mining, and agricultural production. Roosevelt wanted to add justices to the Court who were more amenable to his economic philosophy.[48]

For irreconcilable foes of the New Deal, the court reform plan threatened to eliminate the only constitutional means of containing administration excesses. North Carolina Democrat Josiah C. Bailey warned the Senate that the plan foreshadowed a "political revolution" that would make the president a "dictator." Bailey was soon inundated with sympathetic letters. One South Carolina woman wrote: "Bully for you! Oh bully for you! Don't, don't let that wild man in the White House do this dreadful thing to our country." Writing years later, Smith echoed Bailey's concern, asserting that Roosevelt's court-packing attempt was "a very important chapter in the history of the erosion of constitutional principles" because it brought to the public's attention the president's course of aggrandizement.[49]

Although the proposal was not enacted, Smith believed that it intimidated the Court into endorsing controversial New Deal programs. In one sense, as Smith suggested, Roosevelt lost the battle but won the war. While Congress considered judicial reform, Justice Owen Roberts switched sides, and the Court suddenly reversed direction to uphold a state minimum wage law, the Wagner Act, and social security. Within three years of the packing fight, the Court had five vacancies, which allowed the president to name a majority to its bench. But viewed from another perspective, Roosevelt lost the war. The struggle had sacrificed Democratic party unity and solidified the anti–New Deal coalition determined to block more liberal bills. Historian William E. Leuchtenberg concluded, "The new Court might be willing to uphold new laws, but an angry and divided Congress would pass few of them for the justices to consider."[50]

When Congress erupted over the court-packing scheme, Roosevelt withheld the wage-hour bill in the hope that Democrats would unite and back court reform. It became evident by May 1937 that this strategy had not worked, prompting Democrats Hugo L. Black of Alabama and William P. Connery, Jr., of Massachusetts to set the wage-hour, or fair labor standards, bill before Congress. To hasten action, the labor committees of each house held joint hearings.[51]

By the end of the summer, however, many House members were not receptive to labor legislation. Fearful that the recent successful strikes might spread to their states, southern Democrats like James F. Byrnes of South Carolina had become impatient with the president's reluctance to assist employers who had experienced strikes. These congressmen also resented the House passage of an antilynching bill, as well as the administration's hesitancy to renew commodity crop loans to cotton farmers. Conservatives declared that they had no desire to stay on Capitol Hill if it meant approving more New Deal legislation. Noting the decline in the unemployment rate, they argued that the emergency was all but over, making unnecessary further debate on New Deal bills on wages and hours, farm relief, and tax reform.[52]

The fate of the wage-hour bill rested with the Rules Committee, which had to grant a special dispensation to the measure. But three southern Democratic members saw the bill as a threat to their region. One of them, Cox, savagely attacked the bill's apparent chief beneficiary, organized labor: "I warn John L. Lewis and his communistic cohorts that no second 'carpetbag expedition' in the Southland, under the red banner of Soviet Russia . . .

will be tolerated." His confederates, Judge Smith and Dies, implored two new southern Democrats on Rules—William J. Driver of Arkansas and J. Bayard Clark of North Carolina—to side with them and the Republicans in blocking labor standards. More than 150 northern Democrats attempted to call a party caucus to pressure Rules to release the bill. The plan collapsed when two dozen other Democrats did not attend. The *New York Times* described the legislative history of the wage-hour measure as "that of the triumph of a minority." For the next three decades, southern Democrats and Republicans would hold a hammerlock on the Rules Committee, balking repeatedly at the release of liberal measures.[53]

After Congress agreed temporarily to shelve the wage-hour bill, Judge Smith entered the well of the House to educate his colleagues on the proposal's "many defects and inequalities." Assuming his typical courtly manner, he claimed to be particularly well suited to this task because he was a friend of neither business nor labor. He then suggested the bill needed more than the good intentions of its backers to assist the less fortunate, for the "road to hell" was paved with such intentions. What mattered, he explained, was the bill's language.[54]

Smith then laid out a carefully prepared four-point argument. First, he dismissed the notion that southern representatives opposed the wage-hour bill for reasons of regional self-interest, although the South paid lower wages. On the contrary, he warned of its potential to do "immeasurable injury to labor and to industry in every section of the country," especially because northern sweatshops could easily evade the law. Second, Smith alleged the bill was plagued with inconsistencies that favored some groups over others. For example, the bill unfairly exempted some seasonal work on perishable crops but did not exclude grain threshing or hay baling, which were usually done by independent contractors. Third, he denied that the 1936 national Democratic platform obligated members to support the federal wage-hour bill. Rather, the platform "committed the Democratic Party to joint State and Federal control of wages and hours." Finally, he beseeched the House not to use the excuse of hard times to abandon the system of government framed in the Constitution.[55]

Although Smith and other southern representatives generally

couched their objections to such New Deal legislation as the wage-hour bill in constitutional terms, the arguments often were intended to protect certain local practices and interests. In relying on the seemingly unassailable constitutional defense, Judge Smith continued a long-standing tradition dating to the antebellum period, when the South had sought refuge in the Constitution to safeguard slavery. In a 1940 book, southern-born political analyst Thomas L. Stokes pointed out that Roosevelt's reform program had "endangered the Southern system." To protect their society, southern Democrats naturally listened to their "real masters," whom he defined as "the business, financial and industrial interests which had fattened on the low-wage economy—both in the mill and on the farm—and who, over the years, continued to control the political machines." This analysis particularly fit Howard Smith, a wealthy bank president, an owner of three successful northern Virginia dairy farms and valuable real estate near Washington, D.C., and a friend of coal mine operators. He was also a pillar in the Old Dominion political organization run by Senator Byrd. Beyond economic self-interest, the constitutional defense permitted conservative southern Democrats to attract Republicans who cared chiefly about political survival.[56]

President Roosevelt had heard constitutional objections to his proposals before, so they gave him little pause. In November 1937 he pressed ahead for a strong labor measure, calling Congress into special session. But the Rules coalition of Republicans and southern Democrats continued to block action on the wage-hour bill. At this point, Labor Committee chairman Mary Norton of New Jersey filed a petition to discharge the bill from the Rules Committee, a difficult move that required majority approval, or 218 signatures. The administration tried to secure the signatures by making concessions on pet projects desired by the bill's opponents. But when the American Federation of Labor (AFL) came out for another version, the measure made no further headway. The confusion over which provisions the administration and unions really wanted enabled conservatives to recommit the bill in December.[57]

The labor standards debacle spilled over into the 1938 session. Once the AFL agreed to a compromise, the measure returned to Rules, where conservative committeemen again damned the bill's lack of a regional wage differential. At last, the White House employed some astute political strategy. It decided to delay further action on the wage-hour proposal until a referendum was held on it in Florida. When Claude Pepper triumphed easily in the Democratic senatorial primary, largely because of his wage-hour advocacy, the discharge petition quickly gained the requisite signatures. One conservative Kansas Republican acknowledged that "the Florida primary put the fear of God in the hearts of some of the Democrats" who had not backed the measure.[58]

The bill's final version provided for a single administrator in the Labor Department, the implementation of the forty-cent wage and the forty-hour week over a two-year period, and advisory wage boards that could determine exemptions and wage differentials from the act's provisions. When the bill cleared the House by a three-to-one margin, fifty-two of the fifty-six opposing Democrats came from the South. Smith, Cox, and Dies had resisted to the bitter end. Although the highly visible wage-hour fight failed, Smith's political capital had risen to new heights.[59]

Judge Smith's role in obstructing the Fair Labor Standards Act led the administration to intervene in his 1938 reelection bid. The recalcitrant congressman had already voted against PWA appropriations, court enlargement, coal conservation, and the end to farm tenancy but in hamstringing the wage-hour bill he brought on presidential retribution. By late 1937 Roosevelt had been stung too often by the opposition of such reactionary Democrats as senators Glass and Byrd of Virginia and Walter F. George of Georgia and Representatives O'Connor and Smith. At the urging of presidential aides, including Thomas G. Corcoran and Interior Secretary Harold L. Ickes, the president intervened in Democratic primaries, denouncing New Deal foes and anointing those candidates who had vowed unswerving loyalty to the administration. Against the advice of Democratic National Committee chairman James E. Farley, Roosevelt embarked on a western and southern campaign swing to stump for New Deal champions, such as Alben Barkley of Kentucky and Elmer Thomas of Oklahoma. But after an embarrassing setback in Iowa, the administration moved more cautiously in its celebrated purge of New Deal opponents. Roosevelt therefore chose not to come to northern Virginia to blast Smith personally. Instead, he aided Smith's Democratic primary foe by providing publicity assistance and by granting a leave to Assistant Attorney General Robert N. Anderson, a shrewd, antimachine Virginia Democrat, to serve as campaign director.[60]

Although some doubts remained as to whether William E. Dodd, Jr., Smith's challenger, was receiving full administration backing to purge Smith, CIO president John L. Lewis made it crystal clear that organized labor wanted to dislodge the incumbent. To avenge the delay of the wage-hour bill and the defeat of a contractor-"blacklisting" bill, the Non-Partisan League of the CIO, formed originally in 1936 to rally labor support for Roosevelt, targeted more than forty congressmen for political defeat in the 1938 elections. The list included Smith and nine other Rules Committee members. Because the CIO singled out several congressmen whom the Roosevelt administration also opposed, many people believed that individual congressmen disliked by labor were also picked by the president for political elimination. As a result, Smith seemed stamped for defeat by New Dealers.[61]

Much of the 1938 primary race revolved around the degree of New Deal allegiance claimed by each candidate. Dodd, a young historian and the son of the former ambassador to Germany, declared himself the one true Democrat, a loyal party man who would work for Roosevelt "at all times." But the politically inexperienced Dodd made a critical miscalculation. He thought that Eighth District voters were entirely supportive of New Deal policies because they had voted overwhelmingly for Roosevelt in 1936. This conclusion led him to paint the incumbent as a member of the "grasping reckless minority" threatening "to destroy the President." Dodd further charged in a flurry of press releases that "reactionary" Democrats such as Smith were really "Republicans in disguise" and members of the "I-hate-Roosevelt Club." Lambasting the Judge as a "One-Man-Gang" who committed an act of "high political immorality" in delaying the wage-hour bill, Dodd laughed off Smith's assertions of following the lead of famous Virginians, including Washington, Jefferson, Madison, and Monroe. The truth, the novice politician alleged, was that "the Banker" pursued his personal desires, not the wishes of most of his constituents.[62]

As a veteran politician, Judge Smith expected such allegations. What he had not expected was that his cousin Richard M. Smith, editor of the *Arlington Courier*, would publicize these allegations and promote his sharp-tongued challenger. Like Dodd, the *Courier* editor insisted that an Eighth District voter could not logically support both President Roosevelt and Representative Smith. When Richard Smith endorsed the New Deal and its apologist Dodd, the incumbent sought immediate revenge, ordering his cousin to repay a $500 personal loan. Editor Smith in turn printed the congressman's dunning letter on the front page of his paper and declared that no matter what the cost to his newspaper, he would continue to praise Roosevelt's programs. At the bottom of the page, there appeared a photostatic copy of a bank check which repaid Judge Smith in full. Fifty thousand copies of this July 14 issue were sent to all homes in the district. Within the next week, millions of Americans learned of the incident as the story was repeated by the United Press news service, newscaster Lowell Thomas, and radio personality Arthur Godfrey.[63]

Despite this national notoriety, Congressman Smith tried to maintain his usual low-profile campaign, confident of another primary victory. He circulated his campaign promises of 1930 through the district newspapers, most of which remained pro-Smith, and had his picture taken alongside a large American flag. This photograph had particular meaning as the Judge repeatedly implied that his opponent, who had recently returned from Germany, might have Nazi leanings. To counter the charges of the CIO and the man he dubbed an "unworthy" challenger, Smith insisted he was far from being a reactionary in the ordinary sense of the term. He recalled his broad cooperation with Roosevelt and claimed to have compiled a rather "progressive" record, in line with his beliefs in "sane expenditures" and limited government. Comparing himself with Dodd, Smith declared the chief difference between them was that his young foe planned to be an unthinking automaton instead of an independent-minded representative.[64]

The campaign reached an angry climax on July 28, when Interior Secretary Ickes openly attacked the Virginia congressman. Ickes denounced Smith for pretending to have been responsible for obtaining PWA funds for his home district. The secretary thought it more accurate to say that Smith "has obstructed, opposed and fought every PWA bill and now it looks like he is trying to muscle in and ride into office on the PWA coat tails." Dodd supporters enthusiastically received these remarks because Ickes was the first Roosevelt cabinet member to intervene directly in the primary fight. To them, these comments offered additional evidence that Dodd had New Deal approval.[65]

Smith angrily lashed back at Ickes and Dodd the next evening in a radio address. Originally, his speech "didn't have much blood and thunder in it." But in the midst of a sleepless night, Smith

What Will Pocahontas Say About It?

Courtesy of the *Richmond Times-Dispatch,* July 30, 1938

rewrote the address to condemn the interior secretary. After expressing astonishment at the personal accusations leveled against him, Smith somberly reviewed his congressional record. He claimed to have backed all public works projects in Virginia. The proof of his assertion, he maintained, could be found in the new buildings and bridges constructed during his congressional tenure. He offered no apology for voting against several public works funding measures because after these bills had become law, he had fought for Virginia's fair share. He closed his half-hour speech by accusing Ickes and Dodd's "little group of C.I.O. purgers" of undermining democratic government.[66]

Four days later, in an unprecedentedly large vote, Smith "swamped" Dodd more decisively than anyone had anticipated, 19,734 to 6,555. The energetic challenger lost his home precinct, his home county of Loudoun, the urban areas of Alexandria, Arlington, and Charlottesville, as well as every other county and city in the district. He carried only four precincts out of 219.[67]

District newspapers like the *Midland Virginian* and the *Fauquier Democrat* viewed the election as a repudiation of Roosevelt's administration and a victory for representative government. Ready to begin his fifth term, Smith also believed that he had received a mandate to continue undermining the New Deal. Two Washington papers cited other, more convincing, reasons for the congressman's triumph. The *Post* and *Times* singled out Judge Smith's longtime popularity as a politician, Dodd's political inexperience and unfamiliarity to district voters, and district resentment against the involvement of outside groups as factors in the incumbent's renomination. From the start, the contest had been unequal, and Howard Smith won principally because he was the incumbent in a district that consistently rewarded incumbency. Nonetheless, Smith was pleased and relieved. He had survived purge attempts from both the administration and organized labor, while waging a bitter intraparty struggle with Dodd.[68]

Smith's primary victory was a harbinger of greater conservative strength in the House. In the 1938 general election, Roosevelt suffered his worst reverses since 1932 as most southern Democrats won reelection and the Republicans nearly doubled their seats to 169. As the new session opened in 1939, both conservative groups seized the opportunity to block additional liberal legislation. The wage-hour fight had demonstrated that the Rules Committee could delay liberal bills for months, even if it could not always sink them. Another weapon had to be held in reserve. Massachusetts Republican Joseph W. Martin, Jr., a friend of Cox and chairman of the Republican congressional committee, had risen to House minority leader, and he was especially anxious to build party strength in this bleak political period. He "instituted new discipline" in the Republican ranks. A new Republican whip organization assigned key men in each section of the country to uncover party sentiment on upcoming measures. These legmen could assemble nearly all House Republicans within minutes to vote on critical bills. Martin recalled that whenever issues of mutual concern appeared, he "would go to Representative Howard W. Smith of Virginia, for example, and say, 'Howard, see if you can't get me a few Democratic votes here.' Or I would seek out Representative Eugene Cox of Georgia, and ask, 'Gene, why don't you and John Rankin [of Mississippi] and some of your men get me some votes on this?'" One statistical study of this conservative coalition reveals that in 1939 the group coalesced on six bills and won every time. And conservative clout only grew as the economic emergency diminished and Roosevelt's popularity dipped.[69]

The thirties had been a time of general testing for Smith. At the beginning of his congressional service, he had supported most of the emergency relief legislation of the Hoover and Roosevelt administrations. But as early as May 1933, he showed signs of breaking with Roosevelt to become part of the reactionary bloc opposing nearly all New Deal recovery proposals. By January 1935, with his speech against work-relief funds, he had become one of the early House irreconcilables. According to one analysis of congressional conservatism in the 1930s, "no one was more stringently opposed to the New Deal" than Judge Smith. Most significantly, the liberal Democratic leadership unwittingly had given him the position on Rules that assured his power for more than three decades.

Howard W. Smith was undoubtedly sincere when he found New Deal legislation unconstitutional. In this category, he put the Wagner Act, part of the Public Utility Holding Company Act, and the Fair Labor Standards Act. But these constitutional arguments were exactly those he believed most effective in supporting Virginia's business interests. It was surely no accident that he worked to block bills that would have cut into business profits. Under the guise of constitutionalism, Smith frequently spoke for Virginia employers who steadfastly opposed higher taxes to pay for relief programs, as well as such fundamental gains for workers as minimum wages, maximum hours, and collective bargaining. In the next few years, national preparations for war provided Smith with a new, greater opportunity to narrow his sights on organized labor and to hone his obstructionist techniques to a fine point.

CHAPTER 4

The War Years: Anti-Communist and Labor-Baiter

Early in this struggle I took my stand in opposition to the threatened labor dictatorship, and in retaliation these groups have repeatedly sought with every weapon at their command to eliminate me from public life.

Howard W. Smith (1946)

By the mid-1930s, international aggression combined with domestic economic uncertainty to drive the United States into a climate of antisubversive hysteria. As Europe succumbed to totalitarianism, many Americans began to perceive anything foreign as a threat to democracy. Aliens and Communists—often equated—became the targets of public paranoia; they were blamed for causing the depression and labor unrest and accused of promoting subversive ideologies. In actual fact, aliens constituted just 3.5 percent of the population, which meant their removal would not have affected the unemployment rate appreciably. Moreover, almost half of the aliens were over fifty years of age, and their literacy and crime rates, as well as their ventures into political radicalism, compared favorably with those of the native-born. But such facts as these were ignored or went unrevealed. The Justice Department received three thousand "spy tips" per day from alarmed citizens. Many states passed sedition legislation or enforced dormant criminal syndicalism laws. Virginia and Georgia even resorted to nineteenth-century slave insurrection statutes to harass aliens and Communists. When it became clear that the country supported federal control of suspected saboteurs, Congress responded by proposing more than one hundred antialien bills.[1]

Smith capitalized on the xenophobia by writing one of those proposals in the Seventy-sixth Congress. He stressed the urgent need for legislation because so many aliens threatened American government and society by participating in radical groups and labor unions. In March 1939, after first offering the bill to Chairman Martin Dies of the House Un-American Activities Committee, Smith himself put forward a comprehensive five-title bill to curb, punish, and prevent "some of those flagrant offensive, persistent, and organized subversive movements against our constitutional form of democratic government." The bill's most important elements were a military disaffection provision, the incarceration or deportation of undesirable aliens, the ban on attempts to overthrow the United States government, and the mandatory registration of aliens. Smith conceded that his bill had drawn heavily from others, including those of Democrats John W. McCormack of Massachusetts and Joe Starnes and Sam Hobbs of Alabama; but he believed his measure was more attractive because he had removed the objectionable features of competing bills. Anticipating the charge that his bill was nothing more than "red baiting," the Virginian agreed, saying that he advocated "fighting the devil with fire."[2]

Smith's antialien legislation became known officially as the alien registration bill for its seemingly harmless provision requiring the fingerprinting of all aliens entering the United States. The Judge saw "no reason why anyone should object to that." He even welcomed it for himself if he traveled overseas, though he had never done so. "It seems to me," he said, "if I were going to a foreign country I would like to be fingerprinted for purposes of identification."[3]

The Virginia gentleman saved his more persuasive language for winning the House over in July. Aware of tensions in Europe, Smith emphasized the bill's first part—"the very heart of the legislation"—which prohibited anyone from impairing the armed forces' loyalty or discipline. The military had grown concerned about the morale of soldiers and sailors since the Roosevelt administration had instituted pay cuts for military personnel. With resentment rising among the troops, Communists distributed leaflets calling for improved living conditions, civil trials, the right to receive working-class literature, and equality between officers and enlisted men. One leaflet urged American troops to join the Communist revolution: "You must refuse to fight in the interests of the bosses! When you are called into war, follow the example of the Russian soldiers and sailors. Use your military training against your real enemy, the capitalist class that exploits us and plunges us into wars! You must refuse to fight against the Soviet Union." For Smith, the military's public endorsement of this proposal was sufficient: "That is the request of the Army and Navy, and that is all I have to say upon title I of the bill."[4]

But this "military" section of the Smith bill, as the measure was popularly known, was only the capstone to an entire series of sanctions offered against aliens. The Judge, for example, demanded the expulsion of aliens committing narcotics violations. And of particular concern to the Virginian was an amendment to remove aliens convicted of carrying deadly weapons. "It is," Smith admitted, "a little difficult for me to understand why Members of Congress should object to the deportation of those folk who come here from foreign countries and indulge in the use of machine guns and sawed-off shotguns upon our population."[5]

In the most controversial section of his omnibus bill, the congressman summoned the federal government to deport aliens who had once belonged to a subversive organization. A legislative remedy was needed, Smith claimed, to counter the Supreme Court's protection of Communist aliens. He cited the recent *Strecker* decision, which held that an alien's past membership in the Communist party was not a valid reason for deportation. He wanted "to avoid the situation where a person who, upon being suspected, could resign from that organization and say, 'I was a member of that organization last week but I have resigned and you cannot deport me.'" The Court, Smith cautioned, would shield subversives like Harry Bridges, who epitomized the Virginian's fears. Bridges was an alien from Australia, a powerful labor activist among Pacific coast longshoremen, and a former Communist party member reputed to be still involved with the party. Smith closed his argument with an ultimatum that surely seized the House's attention: "Those who want to keep aliens in this country who favor the overthrow of this government by force ought to vote against the bill, and those who want to throw them out on their necks when they advocate the overthrow of this Government by force ought to vote for the bill."[6]

When Smith first submitted this bill in March, it had provided for the deportation of any alien who "advises a change in the form of the government of the United States," even if that change was supported legally and nonviolently. In addition, Smith strove to expel any alien who "engages in any way in domestic political agitation." Under this provision, an alien conceivably could be deported for attending a Democratic party rally or a union meeting that endorsed higher wages. Aliens abiding by these rules would be safe only for their first year of residence. After that, the Judge originally insisted they either leave America's shores or declare their intention to become citizens. Aliens who had to be deported would, in Smith's scheme, be consigned to concentration camps. The Judiciary Committee was unsympathetic, however, and scrapped these severe proposals.[7]

Despite the tempering of the measure's provisions, a handful of Democratic representatives challenged Smith's bill. Francis Walter of Pennsylvania reminded the House that additional legislation against subversion was unnecessary since McCormack had already shepherded a similar, more effective measure through Congress. Other representatives, such as John A. Martin of Colorado, took exception to the notion that an alien should be removed for having once belonged to an undesirable organization. He told his foe from Virginia that the clause would make Jefferson, Smith's hero, roll over in his grave, and that it was "an invention of intolerance contrary to every principle of democracy and abhorrent to the spirit of Christianity." The most stringent attack came from Lee E. Geyer of California, whose Los Angeles district included many longshoremen. He charged that Congress was being asked to pass, "under the guise of Americanism," this "Hitler measure" denying free speech. In his view, Howard Smith had written a "labor-baiting" bill that singled out labor unionists like Bridges, not because Bridges was an alien or a Communist, but because "he is going to bat for the underprivileged group" of longshoremen who worked for ten cents an hour.[8]

A more scholarly and trenchant criticism of the Smith bill came from Harvard's civil libertarian law professor Zechariah Chafee, Jr. In his 1941 book on the First Amendment, Chafee condemned the military disaffection provision, comparing it to the regrettable Espionage Act of 1917. He pointed out that the Communists had attracted few recruits among American troops. In the 1935 hearings before the House Committee on Military Affairs, General H. E. Knight conceded that there was little danger of disloyalty: "While there has been much effort for several years on the part of the subversive groups to penetrate the armed forces, it appears that their efforts have not met with a great deal of success." Chafee further noted that laws dating to the Civil War already proscribed conspiracy against the United States. These statutes provided up to a six-year jail sentence for conspiracy to overthrow the federal government by force, while the Smith bill punished those who stuffed controversial leaflets in battleship ventilators with ten years. Chafee concluded that the measure "proposes, in effect, to use a twelve-inch gun to kill a gnat."[9]

The antisubversion section also incurred Chafee's wrath. He interpreted this provision as "a full-fledged sedition law," the peacetime sequel to the "ill-fated" Sedition Act of 1798. According to the legal scholar, Smith had cleverly taken advantage of pervasive antialien sentiment to add this "anti-citizen section" to the bill. The Virginia representative had gone further than earlier legislators in limiting subversive action because he introduced as a federal crime the concept of guilt by association. An individual who had once belonged to a group subsequently found to support the violent overthrow of the government would be guilty of sedition, regardless of his own conduct. Chafee dismissed the notion that the section would be narrowly construed against "really dangerous men": "The truth is that the precise language of a sedition law is like the inscription on a sword. What matters is the existence of the weapon. Once the sword is placed in the hands of the people in power, then, whatever it says, they will be able to reach and slash at almost any unpopular person who is speaking or writing anything that they consider objectionable criticism of their policies."[10]

Because Smith best encapsulated the reigning nativist fears, columnist Kenneth G. Crawford of the *Nation* named the Virginian as "the Man of the Hour." According to the journalist, Smith undermined democratic government in ways that escaped all but the trained political eye. Crawford's analysis anticipated Smith's ideology and methods for the remainder of his career:

"Smith . . . is no publicity hound. He is content to work for the cause of social and political retrogression behind the scenes and let [Martin] Dies take the bows. His motivation goes deeper. He is a convinced, sincere, native American primitive who seems to believe with Hamilton, that the populace is a beast. The beast must be caged. Repressive measures against aliens, politically harmless because they have no vote, are a start in the right direction." The Smith bill was so repressive, Crawford wrote, that Jefferson's advocacy of periodic revolution would make the former president a criminal.[11]

In the end, Crawford was right in naming Smith "the Man of the Hour" because the Virginian's philosophy most accurately reflected the frightened atmosphere in Washington. On July 29, 1939, the House passed the bill. A California congressman observed, "The mood of this House is such that if you brought in the Ten Commandments today and asked for their repeal and attached to that request an alien law, you could get it." Another unnamed congressman declared that alien-baiting was "perhaps the best vote-getting argument in present-day politics."[12]

One year later, the Senate passed the bill after just minutes of discussion. President Roosevelt, aware that public opinion supported the bill, signed the measure into law on June 28, 1940. To soften the bill's impact, Roosevelt stressed that alien registration would be no "stigma" and that noncitizens "are entitled to and must receive full protection of the law." The Smith Act's passage did not make headlines, for it was just one among many antisubversive proposals enacted in these years. Other laws barred aliens from employment in the WPA, the Civil Service Commission, the War and Navy Departments, and virtually every other federal agency.[13]

The immediate and enormous task of the Smith Act was to register five million aliens by the end of the year. Every alien over fourteen years old had one hundred days to be fingerprinted at a neighborhood post office and to complete a questionnaire informing the government of his or her name, address, date of birth, sex, race, occupation, employer, relatives, physical appearance, citizenship, marital status, and military or criminal record. Aliens also had to divulge their whereabouts and future residency plans. The crucial question was whether an alien had been a member within the past five years of any organization supporting a foreign

government. Failure to register or false statements were to be punished by six months' imprisonment, a $1,000 fine, or both. [14]

The government went to extraordinary lengths to reassure
"needlessly terrified countless aliens" who feared separation from
relatives or dismissal from their jobs. Under the direction of liberal Philadelphia lawyer Earl G. Harrison, the Justice Department used the mass media, enlisted postal employees rather than
the police, and prodded employers to remind aliens of the registration requirement. Repeatedly, the federal government issued a
comforting slogan, "If you have nothing to hide, you have nothing to fear." The government went so far as to insist that registration was for the alien's "protection" from persecution by
unscrupulous native sons, including vigilantes, spy hunters, loan
sharks, and unprincipled attorneys. To ease the process, the government provided forms in a dozen languages. [15]

The government's registration drive, unprecedented in American annals, was accepted by many aliens but alarmed others.
Most foreigners, according to *Survey Graphic* magazine, regarded
the fingerprinting "merely as a matter of scientifically exact identification and were not upset by it." But grim stories appeared,
too. A middle-aged man who came from Nova Scotia at age four
had never been naturalized by his father. Neither the man's family
nor his employer knew he was an alien. "It was just carelessness,"
he admitted, "and now I am afraid it will spoil my home and my
job." An old Irish woman came to American shores "about 1890,
or mebbe longer." She wept and wrung her hands because she
knew nothing of her entry and had no legal documents to prove
she was a citizen. "Shure, we never bothered with the papers." [16]

Smith took an active role in reporting suspected subversives to
the federal government. In May 1940 he furnished J. Edgar Hoover's Federal Bureau of Investigation with information alleging
that certain employees of the Shenandoah National Park were
engaging in "subversive activities." A month later, the Virginian
turned in a Department of Agriculture employee and a Coast
Guard radio technician as Nazi sympathizers "loud in [their]
praise of the German way of life." In June 1941 Smith submitted
the names of bank employees who appeared to have "Communistic tendencies." The FBI acknowledged Smith's letters but did
little more than forward the names of the accused to other agencies. [17]

Despite Smith's own diligence in helping to round up radicals, the Smith Act unexpectedly served in the short term to soothe hysterical fears that might have erupted into antialien demonstrations. The federal law yanked the alien question from the hands of more intemperate local officials. Moreover, smooth alien registration relieved community tensions through the knowledge that "the federal government is handling these aliens." In effect, the statute for a time channeled xenophobia to acceptable outlets and dramatized alien loyalty. Criticism of the act largely dissipated in the wake of alien cooperation, public apathy, and the swift passage of the compulsory selective service law. The far-reaching consequences of the Smith Act on the Communist party and civil liberties would not be felt until the Cold War touched political nerves in the late 1940s.[18]

As liberal bureaucrats prudently implemented the Alien Registration Act, its author was busy safeguarding his own and his district's substantial farming interests. A probing congressional investigation by Indiana Democrat William T. Schulte had revealed that the twelve-hundred-member Maryland-Virginia Producers' Association had a nearly total "monopoly in the [milk] marketing field" in Washington, D.C. The milk it sold was more costly and below average in quality than milk available elsewhere. Moreover, certain members of the milkshed had been caught bootlegging "uninspected and unlicensed" cream and butter in the District of Columbia "under cover of darkness and by secretive and devious ways." The investigating committee therefore proposed opening the milkshed to higher-quality and cheaper dairy products from Pennsylvania, West Virginia, and midwestern states.[19]

On the House floor, the usually succinct Smith launched a long-winded rebuttal, alternating between counteraccusation and appeals to congressional fairness. He charged his "devious" dairy competitors with the embezzlement of $200,000 from their own companies. All he sought, he asserted, was for all dairy producers to be treated fairly, by which he meant that everyone would be inspected by the District of Columbia's health officer. But midwestern producers were fearful that a double standard might apply. Smith closed his case for the milkshed by describing its suppliers as "just a bunch of poor farmers . . . trying to take advantage of what this administration has been telling farmers to do, namely, to get a cooperative marketing association so that they will have some collective bargaining power." He did not mention the fact that the Maryland-Virginia group included such farmers as Smith himself and others with yearly incomes of up to $75,000. After a four-hour session of name-calling and parliamentary delays, Smith and his associates managed to shelve the bill. Their investment was safe.[20]

To Smith, collective bargaining should be allowed only to such businesses as dairy producers like himself, not to industrial workers. He waged a relentless assault on organized labor, convinced that it presented the second most potent threat—besides revolutionaries—to the American way of life. Publicly, he decried labor's gains on constitutional grounds. No interest group, he thought, including unions, should benefit at the expense of the general society.[21]

Two of his fellow southern Democratic congressmen recently shed further light on Smith's antilabor views. Thomas G. Abernethy, a Smith intimate from Mississippi, believed Smith regarded union activists as a lawless, subversive cancer on society: "They were troublemakers, and they go out on strike, lose that money, and they create trouble and confusion in the community and disturb the peace and shoot at you and burn your house down and anything in a strike." Carl Albert, the Oklahoma Democrat who later became Speaker of the House, thought Smith also had a fiscal motive in restraining, if not abolishing, unions. The Judge, according to Albert, saw organized labor as a symbol of the Roosevelt administration's spendthrift policies. The former Speaker concluded that the Virginian "looked upon labor as the principal force behind government spending. That's why he was against labor primarily. . . . He just looked upon labor as part of a movement that was trying to socialize the country and spend the country into bankruptcy." In Smith's view, labor's ill-gotten gains included the minimum-wage law, unemployment benefits, and an expanding social security program.[22]

After successfully sponsoring the antisubversion bill in early 1939, Smith decided to trim labor's powers by investigating the operations of the National Labor Relations Board (NLRB). He paid no attention to the two-year-old Supreme Court decision that had sustained the board's enabling legislation. He suspected the board had sanctioned such abuses as secondary boycotts and questionable union certification by the radical Congress of Industrial Organizations. Acknowledging bitter opposition to his plan, Smith pledged an unbiased attitude toward the board, even though he had voted against its creation. He promised the House that he would conduct "a careful, impartial investigation" of the nation's labor problem.[23]

Politically, the time was right for an antilabor investigation. Roosevelt's New Deal supporters in Congress had been whipped in the 1938 fall elections. As a result, southern Democrats regained influence in their party and allied themselves with conservative Republicans hostile to the president's emergency program. For the moment, the major labor unions declined to rescue Roosevelt. The AFL resented the board's apparent preference for the CIO and blamed the New Deal for having established the board. Even John L. Lewis of the CIO was feuding openly with Roosevelt. The NLRB investigation might serve, too, as a means to embarrass the president, dissuading him from running for an unprecedented third term in 1940.[24]

Conservatives across the country lauded Smith's idea. A Pennsylvania doctor wrote Smith that the board had unfairly ruled for the CIO and against the rival AFL, which was organized along traditional craft lines. The doctor also counseled Smith to move against the CIO because this more militant industrial union was "full of anarchistic perverts, mostly from the sewers of the South of Europe." Another writer offered to enroll Smith in the True Americans Society for trying to destroy collective bargaining. One of the Judge's longtime friends in The Plains, Virginia, praised his effort to stop organized labor.[25]

However, Smith's pledge of an impartial labor investigation did not reassure everyone. The House applauded when Labor Committee chairman Mary Norton—"a right fiery little gal," according to Smith—chided him as "the last man I would pick to pass on labor legislation," considering his long opposition to labor. She "begged" the House not to create a subcommittee that would infringe on her own standing committee. Other representatives, including Georgia Democrat Robert Ramspeck, termed Smith's proposal "a waste of money" since the Labor Committee had already been holding hearings for ten weeks on Wagner Act amendments. The *Nation* declared that Smith's investigation of the NLRB—"the keystone of the Administration's arch of social legislation"—was part of an organized effort led by the John Garner and Harry Byrd bloc which planned to "unleash its full power to sabotage the New Deal's domestic program." But in July 1939 the House approved Smith's resolution by a nearly two-to-one margin. The majority agreed with Eugene Cox of Georgia, who said that if the House waited for the Labor Committee to correct abuses, "we'll be here until Gabriel blows his horn."[26]

A week later, Smith brushed aside Norton's accusation. He recalled his votes for the Anti-Injunction Act, the Social Security Act, and the Railroad Retirement Act. Admitting opposition to the Guffey Coal and Fair Labor Standards acts, he contended that he had caused no hardship for his district's working people. Rhetorically clothing himself in Jefferson's "liberal" philosophy, Smith promoted himself as an independent congressman, one who had the fortitude to resist special interests like labor. He confidently invited his critics to "let historians of tomorrow say who best served God and man today."[27]

The critical issue before Smith's Select Committee to Investigate the National Labor Relations Board was its own membership. The faction that controlled the committee would write a report sympathetic to its views. President Roosevelt understandably wanted to protect the NLRB by naming three liberals from the Labor Committee, including Chairman Norton, ranking majority member Ramspeck, and ranking minority member Richard J. Welsh of San Francisco. But as usual, Smith was one step ahead of his opponents. When Speaker Bankhead informed him of Roosevelt's committee roster, the Judge issued a threat: Either the president recommend a conservative majority, or he would resign as committee chairman and issue a candid public explanation.[28]

The resulting committee demonstrated Chairman Smith's clout, because two of the remaining four members were antilabor, giving Smith the deciding vote. One of the two Republican members of the committee was thirty-nine-year-old Charles A. Halleck of Indiana, not known as a friend to labor. Although he had backed some New Deal measures, he had also voted for an investigation of sit-down strikes and against the wage-hour bill. The junior Republican committeeman was Harry N. Routzohn, who at fifty-eight was a freshman representative from Ohio. Once a probate judge and general counsel for the AFL's carpenter union,

Routzohn "really hated [the board's] enterprise and was really very nasty," according to NLRB chairman J. Warren Madden. The two New Deal Democrats, Arthur Healey of Massachusetts and Abe Murdock of Utah, voted against the creation of the Smith committee and served primarily as "buffer[s] to prevent the majority of the committee from running away and becoming too troublesome."[29]

Once the committee was appointed, Judge Smith assembled his staff, made preliminary inquiries about the labor board, and acquired pertinent documents. As chairman, Smith dominated this initial phase. The most important staff position was counsel, and at Senator Harry Byrd's suggestion he chose Edmund M. Toland, a forceful, wealthy Boston lawyer and former assistant attorney general who had practiced before the NLRB. Smith later called Toland "a bulldog of a prosecutor" who went after the board "like they were going after industry." With the committee's $50,000 appropriation, Smith hired twenty-two attorneys, opened regional offices, and retained 109 field examiners. He also distributed to employees, unions, and local officials sixty thousand questionnaires that asked police chiefs such loaded questions as whether they believed crime had increased since the NLRB's creation. In addition, Smith seized the board's thirty-eight hundred files. Many of the documents seemed damning. Halleck "couldn't imagine people writing such incriminating things and then letting them sit around there . . . we didn't have to put words in witnesses mouths. Hell, they'd written most of it down, for everybody to see." The committee also laid plans to hold hearings in cities across the country where antiboard complaints were numerous, but funds proved insufficient for travel outside Washington, D.C.[30]

The hearings were delayed for two months by Smith's bout with pneumonia. When they finally convened in the old House Office Building in December 1939, the chairman captivated the media with his distinctive "jet-black unruly hair," piercing dark eyes, and old-fashioned stiff wingtip collar. His first witness, newly appointed board member William M. Leiserson, had conferred at length with Smith in August because Smith had given the impression of knowing little about the Wagner Act. As the "President's messenger of moderation," Leiserson had been a highly respected federal railroad mediator and wanted to paint an honest picture of the board's conduct. But Smith had a completely different objective: "We knew what we were trying to do. We were trying to show up the cases that were extreme, where injustices had been done to people, so as to lay a foundation through this evidence to write an amendment to the law and then have the evidence to go to the floor and support the findings and we did that in the way you'd do it in a law case, for instance. You prepare your testimony and put your witnesses on the stand." When Leiserson tediously defended the agency's general conduct in addressing labor problems, such as labor spies, the blacklisting of nonunion workers, and labor violence, Toland suddenly distributed "juicier" board memoranda to the press for the afternoon newspaper editions. Conservative journalist David Lawrence reported that "the Smith Committee has had a sensational beginning and there are rumors of still further revelation."[31]

For his labor probe to gain additional momentum, Smith calculated that he needed popular support. He therefore adopted an uncomfortable role as speechmaker throughout the East. His first major national speech on the Wagner Act came in a December 1939 radio address aired by the National Broadcasting Company. After carefully establishing his committee's task, the chairman emphasized his desire "to conduct this investigation with the utmost fairness to all parties concerned." He then confessed to opposing the Wagner Act's enactment, but he now claimed that the law, if properly administered, could "perform a useful and a desirable purpose." Smith insisted that he was concerned chiefly with stopping labor disputes that slowed economic recovery, "no matter who is right and who is wrong." To the uninformed, the soft-spoken Virginia congressman hardly sounded like a labor-baiter.[32]

But Smith shrewdly recounted only examples of the board's ill-advised administration. One of the act's more controversial sections authorized the board to decide by an election among the employees which union was the appropriate representative in each collective bargaining action. This section, Smith declared, "looks like a very fair and democratic method." In fact, however, the board abused its trust: "We have been beseiged with complaints as to the practical operation of this provision by both labor organizations and industry, claiming that it is against the interests of the employer, of the employe and of the public, and that it promotes troubles rather than diminishes them." For example, the board on occasion had compelled an employer with two independent plants to accept the union preferred by the larger plant's employees, even if the smaller plant's employees were against that union. Smith also advised his listeners that business criticized the provision reinstating an employee with back pay for the entire time he was unfairly out of work. He ended by pleading for the "cooperation and assistance of all interested organizations and persons" as the only possible means to eradicate all these shortcomings.[33]

During this Christmas recess, Smith also arranged to see Roosevelt before the hearings resumed because "he and the President [were] not far apart in their ideas." Smith hoped to secure a presidential blessing for a modification of the Wagner Act. When the Virginian arrived at the White House at 9:30 A.M. on December 28, the president was still in bed eating breakfast. According to Smith's memorandum of the forty-minute meeting, Roosevelt agreed with most of his suggestions, including personnel changes and "clarifying" amendments to the law. As Smith departed, he told the president that his committee would draft amendments to the act, which prompted Roosevelt to reply, "Well, when you get the bill drawn I'd like to go over it with you." But Smith wondered how far the president "was going to go with me."[34]

The Smith inquiry soon attracted the liberal press, especially because a recent George Gallup poll indicated that for the first time a narrow majority of Americans now favored Wagner Act revisions. In January 1940 Russ Stone wrote in the New Republic that southern "diehard reactionaries" had shifted their reliance from the now undependable Supreme Court to a new method of controlling organized labor, the congressional investigation. After the Dies committee on un-American activities pioneered this technique, Howard Smith and others like him decided to develop this "inquisitorial" power as the means to destroy laws protecting collective bargaining. According to Stone, Smith counted on his investigating committee to allow southern industry to maintain its cheap labor force and, "in one bold offensive, wipe out the New Deal." The journalist noted this technique operated effectively because a committee possessed the power to hold hearings, to compel witnesses to attend, to expose an individual's actions, and to issue contempt citations. The wily Virginian relied on his counsel, Edmund Toland, who was "the gray wolf that lurks in the sheep's clothing of Smith's judicial temperament." As a matter of fact, not once did Toland introduce any evidence favorable to the board, nor did he permit the NLRB's attorney to cross-examine adversarial witnesses.[35]

In just three months of investigation, the Smith committee collected its initial findings on the board's performance. According to Drew Pearson, Washington's leading muckraker, Smith did not secure committee approval for the report easily. Because the committee's two New Deal Democrats flatly refused to support the chairman's suggested amendments to the Wagner Act, the pivotal vote belonged to Indiana Republican Charlie Halleck. But the pugnacious Halleck disliked one provision placing a limitation on strikes because his district had a large steel and railroad union vote. Bluntly calling the amendments "half-baked" and "biased," Halleck thought the report should wait until the investigation was completed. As the outspoken Republican prepared to leave, Judge Smith reminded him: "I'm chairman of this committee, and I insist on staying in session until we finish this report. Tomorrow will be too late." When Halleck questioned what difference a day would make, Smith sputtered that he had promised reporters a story on the amendments that morning. With this implausible explanation, everyone in the closed session burst into laughter, relieving the tension. The chairman then reluctantly agreed to delete the antistrike amendment in return for Halleck's approval of the remaining amendments.[36]

Less than an hour after the committee adjourned, a presidential aide advised Smith to rush to the White House. Before leaving Capitol Hill, the Judge chanced to see Abe Murdock, one of the committee's dissenting members. Convinced that Murdock had been confiding the committee's proceedings to President Roosevelt, he confronted his colleague, asking derisively, "Abe, did you tell Poppa to spank?" Murdock blushed furiously, providing Smith with sufficient proof as to the source of the leaks. Nevertheless, the Virginian went as requested, taking along Sam Rayburn, the new House Speaker, for protection against the "trap" of misrepresentation of his views. For an hour, the three political powers went one-by-one over Smith's sixteen proposals. The chairman observed that "the President seemed to have no final objection to any proposal that I made." Smith once more believed that Roosevelt was "frankly speaking . . . in accord with the view that there should be changes in personnel and that there should be amendments to the Act that would allay some of the public criticism." This judgment, however, proved erroneous. As Smith himself noted years later, the president had a practice of being "pleasant" while at the same time "sticking a knife in your back."[37]

The day before Smith submitted his proposals to the House on March 7, 1940, Roosevelt made one last-ditch effort to sidetrack the chairman. The president, who had been out of town, asked Smith to give him time to study the proposed amendments. Some House Democrats wanted Smith to delay his proposals for a different reason. If Smith could sway at least one other Democratic committeeman to support labor reform, the Democratic party could claim credit for changing the Wagner Act. The Judge refused both requests for delay, concluding that he had wasted enough time attempting to get the New Deal committeemen to sign the report. Roosevelt finally suggested that the NLRB controversy could be resolved satisfactorily simply by adding two members to the board. Smith promised the president that he would try "to work out something along that line," but the proposition went nowhere.[38]

On March 7, Smith stood before Congress, less than a week after his younger brother's death at fifty-two, and delivered a preliminary report on ways to change board practices. With the support of the committee's two Republicans, he issued a list of recommendations, vowing that the country needed "a measure of immediate relief for wrongs that are being perpetrated daily upon industry, labor and the general public." First, he proposed abolishing the present board and replacing it with a new agency with the same name, whose positions would be filled by the president, but only with the Senate's consent. Second, to remedy a common criticism of regulatory commissions, the board's judicial and prosecutorial functions should be divorced by creating an independent administrator with prosecuting responsibilities. The board could never decide cases impartially as long as it held the dual roles of prosecutor and judge. In addition, the board would be prevented from intervening in disputes between competing labor unions, from not allowing employers to speak to their employees about union representation, from conducting hearings without adhering to judicial procedure, or from reinstating an employee who had committed violent acts against his company. To protect employers charged with an unfair labor practice, the committee favored a six-month statute of limitations on back-pay awards.[39]

These recommendations surprised few congressmen, but the committee's plan to redefine collective bargaining proved startling. Chairman Smith believed that an employer should be obliged only to meet with his employees or their representatives, hear their complaints, and suggest ways of resolving differences between them. This recommendation would not compel either party to reach an agreement. Despite its protests to the contrary, the committee wanted to destroy a basic principle of industrial relations; if employers only had to listen to union complaints, they would not have to reach a mutually agreeable solution with their workers. Ingenuously, the Smith committee stated that it had proposed no change "adversely" affecting the Wagner Act's primary aims.[40]

Smith's suggested amendments touched off a fierce struggle in Congress. After accusing Judge Smith of "a vain search for evidence to support preconceived conclusions," Labor chairman Norton blocked his proposals. As her delaying tactics became apparent, a series of parliamentary moves pitted Norton's and Smith's forces on Rules against each other. While this legislative maneuvering went on, New York senator Robert Wagner, the labor law's author, damned the Smith amendments for repealing the Wagner Act just when labor conditions were improving. He lamented that those who advocated amending the act sought "to bring back the company-dominated union and turn labor's Magna Carta into a weapon of labor oppression." At the same time, the president promised to veto any substantial changes.[41]

But while his opponents gathered forces, Smith dropped a "bombshell" in the form of a letter from William Green, president of the AFL, who withdrew all opposition to the amendments. In exchange, Smith promised to include AFL-backed proposals intended to counter the board's alleged favoritism to the CIO. A shocked Mary Norton told the House: "Surprises have come very fast today. . . . The gentleman from Virginia is the spokesman for the President of the American Federation of Labor. Could anything be more perfect?" In fact, however, this superficial agreement represented a well-calculated plan. Green, whom

Smith called a "nice old gentleman," surmised that the Senate would eliminate Smith's antilabor amendments while preserving provisions advantageous to the AFL.[42]

On June 7, 1940, Smith finally persuaded the House to close the debate on his amendments. The Rules committee previously had permitted his measure to substitute for Norton's comparable bill, and now the full House did the same. Nearly 90 percent of the eighty-three southern Democrats voted for Smith's bill. But the Senate did not take action, confining the amendments to Elbert D. Thomas's Labor Committee for the rest of the session. A frustrated Smith always suspected that Roosevelt had asked Thomas to put the Smith bill "in the cooler."[43]

Desperate that fall for Senate action on his antilabor bill, Smith resorted to highly questionable tactics. He first manufactured the charge that David Saposs, the head of the NLRB's Division of Economics Research, was a Communist. Smith committee investigator Roger Robb had examined thoroughly pertinent files in Saposs's office and the division's headquarters and was convinced that "the bushy, rumpled, little expert" was not a Marxist. *Time* magazine reported that Saposs was often denounced as a Communist, when in truth he was "a zealous watchdog of labor rights." But Smith needed a new charge to bring more public pressure on the Senate Labor Committee, and communism seemed tailor-made to his needs; Smith's Alien Registration Act had made him an apparent expert on the subject. When the Saposs investigation sagged, Smith delivered a nationwide radio address that claimed employers throughout the country believed the NLRB had "departed radically" from the law that created it: "I have never seen a more united or extensive protest against a Federal Board as is shown here." Smith failed to tell his audience that his own questionnaire revealed that nearly two-thirds of the employers surveyed found that their business profits, operations, and labor relations were not harmed by NLRB decisions.[44]

At the end of December, just four days before the end of the congressional session, the Smith committee completed its seventeen-month study of the labor board and its administration of the Wagner Act. In "a rushing, wide-swinging attack that required thirty volumes," the chairman and the two Republicans concluded that the board was "grossly partisan" to the CIO and "deplorably biased in its relations to employers and employees." The majority also charged that the board had induced and protracted numerous industrial disputes. In addition, the report accused the board of employing radicals and of engaging in the "invidious practices" of blacklisting litigants before it and seeking to legalize "the infamous, anarchistic sitdown strikes." The committee warned that without considerable changes the probable results would be the utter destruction of industrial peace, the national defense program, and democratic government. As for solutions, the majority recommended the prompt dismissal of radical board employees and Senate adoption of the House-approved amendments.[45]

The final report, which Smith regarded as "just winding up the Committee's . . . real report" filed in March, generated sharp reactions. The *New York Evening Post,* for example, asserted that the Smith committee "merely concludes with the prejudices it had at the start—prejudices which the record of testimony should have dispelled." A study by historian James Gross concludes that Smith's work was "a one-sided and often distorted appraisal of the work of the NLRB" which relied on half-truths, withholding of evidence, magnification of minor events, and "unwarranted generalizations." Earl Latham, another student of the committee, also adjudged its work negatively. According to Latham, the Smith committee's "antilabor animus impaired its ability to discriminate between the fantasy it chased and the fact it ignored." Although the report alleged that board decisions had been unfair, the Supreme Court had overturned just two of twenty-four administrative decisions, and the federal courts had supported the board in 90 percent of the cases brought before them. Moreover, the committee itself revealed that half of the board's cases were settled satisfactorily to both parties and that in the other half the employer received a favorable ruling 92 percent of the time. The *Post* also noted that since the Court had upheld the Wagner Act, the actual number of strikes had been halved and the number of workdays lost had been cut by two-thirds.[46]

The Smith report lay dormant until the Republican party captured Congress after World War II. Although Smith's suggested revisions of the Wagner Act were stalemated for years by the war, his report and the public support it engendered eventually restructured the NLRB. After Roosevelt's election to a third term in November 1940, most liberal staff members lost their jobs. Economic statistician Saposs was dismissed, and his division abolished. Board chairman Warren Madden was replaced first by Harry Millis, a lethargic University of Chicago economics professor, and then by Paul Herzog of the New York State Labor Relations Board. Both men adopted a pragmatic viewpoint, especially Herzog, who listened closely to public opinion—"utterly essential" in his mind. The board thus began an "orderly retreat" from its earlier liberal doctrines. For example, the NLRB abandoned the policy of letting one union control all plants owned by one employer regardless of an individual plant's preference. Millis and Herzog also held that striker replacements could vote along with the strikers to determine union representation. In addition, the newly constituted board granted employers a greater range of permissible conduct during a strike. As long as an employer continued labor negotiations, he could not be charged with an unfair labor practice for making unilateral changes in working conditions.[47]

Smith was "bathed in prestige from his committee investigation," and he became a recognized and influential expert on labor matters despite not being a member of the Labor Committee. Because Congress would not revamp the NLRB, he searched doggedly for other ways to check organized labor. America's ongoing war preparations convinced him to tap patriotic sentiment against strikes in defense industries. In January 1941 he introduced a bill prohibiting "acts of sabotage with respect to the performance of national-defense contracts." Smith especially denounced the union practice of compelling employers with defense contracts to require new workers to become union members. He also counseled Congress to bar strikes in defense firms until workers gave thirty days' notice to their employer and the secretary of labor. But the House rejected his proposal to cut off appropriations to defense contractors permitting the closed shop.[48]

In the spring of 1941, the Judge's repeated warnings about the crippling strikes in aviation and shipbuilding became more shrill. On the House floor he challenged his colleagues: "Do we not realize that when we put these boys in the Army at $30 a month we have got to get them some powder to shoot with? Do we not realize that when we are training these boys at the risk of their lives every day to fly planes, that we must give them some planes to fly?" Smith wondered when the United States would start fighting "dictators at home."[49]

Under the guise of restoring order to the defense program, Smith and the House antilabor bloc sponsored an antistrike bill in war industries. Smith's bill, which was much stronger than five similar measures, prohibited mass picketing, barred strikes for the closed shop, outlawed open strike votes, required unions to list their officials and membership with the government, and created a mediation system that could order a strike-free period of sixty days. The House, upset over a strike by the United Mine Workers, passed Smith's measure. Once more, the Senate proved uncooperative, as Labor chairman Thomas endeavored to replace the Smith bill with a milder version.[50]

Rebuffed by the Senate's inaction, Smith tried to weaken labor by preventing overtime pay. In February 1942 he proposed suspending extra pay for work exceeding forty hours a week. To illustrate his amendment's importance, Smith cited the example of a West Coast union leader who ordered his members not to work on Washington's birthday when their employer refused to pay the required double time for holiday labor. Anticipating prolabor opposition, Smith maintained that his proposal was not an attack on organized labor, for the amendment would only affect labor statutes during the war. In concluding remarks, he stated that he could not understand why any loyal American could "persist in resisting a suspension of those things which are daily, and hourly, and weekly, and monthly handicapping the efforts of this Government to save itself in the hour of emergency."[51]

Smith's amendment provoked a sharp response from representatives with large labor constituencies. The most biting remarks came from Rhode Island Democrat John E. Fogarty, who charged that Smith and the antilabor forces were trying to destroy the union movement:

> The supporters of this amendment proclaim that this is just a suspension of the laws for the duration; well, I fail to agree. I maintain that this is just the beginning of a drive that is being carried out all over the country conceived and sponsored by the manufacturers, the industrialists, the press, and those of you in and out of Congress who hate and fear labor, the ultimate purpose to shackle labor, to take away from them everything they have gained during

the past 50 years, to drive them back to the sweatshop days, back to the cut throat conditions, back to the days of starvation wages and unlimited hours; yes, back to the days of slavery. When the gentleman from Virginia [Smith] or the gentleman from Georgia [Cox] or the gentleman from Mississippi [William M. Whittington] get up on the floor of this House and claim that in the interest of national unity they are sponsoring or supporting a bill that has to do with labor, I question their sincerity.[52]

During the prolonged debate over labor's organization, Smith often seemed unconcerned with events in his home district. But unionists there kept a close eye on him. In fact, his persistent attack on labor sparked an intraparty fight for his congressional seat in the summer of 1942. Organized labor, particularly the Railway Brotherhoods, was strong in Alexandria and neighboring towns, and it now tried to oust Smith. Labor's potential political clout was vast because there were nearly as many union members as voters in the last local Democratic primary four years earlier. The AFL alone had ten thousand members in the Eighth District's building trades and in Alexandria's large navy torpedo station, and the CIO had organized a small local Ford Motor Company plant. Many other anti-Smith union workers, including John L. Lewis, lived in Smith's district while working in Washington, D.C. These unions condemned Smith's bill to outlaw the union shop and to suspend the wage-hour law as a "deliberate sabotage of the war effort."[53]

As the campaign heated up, both Democratic candidates leveled personal charges against the other. The challenger, Emmet C. Davison, secretary-treasurer of the International Association of Machinists and a former mayor of Alexandria, fired the opening salvo. He accused Smith of not backing the president's preparedness program, labeling the incumbent "the Nation's No. 1 disrupter to a 100 per cent prosecution of the war." Davison also reprinted articles from the New York Communist paper, the *Daily Worker*, that implied Smith had profited unethically from real estate sales while a judge and a congressman and had protected importers of impure milk into Washington.[54]

A week before the August primary, Smith blasted these charges in a radio address. He claimed "this disgraceful exhibition of putrid and malicious scandal" was the product of a "crew of hired jackals" in league with his labor-controlled opponent. The veteran politician assured his audience that the slander could be rebutted if the *Daily Worker's* publisher faced libel charges in Virginia. He then reminded his listeners that Davison had been accused of perjury and had once filed for bankruptcy. A Davison victory, Smith suggested, might lead to a "labor dictatorship" which would cut off goods to nonunion southern communities. Actually, Smith had little reason to worry because the Democratic machine was still united behind him. In the primary he trounced Davison by better than four-to-one. The *Virginia Star* described Smith's "smashing primary victory" as "a surprise" and singled out labor's flaccid political muscle as the chief reason for the wide margin.[55]

The local Republican party mounted an even weaker challenge in the coming months. Many Eighth District Republicans supported Smith because of his "stand in relation to outlawing strikes and saboteurs and labor racketeering." When two unknown Republicans nonetheless opposed him in the pro forma general election, Smith captured 87 percent of the vote.[56]

Comfortably reelected to his seventh term, Smith renewed his attack on labor radicalism in 1943. Spiraling living costs had sparked walkouts by San Francisco machinists in March, Akron rubber workers and Appalachian coal miners in April, and Chrysler employees and United Mine Workers in May. The public grew particularly incensed when John L. Lewis led 400,000 coal miners to strike four times within three months, breaking the wartime "no-strike" pledge. What right, asked Smith's friend and occasional houseguest Judiciary chairman Hatton W. Sumners of Texas, did labor have to "leave the [soldiers] at the point of danger and deprive them of the best opportunity to extinguish the fire, save their lives, and preserve the homes of everybody in the community?" After Lewis defied War Labor Board requests to return to work, Roosevelt seized the mines. Then the president coupled a plea for patriotism with the threat to end draft deferments for striking coal miners if production was not resumed. Although Lewis complied, he warned that an unsatisfactory contract would precipitate another walkout in the fall.[57]

As anti-Lewis sentiments flourished, conservatives grasped their long-awaited chance to enact antilabor legislation. Smith

relished the opportunity because his own antistrike measure had
been before the House for two years. On one occasion, he bluntly
admitted his antilabor intention, telling his colleagues, "very
frankly, this legislation would uproot the closed shop for the du-
ration of the war." He ignored warnings that his antistrike bill
would lead to work slowdowns or a "general walkout": "If there is
an insurrectionist spirit in American labor, for God's sake let us
find it out now and meet it before it is too late. Let us see if this
Congress functions or if the labor leaders are going to lead our
country." After months of frustration, Smith awaited Senate action this time. In May the Senate readily approved Texas senator
Tom Connally's bill clarifying the president's power to seize any
vital defense plant afflicted by a strike. Previously, presidential
authority to take over defense factories depended on the actions
of recalcitrant owners, rather than striking workers. Smith then
quietly collaborated with Georgia Democrat Carl Vinson, chairman of the House Naval Affairs Committee, to attach the major
elements of his own antistrike bill to the Connally measure. The
combined proposal gave the War Labor Board formal statutory
authority, required unions to give a thirty-day strike notice, and,
in a move that appeared to have no connection with wartime
production, barred unions from making financial contributions
to candidates in federal elections.[58]

To improve prospects for the bill's passage, Smith resorted to
several adroit parliamentary steps. He managed to shift consideration of the antistrike bill in the House from the prounion Labor
Committee to the Military Affairs Committee, whose chairman,
Andrew J. May of Kentucky, had barely survived a reelection fight
with the CIO. Under May's direction, the committee prevented
top labor leaders from testifying against the bill. Once the bill
reached the floor, Smith outmaneuvered prolabor forces in the
House. He cleverly included two anticlosed shop provisions in
the bill, one clearly stated and the other "a sleeper." The "sneak
play" worked. When the House forced him to remove the plainly
stated provision, Smith acquiesced graciously, leaving intact the
section directing the War Labor Board to ignore closed-shop orders. Sly ploys such as these led his colleagues to call him "the
fox of Fauquier County." On June 4 the House passed the Smith-
Connally bill—officially, the wartime labor disputes bill—the

"Congressional answer to Lewis's strike against the coal industry." After five years of menacing organized labor, Smith delighted in his first major victory.[59]

The president, however, vetoed the bill, primarily because he suspected the measure would stimulate, rather than discourage, strikes. Roosevelt was afraid that unions might misinterpret the thirty-day strike notice provision as official sanction for work stoppages, contrary to the wartime "no-strike" pledge. The editor of the *New York Times* echoed the president's fears, reviling the Smith-Connally bill as "one of the stupidest pieces of legislation ever passed by Congress." But Congress was anxious to maintain armament production and public support for the war. It quickly overrode Roosevelt's veto in what *Time* magazine judged the "most stinging rebuke of his entire career."[60]

The president's concern was well founded. The strike notice clause virtually repealed the no-strike agreement. According to historian Geoffrey Perrett, the act's "legislative intent was turned upside down," as unions used the thirty-day waiting period and the mandatory National Labor Relations Board vote as their "trump card." Whenever labor had a grievance against management, it simply filed a strike notice, thereby intimidating employers with a possible government takeover. After the war, Congress cut off board appropriations for conducting expensive union strike polls. By that time, employers, rather than workers, favored repeal of the Smith-Connally Act since it only encouraged labor militancy.[61]

Indeed, the most famous, or infamous, enforcement of the law was directed at management rather than labor. For months in 1944 Sewell L. Avery, head of Montgomery Ward, fought a War Labor Board directive to negotiate with his employees' CIO union. When the labor board turned to the president for help, Roosevelt declared the Chicago mail-order house "useful" in the war effort and ordered its seizure under the Smith-Connally Act. Avery stole the headlines as he was carried from his office, still seated in his chair. The incident incensed Judge Smith because he thought the administration had willfully distorted the act to justify the takeover of a retail store, which had "not the remotest connection with the war effort."[62]

His "antilabor" act had another, more significant, unintended result. After witnessing Smith's recent antiunion success, CIO president Philip Murray decided unions had to support prolabor candidates more actively. Therefore, in July 1943, he established the CIO's Political Action Committee under the direction of Sidney Hillman, leader of the Amalgamated Clothing Workers. The committee evaded the antistrike law's prohibition against union contributions in federal elections by asking individuals to make "voluntary" donations. Hillman effectively mobilized the urban labor vote against the conservative congressional bloc and made the committee a liberalizing force within the Democratic party. Once more, Smith's attempt to quash organized labor's influence had backfired badly.[63]

With the struggle for antistrike legislation turning sour, Smith moved aggressively against alleged administrative misconduct. Already, representatives on both sides of the aisle were filling the chamber with loud denunciations of "arrogant, war-shirking bureaucrats, infiltrating radicals, and New Deal agencies" misusing

Original drawing presented to Howard W. Smith of cartoon by C. K. Berryman in the *Washington Star*, January 15, 1944

the power granted by Congress to implement further social reforms under the guise of wartime necessity. In late 1942 Eugene
Cox, Clifton Woodrum, and Republican minority leader Joe
Martin, Jr., selected Judge Smith to impugn bureaucratic excesses. These men recently had helped form an increasingly influential conservative coalition of House Republicans and
southern Democrats, who believed "the best way to combat the
New Dealers was to put willing Democrats up to making the
moves and delivering the speeches." The Democratic party's poor
showing in the 1942 election only enhanced the conservative opportunity to undo the "capricious and arbitrary" actions of government bureaus.[64]

Congressional unrest arose from the general feeling that depression and world war had perceptibly shifted the balance of power
between governmental branches to the power-mad executive.
Daily, House mailboxes bulged with citizen complaints against
every kind of real or assumed injustice perpetrated by federal
agencies. The war economy was responsible, these letters asserted, for a myriad of problems, including those raised by price
and wage controls, labor strikes, the elephantine armed forces,
and rationing. Isolationists, many southern Democrats, and
Roosevelt-hating Republicans in Congress exploited the public
frustration to dismantle New Deal agencies, and in 1943 alone
they abolished the WPA, the Civilian Conservation Corps, the
National Youth Administration, and the National Resources
Planning Board. Wartime agencies were obviously the other fertile ground for attack.[65]

With conservative support, Smith drafted what *Time* magazine's Washington correspondent called "a blunderbuss resolution
for an investigation of government bureaus from hell to breakfast."
Some House leaders speculated that the Judge's target was the
president himself, and they insisted that the resolution's vague
language be sharpened. Smith then called for and later headed a
seven-member Select Committee to Investigate Acts of Executive
Agencies beyond the Scope of Their Authority. The committee
included Democrats Jerry Voorhis of California, John J. Delaney
of New York, and Hugh Peterson of Georgia and Republicans
Fred A. Hartley, Jr., of New Jersey, John Jennings, Jr., of Tennessee, and John B. Bennett of Michigan. With his committee,
Smith proposed stripping the authority of bureaucrats to promul-

gate regulations that had the effect of law and returning legislative power to Congress, the constitutionally designated body: "What I propose to do is have the committee call up and put [the bureaucrats] on the carpet, ask them to point out the law by which they acted. If they can't point to the authority at law, we are going to ask them, 'well, where the hell then did you get the authority?' and have them show us. We'll have plenty to investigate, and we'll report to Congress and recommend legislation." "I believe," he concluded, "that when the bureaucrats know that there is a committee ready to look over their doings, and with the power to do the job, they'll be more considerate of Congress, the law, and the intention of Congress."[66]

In the spring of 1943 Smith's principal focus became the Office of Price Administration, a wartime agency charged with slowing inflation. Because the office had been largely successful in limiting price hikes, especially in southern cotton, and rent increases, conservative politicians, businessmen, and property investors pressed for its abolition when its authority expired on June 30, 1944. For example, Ohio senator Robert A. Taft introduced two dozen amendments to weaken the office. These amendments sought to reduce consumer subsidies, permit an independent board to oversee price controls, restore farm parity prices, and allow industries to manufacture unlabeled products of varying quality. If enacted, the amendments would have destroyed the price ceilings limiting business profits.[67]

Smith's select committee on investigating executive agencies assisted the war on price controls. According to Colston E. Warne, professor of economics at Amherst College and president of the Consumers Union, the Judge allowed his committee to be used as "a sounding board for every group wishing to discredit" these controls. In November the sixty-year-old Virginia representative charged the office with usurping congressional authority by invoking a meat-pricing program which deliberately violated the law. The committee found that the agency had used subsidies illegally to control live cattle prices, which required the War Food Administration's consent. By setting meat prices, the office supposedly fostered a monopoly which forced processors to operate at a loss. When they appealed for judicial relief, the office resisted for seven months before unsuccessfully asking administration approval of the subsidies. The office then avoided congressional restrictions by securing the Office of Economic Stabilization's permission. The Smith committee regarded this action as having "nullified" a congressional act.[68]

In June 1944 the Virginian attempted to insert his committee's findings into a bill extending the life of the Office of Price Administration. Ordinarily, the bill would have been reported by the Rules Committee under regular procedures for open debate and consideration of relevant amendments. But Smith astutely sensed in the extension bill a chance to send to the floor his select committee's recommendations. He resorted to the unorthodox tactic because his fifty-seven-page list of amendments dealt not only with price control, obviously germane to the extension bill, but also with laws that were not, such as the Stabilization Act, the Smith-Connally Act, and the Wagner Act. By waiving all points of order, the Rules Committee allowed Smith, one of its own, to submit all of his recommendations. This action motivated Speaker Rayburn to protest Rules' conduct as a legislative, instead of a purely procedural, move. The House vindicated Rayburn, but, according to political scientist Christopher Van Hollen, this was "the only important direct defeat" suffered by Rules between 1937 and 1946, during which time the committee had become an "agent of opposition."[69]

By late November, Smith was worried that his select committee's work might evaporate. He saw the swelling criticism against the Dies committee's "sleuthing and talking" without results as a sign that interest in investigations was waning. Worse, a number of northern Democrats had begun to question his own committee's scope and methods. Realizing he had to act soon, the Judge put forward a comprehensive plan to reorganize Congress. Ostensibly drawing from earlier plans, Smith presented a bill with four main parts. He first proposed the establishment of a joint legislative staff service for all committees of both houses. Second, he recommended the creation of a joint committee on appropriations which would oversee executive branch expenditures. Third, he called for a standing joint committee on executive agencies which would investigate allegations that agencies had exceeded their authority. Finally, Smith requested that a joint committee be set up to study congressional operations in order to recommend improvements.[70]

On the surface, the bill seemed to offer constructive reform.

But writers in liberal publications cautioned that its passage would "be the means of freezing reaction at the controls in Congress." Writing in the *New Republic*, Helen Fuller observed that the bill would lead to Howard Smith's selection as chairman of a more powerful, permanent congressional committee investigating other executive agencies. In fact, Smith's proposal was not widely supported, and the House let it die quietly.[71]

After World War II, the question of removing price controls again became topical. In the fall of 1945 livestock farmers, upset with low meat prices, caused a national "meat famine" by withholding their supplies. As the Office of Price Administration fell further from public favor, business and conservative interests wrote an extension bill shackled with so many restrictions that it amounted to repeal of the agency. President Harry Truman vetoed the bill, but another, equally powerless, one-year extension was approved. The office suffered "a slow and painful bureaucratic death," eventually bringing Judge Smith satisfaction.[72]

By 1945 Smith had earned congressional influence and national prominence fighting both internal and external threats to the United States. Using the circumstance of world conflict as justification, he repeatedly led battles on the home front against alleged subversives and labor unions. His successes included the passage of the anti-Communist Smith Act of 1940 and the anti-strike Smith-Connally Act of 1943. Moreover, he had helped to lay the foundation for additional attacks on unions by serving as chairman of the select committee that investigated the National Labor Relations Board. Although his anti-Communist and anti-labor endeavors rarely had the impact he intended, Smith—convinced he was right—continued to pursue these twin concerns. His opposition to these and other groups seemed vital to "save the South of a bygone age."

CHAPTER 5

Defending the South: Labor-Baiter and Segregationist

*No, we down South do not have any friends. We have
to stand up here and sometimes resort to filibusters,
even, to try to keep you people from imposing upon the
southern people things that you know and we know just
do not comport with the traditions of the South and
cannot work and will not work, and neither race wants
them to work.*

Howard W. Smith on northern Democrats (1950)

After World War II ended in 1945, long-suffering labor unions in
the automobile, electric, and steel industries struck for wage increases to match sharply rising prices. In January 1946 President
Truman blamed Congress for the labor crisis. Smith sarcastically
congratulated the president for urging the enactment of laws "to
correct the evils that have grown up under the present inadequate
and one-sided legislation." He reasoned that the nation had two
alternatives to an impending labor "dictatorship over the economy." Either Congress could perform its essential function of
passing appropriate laws, or industry would have to resist labor's
"unreasonable demands to the bitter end." In Smith's view, the
Senate bore the responsibility for congressional inaction because
most labor bills had passed the House only to stall in the smaller
body. The Judge wondered how long the senators would place
one group of citizens, by virtue of their membership in a private

organization, "above and beyond the reach of laws governing the rest of the people of the United States."[1]

By the end of the month, Smith again took the labor problem into his own hands. Working with his like-minded Rules colleague Eugene Cox, he encouraged South Dakota Republican Francis Case to submit a secretly prepared, drastic strike-control bill which had not been routed to any legislative committee. Its familiar provisions included a permanent mediation board, a prestrike cooling-off period of thirty days, a greater willingness to use antistrike injunctions, the liability of unions and employers for any contractual breach, the revocation of a striker's right to collective bargaining or reemployment after engaging in violence or intimidation, and the prohibition of union boycotts. Smith and Cox then convinced the Rules Committee to incorporate the Case bill into a fact-finding labor bill submitted by the Judge's old nemesis, Labor chairman Norton.[2]

The labor-baiters' tactics were not well received. Rules chairman Adolph J. Sabath of Chicago complained that the Case bill "was never brought before the Committee on Labor, and neither members of the Committee on Labor nor of the Rules Committee had seen the bill before the gentleman from South Dakota appeared before our committee with a typescript in his hand." Although a slim majority of Democrats on the committee approved the rule, several of them explained that they had done so only in order to consider the administration's fact-finding bill. While Smith's irregular maneuver did not violate House rules, it stretched the procedural guidelines beyond their accepted limits. In February the Case bill passed the House, but a majority of Democrats now voted against it. When the measure cleared Congress in late May, Truman vetoed it, arguing that the bill "strikes at symptoms and ignores underlying causes" of industrial strife.[3]

That industrial strife touched Virginia in the spring of 1946, raising Smith's furor at the union officials who had halted the state's coal production. He accused the United Mine Workers of leading a "carpetbagger invasion" of the South calculated to purge recalcitrant southern politicians. It was no accident, he pointed out, that the CIO's Political Action Committee, to which the miners' union belonged, had tried to defeat him in three recent elections. Smith further condemned the union by labeling its leaders as foreigners "impregnated" with communism, whose sole purpose in the United States was to impose a dictatorship on the American people. To prove his case, he recalled the union's "extortion" demand of a ten-cents-a-ton royalty on mined coal. Because Smith believed that labor inordinately influenced Congress, he announced that the only way to avert a union takeover was through public protest. Only concerned people like himself who were dedicated to preserving the American way could pressure other congressmen to counter "radical minority" groups like the CIO.[4]

Although Smith's antilabor stand was acceptable in much of his own district, it cost him any chance of achieving higher office. In May 1946 a Senate seat opened up when eighty-eight-year-old Carter Glass, Virginia's senior senator, who had been an invalid since the middle of World War II, finally died. To fill Glass's unexpired term until the party nominated a successor, Governor William M. Tuck selected retiring congressman Thomas G. Burch, who, at seventy-six, seemed to be only an interim appointee. The fight to succeed Glass would take place at the state Democratic convention in Richmond on September 5.[5]

In the meantime, the party seriously considered three Byrd organization men. Former governor Colgate W. Darden, Jr., was clearly the favorite. Though he removed himself from consideration to get "acquainted" with his family, the organization and state newspapers kept his name alive. Seventh District congressman A. Willis Robertson, known for his wildlife and conservation legislation, twice declined to run, stating unconvincingly that a Senate bid would cause him to "neglect my duties in the House." He told friends of his intention to leave Congress: "This year I had reached the conclusion that I had gone as far in politics as I could get, and had, therefore, decided to retire before the end of another term in the House." That left Howard Smith, who in following the Virginia code of never explicitly seeking a political post, could not declare his candidacy openly, even though his national reputation surely qualified him for the Senate. He admitted coyly to being in a "receptive mood" to a draft.[6]

Smith thus appeared to have the inside track to the nomination, but his candidacy was irreparably damaged by his unremitting archfoe, organized labor. Militant coal miners in southwest

Virginia demanded higher pay to match postwar inflation, a six-hour day, and safer working conditions. They joined the devastating national strike led by John L. Lewis and in the process hampered state railroads, chemical plants, and the Dan River textile mills. Electrical workers also sought higher wages. To avert a power strike in the spring, the governor took the unprecedented step of drafting union workers into the militia. Simultaneously, the CIO had launched a massive southern union membership drive called Operation Dixie. According to the CIO's chief southern organizer, Van A. Bittner, a fierce struggle lay ahead: "We expect a lot of opposition. We don't care how the employer feels about it because he has to put it in his pipe and smoke it." The organizer warned, "If you want anything industrially, you have to take it through the power and force and influence of your union."[7]

This labor ferment soon found its way into the political arena. The upcoming Democratic convention provided the ideal forum for organized labor to express its frustration and perhaps to endorse a sympathetic candidate. Labor delegates represented the naval shipyards of Norfolk and Portsmouth and the coal mines of the Ninth District in the southwest. To them, Smith was anathema because he had long opposed minimum wages and the unrestricted right to strike. One Ninth District delegate explained that it was "asking too much to ask us to go any farther to the right" of Senator Byrd to back Howard Smith. Labor threatened to bolt the party if the labor-baiter Smith was nominated. When questioned how this could be done, a Norfolk delegate smugly replied: "When we get in the election booth no one is going to see how we vote." Ninth District Byrd organization leaders confirmed labor's anti-Smith crusade: "Labor unions [are] ready to pour money into Virginia this fall to fight Smith." The tables had been turned; now labor led an anti-Smith crusade.[8]

Because serving in the Senate was Judge Smith's "cherished ambition," he ignored labor's opposition, maneuvering behind the scenes for the party's nomination. Without an obvious front-runner, the ever-cautious Byrd declared his neutrality and sat "on the sidelines playing the part of the political sphinx." He knew the danger of alienating labor because he had just survived a primary in which, he alleged, the CIO tried to "silence" him. As Byrd kept mum, Smith contacted organization lieutenants around the state to seek their support. The response was not encouraging. Organization Democrats feared Smith's nomination "would be little short of a disaster" to Senator Byrd and the party.[9]

The most candid criticism came from J. Frank Wysor, Pulaski County treasurer and a member of the convention rules committee. Wysor pointed out that Smith was not widely known outside northern Virginia and that those who knew of him did not support his antilabor stand. "Your acquaintance out here is limited," he wrote to Smith, "and this whole section is sensitive to the labor problem." Even if Smith captured the convention's nomination, Wysor explained, the Republicans and antiorganization Democrats would say that "it was forced by the organization when you could not obtain it at a primary." The result might be a tragic intraparty split which would spell defeat. Wysor praised Smith as "a man of ability, courage and experience" but added that everyone he had talked to "has emphatically said he thought it would be a mistake to nominate you."[10]

Undeterred, Smith urged Eighth District delegates—all pledged to him—to attend "the pre-convention gabfests" wearing colorful buttons reading "Smith for Senate." No rival politicked this openly in Richmond. Smith then took an even bolder step. In a move that unmasked his burning ambition, he made a "personal appeal" to Robertson to withdraw categorically so that he could win. Robertson refused, reportedly informing Smith that his candidacy was doomed in any event.[11]

With no candidate receiving Byrd's benediction, the convention became a political "cauldron." Darden remained the logical choice, and despite his disclaimers, his Tidewater supporters nominated him. After one ballot, however, he withdrew. At the time, Smith ran a distant second. Robertson had entered belatedly when Burch stayed out of the race. On the second ballot, Darden's votes went to Robertson, assuring him the lead over Smith. "A wild roar of excitement" erupted in the hall as delegates scrambled to switch their allegiance. Before the third and decisive ballot was officially reported, Smith caved in at 10:35 P.M., asking the convention to make Robertson its choice by acclamation. Except for the still dissatisfied laborites, the cheering delegates agreed and leapt to their feet.[12]

Many Virginia newspapers vigorously applauded Robertson's

convention victory. They shared the belief that Smith was too backward in approaching pressing problems, especially labor relations. The *Roanoke Times*, which had favored Robertson, called Smith "a stark reactionary." And the moderate *Richmond Times-Dispatch* viewed the Judge as a "rabid labor-baiter." A Norfolk paper, the *Ledger-Dispatch*, expressed most forcefully the anti-Smith sentiment, emphasizing his antiurban and antilabor attitudes: "Mr. Robertson may broaden his outlook as opportunity for broader work now presents itself. He is much more likely to do so than his chief opponent, Rep. Howard Smith, who is more of a reactionary and much less desirable. Mr. Robertson will realize, we hope, that Virginia has city interests as well as a rural life; and that industry and labor need understanding, and that the state must continue to move forward."[13]

Howard Smith's failure to capture the Senate nomination was a sharp disappointment, and he privately admitted to holding a "few animosities." Ironically, his career was probably better served by losing at the convention. If he had gained the nomination, labor might well have defeated him in the general election. Indeed, labor did defect from the national Democratic party in the fall, giving the Republicans their first congressional majority since Herbert Hoover. If Smith had reached the Senate, he would have had no seniority on committee assignments. By continuing in the House, Smith became chairman of the Rules Committee within nine years. That position made him the most powerful conservative in Congress—much more so than the recognized leader of the Virginia delegation, Harry Byrd.[14]

In the general election that followed, both Smith and Robertson triumphed easily, but Smith suffered some surprising attrition. An Arlington Republican appealed to local voters when he blamed Byrd directly and Smith indirectly for a state government which was more costly than its neighbors, a high crime rate, an inadequate school system, and, strangely enough, for the national strikes in the railroad and mining industries. Smith lost rural Greene County and came close to losing Stafford County and the labor stronghold of Arlington County. Even in Alexandria, his home base, one of the precincts went Republican for the first time since Reconstruction. The Judge had been hurt by the national swing against the Democrats because of war weariness and unpopular social programs. He had also been hurt by railroad union opposition, which was gaining strength in the northern part of the district.[15]

Bearing the scars of the recent campaign, Smith reaped some revenge by resuming his offensive against organized labor in 1947. He was determined to blunt labor's strength in Virginia and to crush paralyzing national strikes. Assessing the Eightieth Congress, the veteran representative felt that restrictive labor legislation had an excellent chance of passage. The country was agitated over labor unrest that had forced the president to seize hundreds of strike-ridden companies. Many citizens voiced concern over the supposed Communist infiltration of unions, a fear that seemed relevant in view of deteriorating Soviet-American relations. The revitalized Republican party, which had just captured both houses, appeared to be the decisive element in asserting tighter control over labor. For the first time since Smith went to Capitol Hill in 1931, Congress would be in conservative hands. And he was ready.[16]

On the first day of the new session, Smith introduced a comprehensive bill to revise the Wagner Act. He had been "constantly hammering" at the law for a decade and with his colleagues had introduced 169 bills to reverse national labor policy. In this, his tenth, antilabor bill Smith's stated aim was "to restore equality between unions and industry and protect the paramount interest of the general public." But his real purpose was to weaken organized labor so that it posed no serious threat to business profits or conservative politicians. Significant changes included the prohibition of the closed shop, a ban on violence or intimidation in labor disputes, the outlawing of sympathy strikes, the registration of unions with the government, and the separation of judicial and prosecutorial functions. Although the Smith proposal contained no criminal penalties, it recommended that union violators lose the right to bargain for employees and forfeit their exemption from court injunctions. As the weeks unfolded, the bill became the focal point for debate.[17]

To promote his antilabor cause, Smith cemented his alliance with suddenly powerful conservative Republicans, such as House Speaker Joe Martin, Jr., House majority leader Charlie Halleck, and Fred A. Hartley, Jr., chairman of the House Labor Committee. All three Republicans had served with Smith on House committees. Because these Republicans "realized that [Smith] had a pretty thorough knowledge of the subject with all the years work that I'd put in on it," they held "constant conferences" in his office. According to Hartley, the measure that emerged "was basically a rehash of the old Smith proposals that Congress had resisted for the past seven years." "We had," Hartley admitted, used "the early Smith amendments as well as the hearings, investigations, and reports upon which they were based."[18]

After Hartley brought up his own measure incorporating Smith's key provisions, Smith and Eugene Cox skillfully orchestrated a conservative coalition of southern Democrats and northern Republicans. The "Dixie boys"—one representative from each southern state—"met like the apostles of old" with the Judge either in his congressional office or in the tiny, mid-Victorian Rules Committee room just off the House floor to plot strategy on the Hartley bill. Virginia's Watkins M. Abbitt and Mississippi's John Bell Williams became two of the most important members of this inner circle. Working intimately with Smith, they kept their state delegations closely informed on labor developments in the House. Together, thirty-eight southern Democrats represented the "hard core" support for the antilabor measure:[19]

Alabama
George W. Andrews
Laurie C. Battle

Arkansas
Ezekiel C. Gathings
William F. Norrell

Florida
George A. Smathers

Georgia
E. Eugene Cox
James C. Davis
William M. Wheeler
John S. Wood

Kentucky
Joe B. Bates

Louisiana
A. Leonard Allen
F. Edward Hébert

Mississippi
Thomas G. Abernethy
William M. Colmer
John E. Rankin
John Bell Williams
W. Arthur Winstead

Missouri
Paul C. Jones

North Carolina
Graham A. Barden
Robert L. Doughton
Carl T. Durham

South Carolina
  Joseph R. Bryson
  John L. McMillen
  James P. Richards
  L. Mendel Rivers

Tennessee
  Thomas J. Murray

Texas
  Omar T. Burleson
  O. Clark Fisher

  Ed Gossett
  Tom Pickett
  William R. Poage
  Olin E. Teague
  J. Frank Wilson

Virginia
  Watkins M. Abbitt
  Clarence G. Burton
  Burr P. Harrison
  Howard W. Smith
  Thomas B. Stanley

These southern Democrats worked closely, though never formally, with the Republicans. Judge Smith later recalled how the process worked:

> Joe Martin was a very powerful, very partisan leader. He and Eugene Cox worked together on many issues. Our group—we called it our "group" for want of a better term . . . did not meet publicly. The meetings were not formal. Our group met in one building and the conservative Republicans in another, on different issues. Then Eugene Cox, Bill Colmer or I would go over to speak with the Republicans, or the Republican leaders might come to see us. It was very informal. Conservative southerners and Republicans from the northern and western states. A coalition did exist in legislation. But we met in small groups. There were no joint meetings of conservative Republicans and southern Democrats.

Majority Leader Charlie Halleck recalled that he met "clandestinely" with Smith to oversee "the whole damn operation in the House."[20]

The remarkable fact was that Smith, Cox, Martin, and Halleck often could achieve their will without a tightly knit organization. This feat can be explained by examining the structure of the House of Representatives and the convictions of the coalition leaders. The coalition congressmen, most from safe districts, attended floor sessions in higher proportions than the more numerous northern representatives, who were often preoccupied with serving their constituents to win reelection. As a result, the coalition held more power than its membership roll alone might suggest. Moreover, the coalition held the chairmanships of key committees, including Rules, Ways and Means, and Education and Labor, which made easier the flow of information to other members. The legislative process also permitted coalition sharpshooters to wage a "guerrilla" war against liberal bills. At any point in the process—whether in subcommittee, full committee, the Rules Committee, the Committee of the Whole, on the floor of the House, the joint conference committee between houses, or when Senate versions of bills again appeared in Rules or on the floor once more—coalition supporters had only to stop a measure's movement one time. Ideological and partisan convictions also determined the coalition's direction. Smith and Cox were irreplaceable southern Democratic leaders who enjoyed the hearty support of Joe Martin and his successor, Charlie Halleck. When these men stepped down, the coalition was never the same.[21]

In the case of the Hartley bill, the conservative coalition found itself in the unusual position of supporting, instead of attacking, a bill. Northern liberals, finding themselves unexpectedly in the minority, took a defensive position to protect organized labor. Adolph Sabath of Illinois, the ranking Rules Democrat, castigated the proposal as "the most vicious, restrictive and destructive anti-labor bill ever brought before this House." Other Democrats argued that the bill's ban on industrywide bargaining would mean sweatshop labor at subsistence wages. But the opposition proved minimal. On April 17, 1947, the House ignored Truman's request for a prolabor report and passed the Hartley measure by a nearly three-to-one margin. Of the ninety-three Democrats who defied the president to vote for Taft-Hartley, eighty-two of them came from the South. This bill culminated Smith's decade-long antilabor program and represented a major victory for his coalition.[22]

On the same day, Ohio Republican Robert A. Taft, chairman of the Senate Labor Committee, cleared a weaker labor measure. Despite the best efforts of senators Taft, Byrd, and Walter F. George of Georgia, the Senate version did not include Hartley's ban on union political contributions, penalties for mass picketing and labor violence, prohibition of government employee strikes, or regulations of internal union affairs. The Senate preferred the milder language, passing the Taft bill in May 1947. After seven

years of Senate inaction, Smith praised the upper house for having finally gotten "religion over there now."[23]

When the compromise Taft-Hartley bill emerged from a conference committee in June, a number of liberal Democrats and
national organizations expressed vehement opposition. Mary
Norton sourly noted that "at last the labor baiters and labor haters
are having a field day." Shortly after Truman received the bill, the
AFL and CIO, all House Labor Committee Democrats, and the
newly formed Americans for Democratic Action demanded a
presidential veto. On June 20, Truman agreed, concluding that
the Taft-Hartley bill was obviously unfair to workers and "would
contribute neither to industrial peace nor to economic stability
and progress." He therefore vetoed the measure. Within days,
however, each Republican-dominated house overrode it. Only 9
of 115 southern Democrats voted to sustain the presidential
veto.[24]

Despite Smith's high expectations, the Taft-Hartley Act did not
have a profound effect on the labor movement. It did transform
the NLRB from "an expert administrative agency" into "a conservative, insecure, politically sensitive agency preoccupied with
its own survival"; but the courts rendered the act's provisions prac-
tically harmless. The act did not achieve its purposes of promoting rivalries between competing unions and of discouraging
union shop elections. Between 1947 and 1957 union membership grew from 14 million to 17.5 million; it also increased from
23 to 26 percent of the civilian work force. A Yale law professor
concluded that the act had a negligible effect on industrial relations because "equality in bargaining power is largely a product
of economic forces and not legal rules," a truth the legalistic
Smith never understood. Politically, the act had the unintended
consequence of pushing back into the Democratic fold union
members who had slipped into the Republican camp in the 1946
election. For a third time, Smith's antilabor engine backfired.[25]

Besides postwar labor problems, the United States was experiencing strained relations with its erstwhile ally, the Soviet Union.
At the end of World War II, the Soviet Union had expanded its
influence over Eastern Europe and the Mediterranean, much to
Allied consternation. Recalling recent Soviet attempts to domi-
nate northern Iran, the Truman administration reacted sharply to
the British warning in 1947 that it could no longer police the

eastern Mediterranean Sea. The British admission was particularly troubling because the Soviets had demanded Turkish land
for naval bases and apparently were supporting a Communist insurrection against the Greek government. Truman responded by
calling for $400 million in military and economic aid "to support
free peoples [in Greece and Turkey] who are resisting attempted
subjugation by armed minorities or by outside pressures."[26]

Though ordinarily preoccupied with domestic matters, Howard Smith spoke out strongly for the president's anti-Communist
foreign policy. In May 1947 he urged Congress to stop yielding to
Soviet aggression and to follow "the responsible leadership" of
both political parties in approving the foreign aid appropriation
bill. He warned that "a policy of appeasement" such as the United
States followed after World War I would inevitably lead to the rise
of a new crop of land-hungry dictators. Smith asked his colleagues, "In these days are we ever going to learn that we cannot
stick our heads in the sand and hope that these tides are not going
to flow over us?" Though some Republicans saw the aid as an
unwise shift in American foreign policy, the House followed the
Senate in giving Truman the funds he requested.[27]

The so-called Truman Doctrine represented an unprecedented
approach in American foreign relations. The administration had
shown clearly that the United States would not accept unlimited
Soviet expansion, especially while Europe was recovering from
wartime devastation. The president's plan was the first practical
application of Soviet "containment." By drawing sharp distinc-
tions between the two countries, the doctrine had longterm re-
percussions. According to historian Robert J. Donovan, the
Truman Doctrine "lent a rigidity to foreign policy that for a generation inhibited a turn from the Cold War." As for the threats
against the Greek and Turkish governments, American aid helped
turn the tide against Communist rebels by 1949.[28]

When Truman requested billions of dollars to assist war-torn
Western European countries, Smith and most other southern
Democrats concurred. They were alarmed by the sudden Soviet
seizure of Czechoslovakia in March 1948. England, Germany,
France, and Italy hovered on bankruptcy, and the latter two coun-
tries feared Communist takeovers. Secretary of State George C.
Marshall convinced the president to fund the European Recovery
Program with $17 billion, provided the recipients contributed to

their own recovery. To Smith, the Marshall Plan required immediate House action. Despairing of American tardiness in repelling totalitarian threats, he warned in March 1948 that another world war might be the price of opposing the recovery bill. If they did not approve the Marshall Plan and universal military training, Smith told his fellow representatives, they would fail in their responsibility as "custodians" of the civilization "we have been privileged to share." Despite Republican fears that the Marshall Plan was "a plan for sanctimonious, global imperialism and continuous war," Congress approved the unprecedented foreign aid bill.[29]

In less than a decade, American monies helped Western Europe return to its prewar productive capacity. Economic recovery helped to diminish the membership and influence of the French and Italian Communist parties. On the other hand, the Marshall Plan was not selflessly motivated, for aid recipients had to use their grants to purchase American goods. Moreover, by inviting the participation of countries under Soviet control, the plan made the Soviets more suspicious of American intentions.[30]

As the Judge spoke out on behalf of Truman's foreign policy, the president was trying to portray himself as a foe of communism at home. Amid Cold War tensions, the Republicans were making political hay with charges that "the Democrats are all left-wingers and that the New Deal was indistinguishable from communism anyhow." Some congressmen went further, claiming Communists had infiltrated the administration. President Truman responded by initiating a "red hunt." His weapon was the long dormant Smith Act.[31]

In July 1948 Truman directed Attorney General Tom Clark to use the Smith Act to arrest twelve Communist party leaders for advocating the overthrow of the federal government. When the accused were found guilty, they appealed unsuccessfully to the U.S. Supreme Court in *Dennis* v. *United States* (1951). The Court applied Oliver Wendell Holmes's "clear and present danger" formula, ruling that free speech does not mean "that before the government may act it must wait until the putsch is about to be executed, the plans have been laid and the signal awaited." Some newspapers denounced the verdict as "the gravest departure from the guarantee of freedom of speech in our history," but the Justice Department subsequently instigated a series of "red hunt"

Congressman Howard W. Smith in the 1940s. (Tonahill Collection)

Reporter May Craig and Congressman Smith after Smith had added the sex amendment to the Civil Rights Act of 1964 as Craig apparently had requested. (Tonahill Collection)

Chairman Smith and the House Rules Committee in 1966. (Courtesy of the Office of Photography, U.S. House of Representatives)

Smith at his retirement dinner in Warrenton with Governor
Mills E. Godwin in September 1966. (Tonahill Collection)

Howard W. Smith in retirement at Cedar Hill. (Tonahill Collection)

trials from coast to coast. Ultimately, the courts convicted ninety-seven World War II veterans, trade union officials, newspaper editors, black civic leaders, and women of conspiracy. Every defendant tried on the charge of Communist party membership was convicted. Along with badly timed events abroad and weak party leadership at home, these prosecutions under the Smith Act further destroyed the cohesion of the Communist party. In effect, the Court banned the party by judicial fiat.[32]

Although Judge Smith undoubtedly relished this crackdown on communism, his energies were devoted to retaining his seat in Congress and his influential position on Rules. After defeating a politically inexperienced attorney in the 1948 Democratic primary, Smith faced an aggressive Republican challenger, Tyrrell Krum of Fairfax. As usual, the incumbent expected the worst—that labor was behind Krum's candidacy. Smith confided to Governor Tuck that "the radical element will take advantage of the dissension within the Party and hook up with the Republican candidates to beat Democratic nominees," including himself. Krum seemed to bear out Smith's fears when he charged that the congressman had never acted in the best interests of Eighth District residents. Krum pointed out that the incumbent had opposed Republican-backed income tax cuts and had supported a fifteen-cent tax on oleomargarine to safeguard dairy interests—interests in which Smith shared. Taking advantage of the general expectation that Republican Thomas E. Dewey would win the presidency, Krum promised that a Republican congressman would achieve more than a Democrat could. Krum and Dewey particularly stood to benefit in Virginia because President Truman backed an unprecedented civil rights program for blacks that included an end to job and voting discrimination. To reduce the political impact of Truman's shocking proposals, Smith linked his name in newspaper ads to segregationist governor J. Strom Thurmond of South Carolina, a turncoat Democrat who was running for president on the States' Rights ticket.[33]

Although Virginians did flock to the Republican banner in heavier than average numbers, Truman captured the Old Dominion's electors with just 47.9 percent of the vote. Governor Thurmond, whose party was popularly known as the Dixiecrats, had cut heavily into Virginia's Democratic total by lambasting Truman's proposals for civil rights. As for Smith, he retained his

congressional seat for a tenth term but received his lowest percentage to that time, 54.8 percent. He lost Krum's home county
of Fairfax, as well as Greene and Madison counties, and he narrowly won the labor strongholds of Alexandria and Arlington
County.[34]

After Truman's stunning reelection, House Democratic leaders
plotted strategy to advance the president's Fair Deal programs. For
Sam Rayburn, the obvious choice as Speaker, the committee assignments to Rules and Ways and Means presented a critical party
matter. Writing to Michigan Democrat John Dingell, Rayburn
reminded him of "our former trouble with the Committee on
Rules" in denying clearance to administration measures for low-
cost housing, federal aid to education, and a national health program. Rayburn, well aware that he had arranged Howard Smith's
promotion to Rules fifteen years earlier, intended "not [to] make
mistakes this time" by placing Democrats of wavering party loyalty
on Rules. In other party correspondence, administration Democrats singled out Smith and Cox as the major stumbling blocks to
a cooperative Rules Committee, and they recommended not
reappointing reactionary Mississippi Democrat William M. Colmer, a onetime New Dealer now allied with Smith. Some Democrats thought a more effective solution lay not in switching
committee members but in tightening procedural rules to let a
bill's sponsor compel Rules action after fourteen or twenty-one
days.[35]

As a veteran of congressional infighting, Judge Smith took the
lead in trying to maintain the reactionary stranglehold on Rules.
In late November he offered Rayburn a compromise on the impending civil rights and labor bills. But he refused the "impossible" bill making permanent the Fair Employment Practices
Commission, which many white southerners regarded as the im-
position of a second Reconstruction. Rayburn promised merely
to meet with Smith after Christmas. As it turned out, Rayburn
did not attack the seniority system or remove antiadministration
Democrats from Rules. Both Smith and Cox were reappointed,
and when a northern Democrat on Rules died, the new Speaker
reappointed Colmer, as well. The Rules Committee now stood
evenly divided between northern and southern Democrats.[36]

Smith suspected the assault on Rules was not over, so he kept
a vigilant pose in the halls of Congress. Soon he caught wind of

the plan to change House procedures for bills stalled in the Rules Committee. He immediately wrote a letter to his colleagues, asserting that allowing any House member the privilege of springing a measure from Rules was "minority rule of the most vicious sort." Smith noted that a majority of the House already could use the discharge petition to release any bill from Rules, although he did not mention that the House had rarely been able to use it because so many signatures—218—were needed. Smith's plea went for naught, however, when Rayburn supported a compromise twenty-one-day discharge rule which could be invoked by a committee chairman. Smith continued his protest. In a rancorous Democratic caucus on New Year's Day, 1949, he and a small group of die-hard southern segregationists resisted the decision to make the twenty-one-day rule binding on party members. Georgia's Gene Cox warned that the procedural change would mean "a weapon aimed at the heart of the South, her civilization, and the institutions that her people have erected." When Smith opposed the change on the House floor, Rayburn and the usually ineffectual Rules chairman Sabath outmaneuvered him. For the first time since the Cannon revolt of 1910, the House managed to restrict the Rules Committee's jurisdiction significantly.[37]

Liberal editors across the country heralded the dilution of the Rules Committee's power. Generally, their newspapers saw the change as long overdue. They expected the Democratic party would now be able to enact its mandate for reform. The *St. Louis Post-Dispatch* typified the widespread reaction to the new rule: "The blow falls hardest on two of the political relics who continue to occupy seats in the House though virtually everything they stand for has been repudiated at the ballot box. Eugene Cox, of Georgia, and Howard Smith, of Virginia, used to run the [Rules] committee pretty much as they pleased by teaming up with the four Republican members. They are now reduced to life-size."[38]

In the 1949 session the twenty-one-day rule allowed the Truman administration to push its wide-ranging domestic program, including civil rights, with only limited success. But because the president's antilynching and anti–poll tax bills clearly were aimed at the white South, Smith concluded that administration supporters had become apostates to the historic Democratic philosophy. He decided the time was ripe to reiterate the party's long-held beliefs. In October he addressed a *New York Herald*

Tribune forum as "a conservative Democrat," who adhered to the principles embodied in the Constitution and the Bill of Rights. "We are," he declared, "unwilling to surrender our convictions to meet every real or fancied emergency that may arise in a modern world, distressed and torn by the swarms of strange ideologies sweeping over the earth." True Democrats followed the Tenth Amendment, which placed most political responsibility in state and local governments. Accordingly, southern Democrats held the eighteenth-century belief that "Congress has no power to enact legislation or expend the people's money on any subject that it is not given authority to deal with under the Constitution."[39]

With this conviction, Smith denounced as unconstitutional the wage-hour law, the anti–poll tax bill, the permanent creation of the Fair Employment Practices Commission, and the federal housing bill. He argued that these measures would produce a welfare state financed by the taxpayers. Whenever federal monies were awarded, he contended, the federal government imposed restrictions "upon the liberties of the people." The only solution, as Smith saw it, lay with the heretofore "slothful and indifferent people" who have remained "impervious" to the danger signals around them. Until voters ousted representatives who abandoned the constitutional limitations on legislative behavior, Congress would continue to yield to various unscrupulous lobbies.[40]

When a midwestern Democrat, Andrew Jacobs of Indiana, criticized southern Democrats for opposing civil rights, Smith elaborated on his New York speech. On February 1, 1950, he asserted that the Democratic party owed a huge debt to its southern wing for keeping it alive in the nadir between the Civil War and the Great Depression. To his dismay, northern Democrats had forgotten the contributions of their southern counterparts. No greater evidence could be found than the northern wing's support of the permanent Fair Employment Practices Commission, which was created temporarily in 1941 to give blacks defense jobs. The Virginian claimed that the commission would "cut the throats of the people who kept your party alive through the years." After dismissing the charge that southern Democrats often had teamed with the opposition, he urged the House not to force racial integration on a "helpless southern people." Smith proudly admitted he was "a reactionary" because he adhered religiously to the Constitution, something he wished all representatives would emulate.[41]

Smith had turned to speechmaking to rouse southern and other conservative congressmen to the dangers of Truman's civil rights proposals. The administration's bills against lynching, the poll tax, and discriminatory hiring represented a massive assault against white southern society. Truman already had demonstrated his resolve for civil rights by ordering the armed forces to integrate, and many military bases were located in the South. Without southern solidarity in Congress, Smith maintained, the administration could disrupt southern segregation, a principle that formed the foundation of his society.[42]

Efforts in early 1950 to make the Fair Employment Practices Commission permanent seemed particularly threatening to southern racial and business patterns. Originally, the commission forbade firms with more than fifty employees to discriminate on the basis of race in hiring practices. During the war, the agency limped along with emergency White House funds. For political and humanitarian reasons, President Truman reiterated his commitment to the commission. Writing to black leader A. Philip Randolph in early 1946, Truman pledged, "I regard FEPC legislation as an integral part of my re-conversion program and shall contribute my efforts to give the Congress a chance to vote on it." But he often sacrificed his support for the commission to attract southern Democratic votes for his anti-communist foreign policy.[43]

When the FEPC bill finally reached the floor in February 1950, Smith unleashed his parliamentary wizardry to strip it before any vote occurred. First, the Virginia representative objected to a motion to speed the bill's consideration. Then he joined Mississippi Democrat John E. Rankin, a rabid white supremacist, to ask the presiding chairman when a substitute to the bill would be in order. The chairman replied that a substitute could not be brought up until the debate's conclusion. At 7 P.M., Smith suggested an adjournment because House members were tired from a long session. New York Democrat Franklin D. Roosevelt, Jr., denied any fatigue, causing Smith to retort that Roosevelt was younger than many other representatives. Once more, the chairman ruled Smith out of order. The Virginian appealed the chair's decision, but the House sustained it. This legislative maneuvering prompted a Republican supporter of the commission to characterize Smith's efforts as "a travesty on parliamentary law and procedure." The dilatory tactics of House conservatives kept the bill off the floor for five hours, and when the chamber at last agreed to adjourn at 3:19 A.M., the original measure had been gutted. Congress had witnessed another classic performance by the "fox of Fauquier County": Smith publicly denounced the bill as an attack on the Constitution, his region, and his class; and he tried every parliamentary device at his command to sink the hated provisions. The House eventually approved a watered-down version enforcing nondiscriminatory hiring practices only on a voluntary basis, but the Senate refused even this modest bill.[44]

Emboldened by his victory against the FEPC, Smith moved against the bane of the conservative coalition—wasteful government spending. His most celebrated exposé came in May 1951, when he attacked the Interior Department's Fish and Wildlife Service for frivolously publishing an expensively illustrated 150-page pamphlet on raccoon reproduction. To cut the department's appropriation "to pieces," Smith carefully prepared a series of amendments. But without a dramatic presentation, the amendments had little chance of adoption. When he reached the House well to speak, he paused, shuffled his papers, and peered over his pince-nez glasses until he had everyone's undivided attention. Then he used his favorite tool, biting sarcasm, to make light of the government's study of wildlife in Alabama.

> Evidently this Government employee went many hundreds of miles from Washington, presumably in one of these 4,500 cars now owned by the Department of the Interior. Perhaps he had a Government chauffeur. A great many of them do.
>
> He went down to watch the love affair of a pair of raccoons in the swamps. He describes it accurately in the book. He describes the intimate details of the love affair, and the ultimate commission of the misdemeanor which in due course of time was calculated to produce another litter of raccoons down there. That aroused my curiosity to some extent. I think it is all right to watch wildlife and to watch raccoons. Certainly as a private enterprise nobody is going to object to that. No one can criticise or complain about

that except the coons themselves and there is nothing they can do about it.

The House "nearly blew up," one spectator recalled, as Smith reenacted the part of the "Peeping Tom" scientist sneaking around the bulrushes in the hope of catching frisky animals at love-making. More importantly to Smith, the House found his per-formance convincing enough to slash the Interior Department's funding. As a matter of fact, however, Smith did not regard all federal government publications unnecessary, because he later had the government print 110,000 copies of *Diseases of the Horse* for interested farm constituents.[45]

For a firsthand look at wasteful spending, Judge Smith joined the thirteen-member congressional delegation to the European unification conference at Strasbourg, France, in November 1951. To cross the Atlantic, he made his first airplane flight. Con-vinced that Europe had rebuilt sufficiently from the war, Smith now sought to limit American funds for recovery lest foreign countries take further advantage of "Uncle Sap." During his two-week stay, the drawling Virginian's homespun tales in support of unification led the press to hail him as "the American Star." His popular appeal overseas persuaded Smith, who had fought tire-lessly to limit government spending and to curtail organized la-bor, that a biblical adage also applied to him: "A prophet is never without honor save in his own country." But the talks achieved few milestones, and Smith returned to the United States, resolv-ing never again to take a similar junket.[46]

Back in Virginia, Smith confronted an unsettled political situ-ation. He had yet another primary opponent, and he faced the possibility of losing a redistricting battle. Homer G. Richey, for-merly an assistant professor of political science at the University of Virginia, had announced his intention to run for Congress from Smith's district. Earlier in the year, he had been relieved of his teaching duties after making unsubstantiated charges that sev-eral professors in his department were Communist-sympathizers. One of Smith's friends described Richey as "a perfect nut" and reassured Smith that renomination was a mere formality. State newspapers found Richey's candidacy equally incredible. In a De-cember editorial the *Lynchburg News* commented, "We never expected to live to see the day Judge Smith would be appraised by anyone and found on the side of the liberal angels." The paper felt confident that Smith would win easily.[47]

The veteran politician, meanwhile, looked past his opponent to the real danger posed by congressional redistricting. He contemplated retiring from Congress if the state legislature did not design a district to his liking. Seeking a rural, and hence conservative, constituency, Smith asked state senator Robert Y. Button of the Privileges and Elections Committee to help redraw a suitable district. Smith realized that northern Virginia had changed substantially and that, if he ever had, he no longer reflected the wishes of city dwellers, federal government employees, and union workers who now made up a sizable proportion of the district electorate. By early 1952 the General Assembly gave Smith what he wanted. The legislature removed the parts of the old Eighth District that Smith had found unreliable, including the pockets of labor strength in Alexandria, Arlington County, Fairfax County, and Falls Church. It also removed Madison County, an erstwhile supporter. The Assembly added Caroline, Hanover, King William, Lancaster, Northumberland, Richmond, Spotsylvania, and Westmoreland counties and Fredericksburg. The new Eighth was larger in area, more rural, and had a more conservative voting record. To run from this revised district, Smith had only to change his voting residence from Alexandria to his farm in Fauquier County.[48]

The next problem confronting Smith was the method of party nomination. He realized that the new district would have to adopt the convention system because of legal questions and time limitations. Accordingly, in March he worked behind the scenes to name the chairman of the district Democratic committee, an often decisive factor at a convention. To minimize any possible disharmony, the Judge agreed to a compromise plan that retained all of the old delegates from the new counties, giving them fractional votes. On the eve of the state Democratic convention, he felt satisfied with the district committee's composition, remarking privately that it was "now composed of people of the same way of thinking." Faced with almost no chance of beating Smith in a convention, Richey withdrew to run as an independent. In May, as expected, the convention unanimously selected the sixty-nine-year-old Smith as the Democratic candidate for the Eighth District congressional seat.[49]

Smith's reelection bid was still troubled by the unpopular presidential candidacy and platform of Illinois Democrat Adlai E. Stevenson. When Virginia's Senator Byrd declined to support Stevenson over the Republican war hero Dwight D. Eisenhower and maintained a "Golden Silence," Judge Smith faced repeated questions about his own loyalty to the Democratic "house of our fathers." Responding to a constituent's inquiry, Smith reiterated his backing of the Stevenson ticket, just as he had endorsed all previous Democratic candidates. Nevertheless, he informed the writer of his opposition to key party planks, including repeal of the Taft-Hartley Act, "socialistic" public housing, and the Fair Employment Practices Commission, which would "do away with segregation of the races." Undoubtedly, Smith's paramount reason for supporting Stevenson was to retain "the committee assignment that I hold as a member of the Democratic party" in order to block antisouthern proposals.[50]

In the campaign, Smith had little competition from Richey and none from the Republican party. In numerous radio broadcasts, Richey accused Smith of collaborating with Truman and Secretary of State Dean Acheson to lead the nation "down the primrose path" to bankruptcy and the "world saving panaceas" of the United Nations and the Marshall Plan. He also accused Smith of voting to cut defense spending during the Korean War. In addition, Richey belittled the incumbent's attendance at the European unification conference, charging its purpose was "to subsidize French perfume makers and Scotch whisky brewers." Although Richey plastered his accusations on trees and poles throughout the district, few residents found him credible. Nor did Smith take his opposition seriously; he made few campaign appearances, solicited no contributions, and declined Richey's challenge to debate.[51]

When the polls closed on November 4, Eisenhower had captured the Eighth District, Virginia, and the nation by a landslide. He even ran 5 percent ahead of Smith, who crushed Richey by a nearly three-to-one margin. At first, it appeared that Smith's obstructionism on Rules might decline because the Republicans had gained control of the House. But the deaths of outgoing Rules chairman Sabath and Smith's reactionary colleague Gene Cox before Congress met in 1953 left the Virginian as the highest-ranking Democrat on the committee. If he and his party could win in the next election, Smith would become the likely choice for the influential Rules chairmanship.[52]

When the Judge returned to Capitol Hill in 1953, he vigorously opposed Hawaiian statehood. This proposal, dating back to 1919, had encountered congressional obstacles before. Smith's objection to the statehood bill rested principally on racist beliefs. The crucial fact about Hawaii, he warned, was its racial composition: only 16 percent of its residents were white. Never before, he cautioned the House, had Congress granted statehood to a territory "where the Caucasian race was in the minority." His second objection stemmed from the plan to reduce the delegations of other states in order to give Hawaii two representatives. Because Hawaii's delegation was likely to vote for liberal Democratic proposals, southern Democrats were afraid that more civil rights and federal aid bills would be approved. Next, he charged that the Communist cause in Hawaii was a potent force, abetted by union leader Harry Bridges, his old bête noire. Turning to the geographical question, Smith pointed out that Hawaii was not contiguous to the continental United States; no previous state had this liability. Finally, Smith raised the possibility of all-out war. He questioned the wisdom of having a far-flung outpost like Hawaii when all military strength might be needed to defend the American continent.[53]

When Smith doubted the fitness of oriental Hawaiians to become Americans, he overlooked the fact that the Hawaiians were already American citizens. As for the presence of communism on the islands, congressional witnesses disagreed. But California representative Donald J. Jackson, a member of the House Committee on Un-American Activities, asserted that Hawaii had no more Communists than places on the American mainland. In any event, other congressmen pointed out that Hawaiians had proved their valor during World War II. Nor was distance likely to present an obstacle to statehood. Hawaii bought more goods than many mainland customers, and it currently paid more federal taxes than nine states. And last, far from being a defensive liability, Hawaii offered an unsurpassed military outpost to maintain a strong American presence in the Pacific. Ultimately, these facts held sway. For the first time since 1947, the House approved Hawaii's application to join the Union, but the Senate again proved uncooperative. Statehood would not come for another six years.[54]

During the Truman administration, Smith perceived increased threats to his state and region, particularly in the areas of labor and race relations. To combat heightened pressure from northern Democrats and the president for the Fair Employment Practices Commission, repeal of the Taft-Hartley law, and expanded federal aid programs, he delivered House speeches that beseeched his southern colleagues to unite against these proposals. More importantly, he became the leader of the Democratic half of the influential conservative coalition. With the deaths of the two highest-ranking Rules Democrats, Smith bided his time, waiting for the opportunity to exercise greater powers of obstruction once the House returned to Democratic control.

CHAPTER 6

Chairman of the Rules Committee: The Eisenhower Years

It's a perilous business for a nation to thrust by force great social changes upon a part of it determined to resist.

Howard W. Smith (1956)

In 1954 Smith faced his thirteenth congressional campaign, knowing his reelection and Democratic control of the House would mean the Rules chairmanship. He was fortunate that year not to have party opposition. Moreover, his Republican opponent, political science professor Charmenz S. Lenhart of Mary Washington College, received only reluctant backing from party stalwarts who respected Smith's record. Lenhart tried to associate herself with President Eisenhower and to attack Smith for inaction on the proposed Rappahannock River dam. But she made little headway against the incumbent, in part because Smith belittled Lenhart's candidacy on the ground of gender. He remarked dryly, "If I had known this was to be a beauty contest I wouldn't have entered." Besides the handicap of being a woman, Lenhart faced other formidable obstacles, including incumbency and ideology. The voters gave Smith a lopsided two-to-one victory. With the Democratic resurgence throughout the country, Howard W. Smith became the new chairman of the nearly all-powerful House Rules Committee.[1]

Smith's victory and elevated position created few immediate waves. The *Washington Post* called his control of Rules an "anticlimax" because his actual power stemmed from work outside committees, such as his leadership of the conservative coalition. Even House Speaker Rayburn appeared unworried by Smith's new post because the new Rules chairman promised to cooperate with the Democratic party chiefs except on "matters of principle." Rayburn probably was also reassured by the traits he shared with Smith, including long service to the House, party affiliation, a conservative district, advanced age, and a farming background. Moreover, Smith had been a party loyalist on minor legislation during his whole career in Congress.[2]

But these two southern titans were on a collision course in the late fifties because their political values diverged so sharply. In Washington, Smith often studied and worked alone, defying the party leadership on almost every important issue. Smith would not, to use Rayburn's phrase, "go along" with the party's wishes. The Speaker, on the other hand, voted with the party even when he disagreed and on the rare occasions when his constituents disagreed. Smith was ruthless in the exercise of power—"a hard, mean old man," an unnamed Rules member once said. Speaker Sam preferred to "persuade" colleagues, avoiding pressure tactics whenever possible. Journalist Tom Wicker noted that "the Gentlemen of the House loved and respected Rayburn and coveted his favor; they feared and respected Smith and deferred to his power."[3]

On the role of the federal government, these preeminent southern Democrats were especially far apart. While Rayburn saw the federal government as a valuable aid to his district, Smith was alarmed by it. Smith seldom took stock of what his constituents wanted from Washington; he believed they were better off unfettered by its demands. By contrast, Rayburn returned frequently to Fannin County, Texas, declaring himself to be a responsive legislator for local concerns. There, he shed his slick Washington manner, and like his constituents he wore khakis, an old shirt, and a slouchy hat, chewed tobacco, drank whiskey, and drove a dented pickup truck. He thought that his farming district needed public works projects that only the national government could provide. He consequently delivered a dam, four military air bases, six man-made lakes, a veterans' hospital and domiciliary, farm-to-market roads, rural electrification, and soil conservation. Smith boasted of having done none of these things. Indeed, he had resisted federally financed roads in front of his own farm and had switched to cattle raising when the government controlled corn production by offering lucrative farm subsidies. Smith's reactionary ideology served him well until national and Eighth District problems could no longer be ignored or suppressed. At that point, Rayburn and Smith engaged in a parliamentary death match.[4]

In the interim, Smith was able to block many civil rights and social welfare measures, despite the clear evidence of public and congressional opinion that favored such measures. How was one man able to defy congressional will? The answer can be found in his adept use of the Rules Committee, which the *New Republic* labeled the "right-wing minority's secret weapon." The committee possessed certain powerful privileges, including the right to sit while the House was in session, to send a rule to the floor at any time, and to have its reports on rules and order of business considered immediately. Generally speaking, a bill from another committee had to be given a rule from Rules to reach the floor for deliberation. The rule granted to a bill could sharply affect its final form. For example, if the Rules Committee disliked a bill, it could keep the measure indefinitely or call for open debate and permit an unlimited number of amendments; conversely, a bill viewed favorably would be cleared quickly and face little debate and no amendments.[5]

Because the Rules Committee, unlike most others, operated without written guidelines, its chairman also possessed unusually broad discretionary powers. The chairman often unilaterally determined when the committee would meet, the order of its agenda, and the timing of committee votes. Without his consent, committee business ground to a halt. The chairman also decided the fate of Rules Committee resolutions. He could call them to the House floor himself or assign that chore to other members.[6]

Under exceptional circumstances, there were three ways to bring a bill to the floor without a rule. The House of Representatives could suspend ordinary procedure by a two-thirds vote, the Calendar Wednesday device that mandated same-day action on a bill could be used, or majority approval could be obtained for a discharge petition. These devices had proved extraordinarily difficult to invoke. Indeed, the discharge petition had been used successfully only once, circumventing Smith's blockade of the minimum-wage bill in 1938; the Calendar Wednesday device had last worked in 1950. Hence, for all practical purposes, Rules Committee action dictated the fate of bills.[7]

During Smith's tenure, the Rules Committee became a "star chamber" for dozens of reform bills that the chairman opposed. It blocked or changed more important legislation than at any time since the New Deal. In so doing, the committee worked at cross-purposes with the majority party and its leadership. This occurred for three reasons. First, liberal northern representatives wrote more far-reaching federal aid bills in the late fifties and sixties to attack pressing urban problems. Congress now routinely considered bills on public housing, education, and civil rights, all of which reactionaries such as Smith fiercely opposed. Southern Democrats and Republicans turned to the Rules Committee to slow the legislative flow to a trickle.[8]

Second, during the period from 1955 to 1960 the Rules Committee maintained a balance between liberal and conservative forces. The twelve-member committee divided roughly along party lines, with Democrats Smith and Colmer joining the four Republicans. The other six Democrats, including Richard D. Bolling of Missouri, Homer Thornberry of Texas, and Thomas P. O'Neill, Jr., of Massachusetts, remained steadfastly loyal to the House party leadership. Because a tie vote prevented legislation from reaching the floor, the Rules Committee delayed, weakened, or killed many federal aid programs sought by liberals for their urban districts.[9]

The most important reason for Rules Committee obstruction in the Eisenhower years was Smith himself. Not only did he inherit the chairman's extraordinary powers, he understood their use and employed them to their fullest extent. Carl Elliott, the father of the National Defense Education Act, pointed out that unlike most politicians who shy away from power, Smith "exercised power completely, as fearlessly as anybody could possibly do." To supplement his unexcelled skill as a parliamentarian, Smith often overcame the liberal majority in the House by becoming a "storehouse of political wisdom." Bolling, Smith's archfoe and a man praised for his own parliamentary brilliance, recalled Smith as the legislative master: "Anytime he was working on a piece of legislation, he knew everything there was to know about that piece of legislation, which . . . involves so many bypaths. Almost all bills are full of references to other laws, and he would go back and look at the references and then look at the references cited in the references. He was as good a student, as good a researcher, as I ever saw. And I never could find anybody who did much for him except look up little bits and pieces." Bolling conceded that the soft-spoken Smith "made a fool out of me quite a few times before I learned, and I never did learn enough to keep him from making a fool out of me." The latest study of the Rules Committee concluded that Smith "possessed an almost unique ability to address a problem of the moment without losing sight of the overall plan." Michigan Republican Clare E. Hoffman once summed up Smith's powerful ability, calling him "one of the wisest, foxiest, smoothest, soundest operators that ever came to Congress in my time." Smith's parliamentary talent was so immense that even his foes "enjoyed watching how he finessed things."[10]

Judge Smith's personality and political style contributed to his success on Capitol Hill. He preferred to block federal aid and civil rights measures without arousing the liberal majority in the House. "Tiptoeing" around the corridors in a cutaway coat and wing collar, Smith usually shunned publicity and referred controversial legislative actions to other southern Democrats, such as Graham Barden of North Carolina. Smith's secretary Virginia Mitchell suggested a low profile "was his middle name." Bolling, a shrewd but acerbic political operator, observed the same pattern: "Smith wasn't the least bit interested in making a noise. He found out something a long time ago that a lot of people in this town never discover. You can do damn near anything in Washington if you don't insist on getting credit for it." Even when Smith became angry, which was "very rare," he would dictate a sharp but unsigned rejoinder to the congressman who irritated him. Then, according to his secretary, "he'd think it over, smoke it over, and sleep it over." The next day, he usually destroyed the unsent letter. Unlike most of his peers, Smith had no time for socializing or glad-handing. He avoided two-martini lunches with colleagues and lobbyists and was not burdened with time-consuming visits to a distant or unpredictable district. Instead, he kept watch over the House nearly all the time it was in session.[11]

House Democratic whip Carl Albert of Oklahoma, who knew Smith well, painted a Janus-faced portrait of the Rules chairman. Smith, who looked like a nineteenth-century Virginia squire, had a courtly demeanor, Albert recalled, but this behavior masked a sharp intellect and his unswerving dedication to "deep, sinister ideas."

> He was very soft-spoken, reserved, friendly, very much an old-fashioned Virginia gentleman, very conservative. He was friendly with everybody. I never saw him lose his temper in my life, I don't think. He was low key, but he'd cut your head off if he wanted you out of the way. . . . He was a tough hombre. He was tough as a legislator. He was tough as a parliamentarian. He had a determination that you hardly ever see in people. He knew what was happening all the time. He had a great sense of what was going to take place and what was going to be his problems. More than anybody else in the Congress for thirty years he was the guardian of archsouthern conservatism—more than anybody, far more than anybody. [12]

Typically, the frail-looking Smith began his closely scheduled day with his only large meal, a breakfast of oatmeal smothered with his dairy's Guernsey cream, corn muffins, and eggs and ham from his farm. His daughter remembered that "he loved breakfast. You could not believe an old man could eat the amount of breakfast that he ate . . . but he had it firmly fixed in his head that the breakfast was the most important meal—being a farmer." He then arrived at his congressional office in the Longworth Building shortly after nine o'clock. For the next hour, he answered the nearly hundred letters that arrived daily and personally returned telephone calls to assure control over every event, every detail. Smith's secretary remembered his attention to his correspondence: "Boy, he wanted to see that mail first crack out of the box. We'd have to have that on his desk. Any phone calls, and I'd just make him little memos. He would go over his mail. He was very meticulous, and he wanted to keep up with everything." Despite the closeness of his district, constituents seldom intruded. [13]

At 10:30 A.M. about three times weekly, Judge Smith convened the Rules Committee in a small, chandeliered room just off the House floor. The meetings were "prearranged" but appeared routine. One observer likened Smith to "an auctioneer," who with an economy of movement nodded or pointed to likeminded colleagues to bring up acceptable matters. As "billows of blue smoke rose slowly" from his well-gnawed cigar, Smith ordinarily kept discussion to a minimum around the crowded rectangular table. The surface calm hid, in the view of a Rules member, the presence of power "so thick that one could slice it with a dull knife." Chairman Smith possessed "a sixth sense about how and when to exercise [power]. He nearly always took the long view and cannily calculated what would later best serve the position he took at a given time."[14]

As noontime approached, the lean congressman slipped quietly downstairs to the House cloakroom to drink his daily lunch, a chocolate milkshake. At the same time, he coolly observed which congressmen were making compromising deals, while studiously evading the omnipresent lobbyists himself. Afterwards, the septuagenarian Smith ambled into the House chamber as it convened. His huge, floppy ears pricked up then, and his steely dark eyes darted around the room, sizing up the proceedings. Once in his seat, he usually sat with hands folded, "peering benignly over his Andy Clyde glasses." But his apparent disinterest fooled few. From all sides, trusted southern legmen flocked to him for his soft-spoken instructions. When House business became routine, Smith returned to his office. In the late afternoons, he outlined legislative strategy with members of the Virginia delegation and conservative coalition. If no one stopped by, he began perusing upcoming bills. At 5 P.M., Smith waited for a secretary to drive him to his Alexandria home, some twenty minutes away, where his wife Annie awaited him. For years, Smith, easily a millionaire, had driven "the plainest of the plain cars," a two-door Chevrolet without a radio or an air conditioner; but advancing age had contributed to a couple of minor accidents, convincing him to abandon driving altogether.[15]

For a workaholic like Smith, his two-story brick home was simply a more pleasant office. Despite his political power, he was "sort of a lonely man in many ways," according to his closest aide. He refused nearly all social invitations, except for the yearly Jefferson-Jackson Day dinner that Democrats were obliged to attend. Seldom did he venture out at night, even for food or entertainment. According to his daughter, Smith "was not a party person—absolutely had to be dragged to a party." Outside of receiving a few close friends and feting Rules committeemen once a year, Smith had no company beyond his family. After eating dinner, he resumed reading "bills over from cover to cover that were to come before the Rules Committee." Smith studied legislation so intently, Alabama Democrat Carl Elliott recalled, that he "often displayed as much or more knowledge of a particular bill than did the chairman of the legislative committee who brought it to Rules." At the close of the day, Smith watched the ten o'clock news on television, listening closely to his favorite Capitol Hill reporter, Roger Mudd, a skilled but unpretentious professional, much like himself. Thus prepared, he went to bed, ready to begin another day that would be almost identical to the one that had just passed.[16]

As Rules chairman, the Judge saw himself as a national statesman, not the representative of a small bailiwick. It was only natural that he took his work so seriously. An essential element in statesmanship, he believed, was ignoring parochial interests when they contradicted the national good. On one occasion, a group of rural mail carriers from his district asked Smith to support a bill raising their pay. Smith listened quietly and then told them directly, "You certainly have my sympathy, but you will not have my vote." True to his word, he voted against the wage increase, though it passed anyway. Most congressmen, the Rules committee counsel pointed out, would have pacified local concerns by saying, "Oh, gee, I'm all for it," only to miss the roll-call vote. "But the Judge was very frank, not only with them, but with any group like that. He didn't side—he didn't play politics in other words." Smith adhered to the view that a representative was elected on the basis of his fitness to make wise decisions, not to be a mouthpiece for organized local interests. While this was antidemocratic, it was also "true republicanism" and consciously not democratic. When asked why he had turned the postal workers away, Smith brusquely replied in his customary low voice, "If that's the kind of people I gotta represent, then damned if I want to be up here."[17]

Smith could, in fact, afford a cavalier attitude toward organized interest groups in his district. He had faced only token opposition since his first race in 1930, and under Virginia's political tradition, he could expect the trend to continue indefinitely. All he needed to do to win reelection was to contact "key people in his district" a few weeks before the voting. A Smith campaign aide explained how the process worked. In every important town, Smith "would have a person there—a good substantial business person—who was always, particularly around election time, boosting Judge Smith around the whole area." With the electorate held in check by the poll tax and influenced by prominent local officials and businessmen, Smith wore the clothes of statesmanship comfortably.[18]

Early in his chairmanship, the Virginian set forth the political principles that would guide his actions. Simply put, he subscribed to what he believed was a Jeffersonian precept, namely, the best government is the one that governs least. To Smith, this notion was best expressed in the Tenth Amendment, which reserved nondelegated powers to the states or to the people. Declaring his hostility to government "compulsion" over individuals, he asserted his opposition to minimum-wage increases and desegregation.[19]

He viewed his own rule as steering the country back to these constitutional ideals. His task was made immeasurably more difficult by public apathy. When Smith received the 1955 George Washington Award from the American Good Government Society, he roundly condemned acquiescence in unconstitutional government, suggesting it had profound implications: "Each such departure from Constitutional standards had directly or indirectly deprived the citizen of some constitutional liberty until today the individual American citizen is gradually being placed under compulsion and his daily life and activities controlled by the judgment of the Federal Courts, the acts of Congress, and the edicts of the Executive Department to an extent never remotely conceived by the authors of the Constitution." The end result, he estimated, signified "government by delegation of authority." Worst of all, centralized government had swallowed up the reserved rights of the states, and the administration of justice had been transferred to the "faraway lands of the Federal Courts." With public support, he hoped to lead the country out of this wilderness.[20]

To counter the trend toward judicial "dictatorship," Smith in early 1955 introduced a brief bill (H.R. 3) innocuously entitled "To Establish Rules of Interpretation Governing Questions of the Effect of Acts of Congress on State Laws." This bill obliterated the doctrine of "pre-emption." He was outraged by the 1954 *Nelson* decision of the Pennsylvania Supreme Court, which overturned state laws against subversion on the ground that the federal Smith Act "pre-empted the field." Smith argued that no court should construe congressional intent as withdrawing state powers unless the laws said so specifically. Without remedy, he believed this "dangerous disease" could "destroy completely the sovereignty of the States." To rally support for his states' rights bill, Smith corresponded with Virginia state officers, including his close political ally Governor Thomas B. Stanley. But Smith was unable to arouse much public backing for H.R. 3, and the Judiciary Committee suspended hearings on the proposal after just two days.[21]

This setback did not deter Smith from sponsoring another bill to restrict judicial dominion when the Warren Court permanently neutralized his Alien Registration Act in the middle fifties. In *Page* v. *Nelson*, the U.S. Supreme Court upheld the state court's decision: The Smith Act had indeed preempted sedition prosecutions on the state level. This decision allowed fourteen members of the California Communist party to appeal their conspiracy indictments. The next year, the Court ignored the *Dennis* precedent to reverse their convictions in *Yates* v. *United States* (1957). Speaking for the Court, Justice John Marshall Harlan argued that the Smith Act did not prohibit the mere advocacy or teaching of violent subversion; rather, the act barred only overt actions to overthrow the government. He warned, "We must be careful that measures designed for legitimate ends are not made instruments of oppression." Because the Court relied on a statutory interpretation in the *Yates* case, it avoided a constitutional attack on the Smith Act. At the same time, the Court stripped the law's threat to civil liberties. Across the nation, charges were dismissed against alleged conspirators, and prosecutions under the Smith Act ceased. Angered at these decisions, Smith worked tirelessly for years, though unsuccessfully, to win congressional approval for limiting the Court's jurisdiction in subversion cases.[22]

While the Judge damned the Supreme Court for overstepping its domain, he also assailed Congress for overspending its budget on extravagant social reforms, such as public housing. Congress had authorized 35,000 public housing units in 1954, but because of statutory restrictions only 142 had been started by the following year. In his State of the Union speech of January 1955, President Eisenhower sought a bill that tied public housing aid to workable slum clearance and urban renewal programs. To provide "decent, safe and sanitary housing for low-income families," the president called for 35,000 public housing units in each of the next two years. [23]

Estimating the bill's total cost at $18 billion, Smith designated the proposal as a wasteful and "purely socialistic project." In early July six Rules Democrats disagreed, most notably Bolling and O'Neill; but their opposition was insufficient. When Smith and Colmer sided with the Republican committeemen, the bill remained bottled up. The *Washington Post* commented that "hatchet man" Smith had misled the Rules Committee into the "legislative massacre business." His proper role, the *Post* claimed, was merely to regulate legislative measures so that members had "a chance to vote on all major policy bills." More politic than the newspaper, Speaker Rayburn blamed House Republicans for blocking their administration's own bill. [24]

At this point, House minority leader Joe Martin applied enough pressure to change three Republican minds. As the chamber readied for a vote, Colmer, speaking for Smith as well as himself, decried the bill's prohibitive cost and its stifling effect on individual initiative. He warned that the Supreme Court's recent desegregation decisions in education might be extended to public housing. Colmer consequently urged the adoption of an amendment offered by Michigan Republican Jesse P. Wolcott which would emasculate the bill by removing all public housing provisions. The House narrowly agreed. The final bill represented a compromise, with 45,000 housing units to be built in a single year. Although Eisenhower had "serious objections" to the bill, he thought the lower classes needed some form of immediate housing assistance, and he signed the measure in August. [25]

Throughout his Rules chairmanship, Smith fought costly federal programs, such as public housing. But he was increasingly occupied by the black civil rights movement that was boiling over on Capitol Hill and in Virginia. In 1954 the Supreme Court dropped the first bombshell when its *Brown* decision forbade the separate-but-equal formula in public schools. The South was caught largely unawares despite earlier desegregation rulings in higher education. The epic decision particularly affected Virginia because one of the companion cases involved the Old Dominion's Prince Edward County.[26]

On the surface, Virginia might have been disposed to accept desegregation. Its black population was not nearly as large as those in the Deep South states. In fact, Virginia's black proportion of 22.2 percent in 1950 was falling and barely exceeded that of Maryland, which obeyed the Court's edict. Within Smith's district, the ratio of blacks to whites was comparable to the state's average, ranging from less than 13 percent in Alexandria and Prince William County to 40 percent in Louisa County. Moreover, a few blacks already had integrated state institutions. In Richmond a black joined the city council in 1949, and blacks had entered the University of Virginia and Virginia Polytechnic Institute. Since Harry Byrd's governorship in the 1920s, no black Virginian had been lynched. In 1949 V. O. Key, Jr., an acute student of the South, pronounced the Old Dominion's race relations as "perhaps the most harmonious in the South."[27]

As it turned out, however, the prospect of integration sparked three highly divergent reactions among Virginians. Two of these groups initially occupied the political backstage. The smallest, least significant group welcomed integration as long overdue. Its few adherents included the state NAACP, clerics, and such outspoken white liberals as Sarah Patton Boyle. The moderate group, led by former governors John S. Battle and Colgate W. Darden, Jr., lamented the *Brown* decision but reluctantly acquiesced in it to save public education. Darden, as president of the University of Virginia, believed that "the people in many areas in Virginia will not consent to having their schools closed in preference to the limited integration which will occur where the Negro population is light." But because the moderates still preferred segregation, they supported two proposals recommended by a state commission. The proposals would permit white students to attend segregated schools by authorizing state tuition grants and a locally administered pupil assignment plan.[28]

The momentum and popular opinion, however, belonged to the diehard segregationists. Dominated by Byrd politicians, this group demanded complete disobedience of *Brown,* in what was called "massive resistance." Its chief exponent in the media, James J. Kilpatrick, editor of the *Richmond News Leader,* drew upon the antebellum doctrines of states' rights and interposition, explaining that "the answer lies in establishing one policy, unyielding, for the State as a whole: No integration in Virginia's public schools, now or ever." To maintain segregation, the stalwarts formed ad hoc cells innocuously called the Defenders of State Sovereignty and Individual Liberties. In reality, this twelve-thousand-member organization was little more than a respectable and nonviolent Ku Klux Klan, subscribing to the belief that "the segregation of the races is a right of the state government." In addition, the segregationists pressed for a state constitutional amendment repealing the compulsory school attendance law and supported sympathetic candidates for statewide office.[29]

Smith sided with the ultrasegregationists. Ordinarily, he regarded himself as a national statesman resisting a steady barrage against the republic's constitutional pillars. But integration affected the federal and state levels at the same time and required his attention in both areas. He counterattacked with every weapon in his arsenal. In Congress he devised remedial legislation to weaken the Supreme Court and tried to gut civil rights bills. He also defended segregation in Virginia, even lending his name and contributing small sums to the segregationist cause. He spared no effort because "the outcome is going to depend very largely upon how deeply the people of Virginia feel about it and how far they are going to be willing to sacrifice in order to maintain segregation."[30]

Like many other white southerners, Smith's racial views were paternalistic at best and racist at worst. He claimed to have helped blacks occasionally at his farm. He would sometimes provide them with loans or untangle bureaucratic snarls. Once, he assisted a black farmhand who was falsely accused of sending live animals through the mail. At his Capitol Hill office, Smith had a policy of seeing black constituents quickly. Of course, few blacks had the political astuteness, time, or money to visit their representative in Washington.[31]

On the other hand, Smith thought blacks were inferior beings. At one point, he justified slavery as an institution on the grounds that the Romans and Egyptians had used slaves to develop incomparable civilizations. On another occasion, the Judge declared that "the Southern people have never accepted the colored race as a race of people who had equal intelligence and education and social attainments as the white people of the South." He insisted that integrated schools were opposed by blacks because "they've got better schools than the white children" and by southern whites because "racial intermixture is abominable to us." To his close friend Luther Dudley, Smith's racial views were understandable because segregation was the normal pattern of race relations when Smith was born, just eighteen years after the Civil War. As a result, Smith assumed that blacks were incapable of assuming the political and financial responsibilities that whites bore. Smith's cousin the Reverend Samuel Chilton put the congressman's racial views in a nutshell: "I think the Judge had a real feeling of kindness toward the black people he knew, but he did not respect the race." Indeed, when the liberal minister at Smith's church in Alexandria publicly endorsed desegregation in 1955, the Judge stopped attending and switched churches.[32]

Smith's first salvo against integration came in January 1956 when he reintroduced his antipreemption bill, H.R. 3. This time, he addressed the entire issue of state power rather than the immediate problem of sedition. After the Supreme Court upheld the *Nelson* verdict in April, Smith pushed harder than ever for legislative approval. Now that the Court had overthrown state sedition laws, it could also strike down local segregation ordinances. Smith's bill had the support of the Southern Regional Conference of Attorneys General, the National Association of Manufacturers, and the editorial backing of many Virginia newspapers. All of these groups believed Smith's measure would curb judicial usurpation of state powers and prevent state submission to a "dictatorial centralized government."[33]

A number of other groups found H.R. 3 totally unacceptable. The *Washington Post* cast a suspicious eye on the Virginian's motivation, rejecting his claim that the bill "has nothing to do with" race relations. Clarence Mitchell of the NAACP's Washington bureau similarly suspected Smith wanted "to destroy the constitutional rights of colored citizens and to attempt to reverse recent Supreme Court decisions in the field of civil rights." Organized labor also voiced alarm at the proposal, exposing it as a camouflaged attack on unions. Labor spokesmen contended the bill would produce "chaos and confusion" by giving states new powers in fields currently regulated by the federal government. Some opponents worried that the bill might apply retroactively to all legislation, thus opening a legal nightmare. Despite some progress in the House, the bill did not reach the floor.[34]

With the legislative avenue blocked, Smith pursued a second approach to preserving segregation. Along with other southern Democrats, he decided a congressional resolution would rally white public opinion, in the words of Rules partner William Colmer, against "the do-gooders and Northern demagogues, who are trying to ram integration down our collective throats." Smith's Virginia colleague in the Senate, A. Willis Robertson, explained this new avenue to Governor Stanley:

> The unfortunate fact remains that any way we may turn to get legal relief from the unjustified decision of the Supreme Court we are blocked by an overwhelming majority which is in favor for political or other reasons of enforcing desegregation upon the South. But we in the South can publicly discuss our allegiance to the principles of States' Rights through resolutions of interposition and we in the Congress can discuss improper interpretation of the Fourteenth Amendment by the Supreme Court; and by constantly appealing to the bar of public opinion we can at least hope that there may be some slow down in the enforcement of the Supreme Court's action and ultimately, of course, some reversal of it.[35]

In response to the desegregation ruling, Senator J. Strom Thurmond of South Carolina prepared a defiant resolution, which Senator Byrd declared to be "a part of the plan of massive resistance we've been working on." On March 12, 1956, Smith alone laid this so-called Southern Manifesto before the House and denounced the *Brown* decision. He decried recent judicial interpretations of the Constitution "reversing long established and accepted law and based on expediency at the sacrifice of consistency." Because the Constitution had limited the federal judiciary's powers, Smith concluded that the Supreme Court's recent deviations subverted the government. But in contrast to the Senate, the manifesto sparked no outcry in the House.[36]

Smith could afford to attack civil rights openly because his views coincided with the views of his voting constituents. This was also the case for nearly every other southern Democrat. It was not true for Rayburn, who, along with Senate majority leader Lyndon Johnson of Texas, was not asked to sign the document. The Speaker found himself in a ticklish political situation. Although he endorsed civil rights privately, his conservative white constituents, who greatly outnumbered blacks who voted, were as fiercely segregationist as Smith's. Nevertheless, Rayburn lent northern liberals important tacit support for political and personal reasons. He realized that blacks represented a potent voting bloc in northern cities whose support of Democratic candidates would strengthen the national party. He also sincerely believed that blacks were granted equal rights under the Constitution. On one occasion, Rayburn confided to another southern liberal, Oklahoma's Carl Albert: "These people are entitled to this." But to retain his congressional seat, Rayburn remained publicly tight-lipped on the manifesto.[37]

To Judge Smith and the other one hundred southern congressmen who did sign the declaration, the manifesto registered their distress over antisegregation decisions. These politicians regarded integration as a potential catastrophe to race relations and southern society generally. With the 1956 Democratic national convention five months away, southerners also wanted to prevent a party plank favoring integration. Their target was Adlai E. Stevenson of Illinois, the apparent front-runner. Unlike his rivals, Stevenson had adopted a moderate stand in race relations. In part, the manifesto was intended to demonstrate that he would lose valuable southern support if he changed his views. But its effect proved negligible, for Congress did not nullify *Brown*, and subsequent presidents endorsed integration.[38]

With his opposition to the civil rights bill of 1956, Smith strained his relationship with Sam Rayburn and antagonized

House liberals. The momentum for black civil rights had been building for months. Although Virginia and the Deep South defied the *Brown* decision, school districts in Baltimore, Louisville, St. Louis, and Washington, D.C., integrated quietly. Then, in 1955, blacks in Montgomery, Alabama, organized a yearlong boycott of city buses to protest the city's segregation ordinance. Martin Luther King, Jr., spearheaded the drive for integration, only to see black homes and churches bombed. In mid-March 1956 President Eisenhower's attorney general, Herbert Brownell, tried to use the volatile situation to partisan advantage. Despite Eisenhower's lukewarm attitude, Brownell proposed a civil rights bill to pull blacks away from the Democratic party.[39]

Congressional reaction to the administration's civil rights bill predictably divided along sectional lines. Smith, for example, regarded the measure as a "very dangerous and ill-advised piece of legislation." He thought that the bill undercut state responsibility for local infractions because it would create a federal Civil Rights Commission to investigate charges of voting irregularities and enable the U.S. attorney general and federal judges, rather than southern white juries, to protect individual voting rights. To northern Democrats, however, the administration's bill appeared too mild, for the bill did not prohibit discrimination and segregation in interstate transportation, threaten criminal proceedings for those who violated black civil rights, or provide an institutional base within the Justice Department to receive and resolve civil rights complaints. Judiciary Committee chairman Emanuel Celler of New York criticized the Eisenhower measure, comparing it to "a bean shooter when you should use a gun." But Celler's efforts in Judiciary to attach severe penalties for civil rights wrongdoing proved unavailing. After days of deliberation, the committee cleared the bill over conservative opposition. Seven Judiciary members, including former governor William M. Tuck and Richard Poff of Virginia, warned that the bill would "bring new and novel principles which, when fully appraised, are absolutely shocking. [It] would be a Frankenstein and a constant threat to any state or local government."[40]

For three weeks after the bill reached the Rules Committee in May, Judge Smith acted as if the bill did not exist. Finally, in mid-June, California Democrat James Roosevelt mustered two-thirds of the required signatures to bypass Rules deliberation. Smith undercut the momentum to dislodge the bill by permitting committee hearings. On June 21, however, his lieutenant Bill Colmer raised the point of order that a committee quorum was not present. Smith agreed and quickly adjourned the hearings. The Virginian asserted that it was his prerogative to call additional hearings but noted, "I'm not interested in calling a meeting." Eventually, longtime supporters in the Republican camp deserted him. With the Republican administration officially behind the civil rights bill, House majority leader Joe Martin pressured the four Republicans on Rules to vote for the bill's release. With their support, the measure finally reached the floor.[41]

As the House considered the bill, Smith organized his fellow southern representatives. As in March, he endorsed, if not directed, a public declaration opposing federal support for civil rights. His good friend Bill Tuck submitted a Civil Rights Manifesto to the House on July 13 which denounced the proposed measure as "a flagrant violation of States' rights [that] would result in further concentration of power in the Federal Government and vest unprecedented powers in the hands of the Attorney General." The manifesto warned that the bill "could only result in deterioration of the goodwill and the harmonious relations existing between the races and grievous injury to the steady progress and advancement of the very people whom the proponents profess to assist." Tuck, Smith, and eighty-one other southern congressmen called on their colleagues in both houses to use every "available legal parliamentary weapon to defeat this sinister and iniquitous proposal."[42]

One of those powerful weapons was the conservative coalition. In the 1930s and 1940s the coalition had attacked organized labor; now, it was a principal southern Democratic weapon against federal encroachments on white supremacy. In both periods, the informal group's approach remained the same. One of the coalition's members, A. Sydney Herlong, Jr., of Florida, described how it functioned. When the bill moved to a critical stage, a conservative Democrat telephoned the "hard core" of about fifteen members—with at least one from each southern state, including George W. Andrews of Alabama, Oren Harris of Arkansas, Herlong of Florida, James C. Davis of Georgia, Noble Gregory of Kentucky, F. Edward Hébert of Louisiana, William Colmer and John Bell Williams of Mississippi, Graham Barden of North Carolina, James P. Richards of South Carolina, Tom Murray of Tennessee, O. Clark Fisher of Texas, and Smith, Watkins M. Abbitt, and Burr P. Harrison of Virginia—to say: "Okay, we got a bill coming up. Let's all get together and see what we're going to do on it." The Democrats met in one of their offices, and Judge Smith "was in charge. He was the man we all looked to for leadership." The small group, Herlong recalled, then dissected the measure line by line, stopping at unacceptable sections: "They would just say, 'Now wait a minute. What are we going to do about this? We can't have this section in here,' or something like that. 'Who's going to put the amendment up?' Then somebody would offer to do it."[43]

Once the southern Democrats reached a consensus, they contacted other congressmen in their state delegations. Herlong, for example, would "feel them out on the thing first and see how they felt about it." If a representative supported the proposed action, Herlong advised him to be present for the floor debate. After the southern Democrats were organized, Smith or Colmer met or called the Republican conservatives led by Indiana's Charlie Halleck. Halleck, a testy, abrasive "drill sergeant," had ingratiated himself with many senior southern Democratic leaders besides Smith by fishing and drinking bourbon with them. But the dominant figure was Smith because he controlled the more important southern Democratic bloc and because Halleck was an alcoholic. While Halleck used the coalition for political ends, his Virginia counterpart was prompted by more potent ideological considerations. Alabama's Carl Elliott, a coalition enemy, believed that Judge Smith breathed life into the coalition because for him "it was a matter of hard-core philosophy—deeper than political parties. It was somewhat like a religion, with the Judge being the chief missionary. His fervor for his cause was akin to that of old Paul as he tried to spread Christianity over the known world."[44]

In the House, Smith skillfully executed the coalition's strategy. Often, he simply forced frequent half-hour quorum calls, the House version of the filibuster, by "hiding in the cloakrooms." Sometimes as many as thirty quorum calls plagued the House leadership in a single day. Smith also persuaded sixteen mem-

bers of the coalition to propose twenty amendments to weaken
the civil rights bill, four of which were attached. When liberals
tried to blindside him, Smith usually avoided the attack. Bolling
acknowledged that the Rules chairman "was absolutely inge-
nious at recovering because he knew everything. . . . He was
that tough; he was that good." At the first sign of trouble, Elliott
remembered, "generalissimo" Smith, who "enjoyed pulling the
strings and then watching the ripples flow out for a while," mo-
tioned to Halleck to discuss the problem. Within a couple of
minutes, the coalition began the countermaneuver. As Bolling
unhappily discovered, "You constantly had it just ground into
you, and you learned that unless you did your homework as well
as [Smith] and knew the bill better than he and had all the
advantages of having the Speaker on your side, there wasn't
much you were going to do."[45]

The morning after key votes on the civil rights bill, Judge
Smith carefully studied how well the coalition had held up. His
secretary Virginia Mitchell informed him of the southern Democratic performance.

> We had a list by states of the members of Congress, and we had
> marked in red—we had some way of knowing which members
> that Judge had under his finger, so-called, and how they voted—
> whether they actually voted the way they said they were going to.
> On civil rights we did that a lot, and H.R. 3. That was one way
> we'd keep tabs for Judge. We'd make one up for him, and he'd
> keep that in his inside pocket. He used to go around so slouchy,
> with papers here and papers there. He was a walking encyclope-
> dia. A lot of it was in his head though.

Any apostate southern Democrat incurred Smith's wrath.
Thomas G. Abernethy, a Mississippi Democrat and coalition
insider, recalled, "If you didn't go along, you knew damn well
he didn't like you." When the next coalition meeting occurred,
Smith often withheld the olive branch from the recalcitrant
southerner.[46]

When the coalition could no longer delay House consideration of the civil rights bill, southern Democrats bitterly attacked
the measure. Harold D. Cooley of North Carolina announced
that the measure would "perpetuate McCarthyism [and] estab-

lish a Gestapo with snoopers, going into all the homes of this country." Mississippi congressman Abernethy thought Americans had a "right to practice" discrimination. In late July 1956 the House passed the bill by a better than two-to-one margin. But the Senate Judiciary Committee, chaired by James O. Eastland, an archconservative Mississippi Democrat, refused to release the House bill in the closing days of the session. Senate liberals, including Paul H. Douglas of Illinois, were unable to pry the bill loose because the special parliamentary rule required unanimous consent.[47]

Smith also tried to safeguard Virginia. He advocated state laws that appropriated funds "for segregated schools only." To rouse grass-roots backing, Smith traveled to the heart of segregationist sentiment in Virginia, Prince Edward County, whose schools had illegally avoided integration. In August he spoke to angry segregationists at the home of J. Segar Gravatt, counsel to the county supervisors. There, he rejected the moderates' tuition grant proposals, preferring instead state monies for segregated schools. The local segregationists agreed, with Gravatt calling state funding "the ultimate power to protect the people of the Commonwealth against the integration of the schools and against the constitutional rights reserved to the states." Having demanded state action, county officials closed all their public schools, white and black, for four years beginning in 1959. It was the only southern school system shut down for that long, and the county relented only under another federal court order.[48]

To fashion an acceptable anti-integration state law, Smith worked closely with Governor Stanley. As was his custom, the aging Judge relied on a legislative answer to a social problem. He recommended two bills, one extremist and the second moderate. The first provided "that when any Negro child was enrolled in a white school no state funds would be available for that school or the school from which the Negro child was transferred." The second bill proposed administrative remedies to handle disputed student placement. The principal objective was to delay, if not dissuade, litigation in federal courts pledged to uphold integration. Once the governor agreed to the legislative drafts, Smith lobbied assemblymen for their support. Both bills eventually passed, and the state paid $275 to the parents of each high school student attending a nonsectarian private school.[49]

The race question complicated the 1956 election for all Virginia Democrats. Stevenson, once again the Democratic presidential standard-bearer, alienated white Virginians by advocating integration when federal funds were used. Smith was so worried that the state would turn Republican for a second consecutive time that he implored Byrd to endorse Stevenson anyway: "I greatly fear that if Virginia goes Republican again it will mean the end of the Virginia Democratic organization as we have known it and that we will be in grave jeopardy in the election for Governor in 1957." A Democratic defeat nationwide also would dislodge Smith from the Rules chairmanship and might pave the way for his ouster from Congress altogether.[50]

With these high stakes, Smith appealed to voters on the segregationist theme. Turning to his loyal supporters, he asked them to contact friends and insert political advertisements in district newspapers. These ads credited Smith with pigeonholing bills for civil rights and federal aid to education. The incumbent promised to continue these roadblocks to preserve self-government. Speaking to a local white supremacist group, Smith labeled the pending federal civil rights bill as "a deliberate attempt to fasten a Gestapo on the people of the South." He implied that his work for states' rights was essential to maintain segregation in the Old Dominion. At Smith's request, W. Tayloe Murphy of Warsaw reminded his radio listeners that Smith's reelection would help preserve racial segregation: "When the next Civil Rights legislation is introduced, as it surely will be, let us make sure that Howard Smith of *Virginia* is Chairman of the Rules Committee and not the senior Republican from Illinois." The *Charlottesville Daily Progress* concurred, advising district voters to keep Smith in his "strategic position" to preserve the "southern viewpoint" on race relations. With the outcome never in doubt, the incumbent handily defeated Horace B. Clay, his inexperienced Republican opponent. Although Eisenhower again carried Virginia and the nation, Smith retained his chairmanship because the Democrats captured the House.[51]

The 1956 elections electrified and encouraged the national Republican party. Large numbers of black voters unexpectedly left the Democratic party to vote for President Eisenhower. Blacks explained their political shift by pointing to the *Brown* desegregation decision, which was written by Eisenhower's appointee, Earl Warren, and to Vice-President Richard M. Nixon's campaign pledge in Harlem that the Republicans would bring "action, not filibusters," on civil rights. When blacks delivered votes for Eisenhower, the Republicans concluded, as Attorney General Brownell had earlier, that civil rights legislation might wean blacks permanently from Democratic allegiance.[52]

As was the case in 1956, the civil rights bill of 1957 took months to clear the obstacles that preceded full House action. Smith was at the center of southern resistance. To scuttle the bill that Smith called "civil wrongs," the Judge worked more closely with the Byrd organization than ever before. As lord of his own fiefdom in the House, Smith seldom had needed Senator Byrd's aid. Unlike many other Old Dominion politicians, Smith did not pay homage to Byrd or to the organization. Many times, the situation was reversed, as Oklahoman Carl Albert once discovered. At a dinner in Richmond, Albert sat next to Byrd and discussed Smith's role in the organization. Albert "told Byrd, 'You've got a very strong man there.' I said, 'Does he follow the party organization?' He said, 'No, he tells the organization.' The organization didn't tell him what to do. Smith was the one who told the organization what to do. That's what he said; that's what Byrd said to me. Of course, Byrd had tremendous admiration for him." But this bill was so threatening that Smith met in "little huddles" with Senators Byrd and Robertson and Congressmen Tuck and Vaughan Gary of Richmond. They conferred frequently and secretly in Smith's committee office because Smith was now the most powerful Virginia legislator and because his office was so close to the House floor. Since all Senate-revised bills, including civil rights, had to pass through the House Rules Committee, Smith held more power as chairman than one hundred senators, a fact lamented by Joseph S. Clark, Democratic senator from Pennsylvania. In conference with the other Byrd machine leaders, Smith tapped Governor Stanley and Virginia attorney general J. Lindsay Almond, Jr., to write Speaker Rayburn and Judiciary chairman Celler to insist on committee hearings. Testifying before the Judiciary Committee in late February, Almond denounced the civil rights legislation as "incongruous, inconsistent and self-defeating" and "aimed directly and insultingly at the southern states."[53]

In the Judiciary Committee, southerners managed to remove the U.S. attorney general's authority to sue for damages in civil rights cases, but the bill cleared largely intact on April 1. The wily Rules chairman then laid plans to keep the bill under wraps. Congressman Bolling, a frustrated liberal member of Smith's committee, warned the House of a "deal" between committee conservatives of both parties to stall civil rights action until after the long Easter recess, leaving little time for Senate consideration. Bolling proved prophetic. After the House reconvened, Smith used his powers to delay further action until May 21. At that time, Rules sent the administration bill to the floor but authorized four days of debate and unlimited amendments. On the floor, Smith and Colmer persuaded New York Republican William Miller, who had helped introduce this civil rights bill only a year earlier, to attach hamstringing amendments and to seek its recommittal. In return, the southerners promised to obstruct a federal waterpower bill for Niagara Falls which would hurt private utilities supporting Miller. Backed by Tennessee Democrat Jere Cooper, Smith then led a fight to send the bill back to Judiciary. Smith claimed that the accompanying report did not specify every change it would make in existing law. If sustained, his argument would have rerouted the bill through Rules, meaning certain death. Here, Rayburn stepped in, overruling Smith on the ground that the disputed sections were only additions to existing law.[54]

Next, southern Democrats offered an amendment requiring jury trials in civil rights contempt cases, on the premise that in the South jurors would be the white peers of the defendants on trial. In large measure, the struggle over jury trials dated from the Reconstruction period when trial by judge had prevailed. When their first attempts failed to convince northern representatives to champion the jury trial amendment, southern Democrats convinced a conservative freshman Republican from Illinois to present the amendment. Smith promised southern support to kill the school construction bill that conservative Republicans opposed if those Republicans voted for trial by jury. But the amendment did not survive. In mid-June the House passed the civil rights bill by more than two to one. The bill became law with the help of northern Republicans, especially Joe Martin of Massachusetts, Leo E. Allen of Illinois, and Hugh Scott of Pennsylvania. Resentful, Smith denounced the deliberations as a "disgusting" spectacle by the two political parties "to win votes of the negro race by getting the credit of this assault upon the white race."[55]

Smith's most blatant act of obstruction came two months later. In August the Senate returned an amended version of the civil rights measure to the House which proceeded automatically to Smith's bailiwick at Rules. This time, Smith took matters into his own hands and brought House deliberations to a halt. Just when pressure for the bill's release reached the breaking point, the chairman was nowhere to be found. Word quickly spread through the House corridors that one of Smith's Virginia dairy barns had burned down and that he had left the Capitol to inspect the damage. Leo Allen, senior Republican on Rules, shook his head ruefully and said with a wink: "I knew the Judge was opposed to the civil rights bill. But I didn't think he would commit arson to beat it."[56]

With the civil rights bill locked in the Rules "cooler," Smith anticipated that his sudden departure would frustrate the party leadership. He told his committee counsel, T. M. Carruthers, "I'm going away for several days, but I'm not going to tell you where I'm going so then you won't have to lie because I know Mr. Rayburn will be calling you before I get out of town to see where I am." As predicted, Rayburn came by Rules every morning for days, asking, "You hear any word from the Judge?" Years later, Smith offered this justification for holding up urgent committee business:

> I reckon, I spend more time in Washington than any member of either the House or the Senate. I normally don't take vacations. It happened that my daughter and her family from Texas were spending their summer vacation down in Nags Head, North Carolina, and things were pretty hot up here, I'll admit that, and they were sort of getting under my skin and everybody else had had a vacation—I hadn't had any and I just up and left here and I didn't want to be bothered—so I went down—visited my family in North Carolina, at Nags Head for just one week and then all this furor arose. . . . [It was] a lot of good fun.[57]

After ten days, Smith finally returned as the Rules potentate to negotiate with a flustered Sam Rayburn. The Speaker, liberal Democrats, and the Eisenhower administration all demanded that the civil rights bill be released from Rules. But Smith laid down his inflexible terms. He would release a weakened civil rights bill only in exchange for Rayburn's consent in axing pending federal aid bills. As Smith left the meeting, he turned to Carruthers, who had accompanied him, and proudly declared, "Guess I did pretty good, didn't I?" Carruthers agreed: "I don't see much more you could have done."[58]

After a record twenty-four-hour filibuster by Senator Thurmond, the civil rights bill passed Congress, and the president signed it in September 1957. The law created a weak Commission on Civil Rights to investigate voter registration abuses. It also authorized the Justice Department to obtain injunctions preventing interference in voting. But Senate majority leader Lyndon B. Johnson of Texas had removed many sections that his fellow southerners found objectionable. In particular, he limited the act to voting and required a jury trial for registrars accused of violating a voter's rights. Although the law did not increase southern black voting, it still marked crucial progress. For the first time since 1875, southern Democrats had been unable to block civil rights legislation. The precedent proved enormously significant to the civil rights movement. As Bolling later remembered, "I think our passing the bill gave greater strength to the Court's [*Brown*] decision, which of course preceded that, and gave the activists an umbrella that they would not have had."[59]

At the same time the Civil Rights Act passed, President Eisenhower sent federal troops to integrate an all-white high school in Little Rock, Arkansas—a startling "breach" of state sovereignty. Smith labeled the action as wielding "the mailed fist of the United States Army" and decried the Supreme Court's practice of issuing legislative fiats like the desegregation decision. Smith thus held to the strict constructionist view of the Constitution he had learned in law school. But time had long since passed him by. Answering a private challenge posed by Smith, F. D. G. Ribble, a constitutional law professor and dean at the University of Virginia, argued forcefully that literalism was outmoded. In a rebuttal to Smith's letter, Ribble contended that no single interpretation was correct, whether his own or that of Smith and his teachers. "I do not insist that students accept my beliefs or those of Raleigh Minor, great as they were." Instead, the law dean believed the courts should use the Constitution to assist "in the change in our country from a small rural population to a highly industrialized society." As a child of the earlier era, Smith could not accept Ribble's innovative notions.[60]

The latest federal civil rights defeat spurred Smith to resume the contest for segregation on the state level. On January 25, 1958, he delivered a major anti-integration address to a joint session of the Virginia General Assembly at the reconstructed Capitol in Williamsburg. Placing the quarrel over race relations in a larger framework, Smith told the legislators that judge-made law portended not only racial integration but the greater evil of autocracy. Speaking with a heavy cold, he blamed a right-thinking but apathetic populace for this unfortunate situation. "It is my sad conclusion that the present generation of the American people has not kept the faith, has not fought the good fight to preserve . . . the precious heritage left us by those who have gone before. . . . We have hesitated and vacillated in denouncing the invasion of State's rights and other constitutional limitations by the Supreme Court of the United States." An aroused public could reverse this course in one of two ways. Either the people could persuade Congress to restrict the Court's jurisdiction, or failing that, they could pressure their state legislatures to convene a constitutional convention to ratify appropriate amendments.[61]

This speech, which Smith regarded as truly momentous, contained several concepts held by many southern whites. He assumed that segregation had been accepted in the South until liberal northerners had recently begun their agitations, but in fact the NAACP, with white liberal help, had been quietly removing legal inequality for decades before *Brown*, and the Court in 1954 had demolished only one more racial wall. In calling on "the people" to defend states' rights, ever the South's last resort, Smith stripped blacks of their citizenship. He assumed that through political resolution the late nineteenth-century world he knew so well could be restored.[62]

Within his district, Smith sided with segregationist groups.

When the Defenders of State Sovereignty and Individual Liberties met in Bowling Green to protest school integration, the congressman dispatched his personal secretary, Calvin H. Haley, to represent him. The Defenders called on the new governor, J. Lindsay Almond, Jr., to restore state sovereignty and local school district control over pupil assignment. Smith also expressed his opinion to interested constituents. "I am," he insisted, "violently opposed to any integration," though he never advocated violence per se. In Charlottesville, which had closed its schools in 1958 rather than integrate, Smith publicly endorsed the private all-white schools. He also contributed $100 to the Charlottesville Education Foundation, a white organization building such schools. The fact that he was then serving on the Board of Visitors of the publicly supported University of Virginia did not deter him.[63]

In retrospect, Virginia's massive resistance was futile. The federal government demonstrated repeatedly and in unmistakable terms that integration was the law of the land. The president used federal troops in Arkansas to force compliance to *Brown*, and the Supreme Court delivered antisegregation decisions for the next two decades. On the local level, massive resistance only deprived some school children of quality instruction. Eventually, the Old Dominion's public schools consented to at least a certain amount of actual integration, although 6 percent of the white children had transferred to the new private Christian academies by 1970. While Virginia retreated grudgingly on integration, Smith was not so compliant, and he would later carry the battle to Capitol Hill.[64]

Now that this first civil rights fight was over, Smith tackled the issues of unemployment relief, Alaskan statehood, and judicial usurpation in 1958. Reacting to the deepening recession, Massachusetts Democrat John F. Kennedy introduced a sweeping expansion of the unemployment compensation program. President Eisenhower had recommended a much smaller plan, providing temporary government loans to individual states. Smith was repulsed by Kennedy's measure, calling it a "dole." Although the Rules chairman could not strangle the bill in committee, he did attach a potentially crippling rule: House members could add any floor amendment they chose during the six hours for debate.[65]

When the Kennedy bill reached the floor in April, the "cigar-chewing, face-screwing" Smith went into high gear. Denouncing the measure as "pure, unadulterated, undisguised, unabridged and unabashed socialism," he coordinated nearly sixty dissident southern Democrats with Republican leaders to support the administration's proposal. Then his coalition ally, Florida Democrat Sydney Herlong, introduced a substitute plan, calling for a smaller program than the president had asked for. More importantly, the Herlong substitute stipulated that states could refuse to match costly federal unemployment funds. With Smith at the forefront, the House accepted this plan, and the president signed the temporary measure in June.[66]

The second major issue in 1958 was Alaskan statehood. Since the early 1950s, both parties had gone on record as favoring its admission because of the region's strategic and economic value. But Smith, noting the government's willingness to relinquish one-third of its land to the new state, criticized the measure as the "greatest giveaway of potential natural resources in the history of our country." To prevent that from happening, he delayed convening the Rules Committee until fifteen minutes before House proceedings were to begin. He then observed that there was insufficient time to conduct hearings, promptly adjourning the committee until early afternoon. At that time, the committee lacked a quorum. Later, he produced a parade of hostile witnesses to delay House consideration. The chamber finally agreed to bypass Rules to act on the bill. This extraordinary move was possible after Speaker Rayburn decided the bill was a privileged matter which could circumvent Rules.[67]

Until debate eventually was limited, statehood opponents forced frequent quorum calls and repeated several of the arguments used against Hawaiian statehood. They argued that Alaska was too distant to be integrated into the nation, that its defense would be difficult, that its population was too small, that the senatorial allotment would unfairly dilute the representation of more populous states, and that its weak economy would require massive infusions of federal funds. But the underlying motive of Smith and his southern Democratic colleagues remained the fear that Alaskan representatives would further weaken southern control of Congress. The result would be more anathematic civil rights legislation. Despite southern bloc voting, Alaskan statehood passed the House, and Eisenhower signed the bill in July.[68]

One other issue attracted Smith's attention in 1958—judicial usurpation of states' rights. To him, U.S. Supreme Court decisions against school segregation and state sedition laws were glaringly illegal actions. The fundamental solution lay in his court-curbing proposal known as H.R. 3. In previous years, the bill had been amended by the Judiciary Committee to allow states to have concurrent powers with the federal government in outlawing sedition. When Chairman Celler held up all court-restrictive bills in 1958, Smith was more than equal to securing committee approval. In the first place, he told Celler, there was an almost forgotten House rule that entitled the Rules Committee to bring H.R. 3 to the floor. He also informed the Judiciary chairman that until H.R. 3 was reported, Celler's pet bill requiring government notification of planned mergers stood no chance of clearance. By the end of May southerners on the Judiciary Committee combined with a few Republicans to approve the measure over Celler's opposition.[69]

Before the full House, Smith continued his anti-Court campaign. When the Justice Department and the NAACP attacked the measure's implied retroactivity, he beat back attempts to make H.R. 3 apply only to future congressional actions. Smith heatedly denied northern allegations that his bill would protect racial separation. In July the House passed the measure with the overwhelming backing of southern Democrats and Republicans. Only two Texans had strayed from Smith's southern Democratic fold.[70]

Senate prospects for the bill's passage looked bright. Forty-six senators had announced for it, while liberals could count only thirty-nine against. But Senate majority leader Johnson limited floor consideration to major appropriation bills, including foreign aid. In a virtuoso performance of arm-twisting, Johnson, who now had presidential ambitions, managed to kill the bill by a single vote, returning it to committee. Embittered, Smith promised to "renew the fight at the beginning of the next Congress," which he did. The *Washington Post* commented that the Supreme Court had escaped the ordeal this time but wondered about its future.[71]

By the end of 1958, liberal resentment of Smith's persistent,

Kamikaze Pilot

From the *Washington Post*, June 24, 1959 (copyright 1959 by Herblock in *The Washington Post*)

and often successful, obstructionist tactics had mushroomed. These northern Democrats began searching for ways to weaken the Rules Committee, which had annually blocked about twenty bills since Judge Smith became chairman. The matter seemed all the more urgent because Smith was unopposed for reelection and because two liberal Republicans were not reappointed to the committee. Meeting secretly, Democratic congressmen Sidney Yates of Illinois, Frank Thompson of New Jersey, Henry S. Reuss of Wisconsin, Lee Metcalf of Montana, and Charles A. Vanik of Ohio committed themselves to cultivating the Speaker's support. These liberals wanted Rayburn to endorse either the twenty-one-day-rule, allowing a committee chairman to spring a bill from Rules after three weeks, or a change in the party ratio on Rules giving the Democrats a nine-to-three edge. If the ratio was changed, the Democrats would drop a Republican in favor of a liberal Democrat, such as Minnesota's John Blatnik. Whatever course was taken, House liberals knew something had to be done to sidestep legislative delays by Rules. As Wisconsin Democrat Lester Johnson said, "I've seen Howard Smith go fishing too many times while important liberal bills languished in this committee. I feel that I was given a mandate . . . to lift the Smith embargo on liberal legislation and I won't rest until something is done about it."[72]

The 1958 election results boded ill for Smith's obstructionist efforts. A record number of voters gave the Democrats, especially liberal, northern Democrats, control of both houses. The Democrats gained thirteen Senate seats, all from northern states, for a total of sixty-two, their highest number since 1940. In the House 282 Democrats were elected, which was forty-nine more than the previous session; this figure was the highest total since 1936. All but one of these freshmen Democrats came from northern states. One political scientist noted that "this new group of Congressmen were more liberal than the Republicans who left in 1958, and markedly less dependable for Congressman Smith." As always, Smith was well aware of the liberal composition of Congress and doubted "if we can stop" further "extravagant spending."[73]

When the Eighty-sixth Congress convened in January 1959, thirty liberal freshmen Democrats joined Metcalf, Thompson, and Chet Holifield of California to revive the twenty-one-day-rule. Holifield conferred privately with Rayburn in the hope of reviving the Speaker's deeply imbedded populist instincts. The Californian also urged revision of the House rules to expedite legislation: "The Rules Committee now seeks to write legislation, not merely schedule the order of voting on legislation." Seeking to mollify the insurgents, the taciturn Rayburn promised major bills reported by legislative committees would be brought to the floor within a "reasonable time." He added, "Howard Smith will have to play ball like everyone else." When asked about Rayburn's pledge, the Judge removed his long, black cigar and commented, "I'm not bound by it. I didn't make an agreement with these men or give assurance to anyone."[74]

As time passed, it soon became apparent that Smith often held more power than the Speaker of the House. In part, Rayburn was unable to keep his promise because the Republicans had recently deposed the aging but cooperative Joe Martin as party leader in favor of Charlie Halleck, a highly partisan politician who would hold "you with one arm around the neck while stabbing you in the stomach with the other." "I could," Rayburn complained, "always manage to get a bill out of the Rules Committee while Joe Martin was the Republican leader. I could work along with Joe. . . . Charlie Halleck is different, a hard man to deal with."[75]

The public housing bill illustrated Smith's influence over liberal-backed legislation. In February the Senate's $2.7 billion federal housing bill reached the House Rules Committee. Once it was in his hands, Smith declared to a supporter that he was "in no hurry about bringing it up." Not surprisingly, Majority Leader John W. McCormack's pleas to "expedite action" fell on deaf ears. Finally, in April the Rules Committee met behind closed doors to vote on the omnibus housing bill. Teaming with Colmer and the four Republicans, Smith prevented its release.[76]

Just a fortnight later, the Rules chairman engaged in some skillfully deceptive legislative maneuvering. He sought out the southern sponsor of the Tennessee Valley Authority self-financing bill and asked him to request a rule for floor action. Smith then sent the bill through Rules. Two factors motivated him. On the one hand, he hoped to silence liberal discontent over his bottling-up tactics by releasing an important proposal. On the other, he planned to forestall House action on the housing bill by acquiescing in the less offensive financing measure.[77]

But liberal pressure for federal housing forced Rayburn to promise anew to squeeze the bill out of Rules within a "reasonable time." During the Easter recess, Rayburn wrote Smith an open letter that blamed Rules for damaging the nation's economy. The Speaker also claimed—falsely—to have enough votes to spring the housing bill from the committee. His bluff worked, intimidating two committee Republicans. In May the Rules Committee granted the housing proposal an open rule. The vote was split along party lines, with Smith supporting the rule along with the other Democrats. He admitted, "I'm eating crow today." The vote was only a partial defeat, however. The *Richmond Times-Dispatch* recognized that Smith agreed to forward the housing bill only to prevent the use of the discharge petition. The veteran Virginia legislator realized that the successful use of the petition would provide a dangerous precedent for other, less desirable bills.[78]

Opposition to the housing bill continued on the House floor. Again, Florida's Sydney Herlong offered a substitute that sharply reduced federal funding, prohibited new public housing units, and required Appropriations Committee approval for additional monies. Though the president endorsed the Herlong substitute, northern Democrats overwhelmingly rejected it. A discouraged Smith watched as more than 40 percent of the southern Democrats deserted the principle of conservative spending, but he felt confident of a presidential veto. True to form, Eisenhower did veto it, saying "the bill is extravagant." On the third try, a compromise federal housing bill emerged, and the president signed the measure in September.[79]

With the housing battle behind him, the seventy-six-year-old Smith did not slacken his pace, especially where his old nemesis organized labor was concerned. In 1959 Arkansas senator John L. McClellan's Select Committee on Improper Activities in the Labor or Management Field unearthed shocking stories of union corruption in James R. Hoffa's International Brotherhood of Teamsters. In suggesting ways to stop these abuses, House members divided into three camps. Rayburn and the moderate Democrats supported Senator Kennedy's reform bill concerned primarily with union official misconduct. The second group, headed by George Meany of the AFL-CIO, gathered behind a weaker version of the Kennedy measure called the Shelley bill after California Democrat John R. Shelley. The last group, led by Smith and Minority Leader Charlie Halleck, chose Georgia Democrat Philip Landrum and Michigan Republican Robert Griffin, respectively, to present a tough antilabor proposal. The Landrum-Griffin bill tried to strengthen the Taft-Hartley Act by restricting picketing and secondary boycotts and by providing criminal penalties for union violations. According to William Colmer, the bill was designed to safeguard the public "from the gangsters and goons who have wormed their way" into union leadership. With the aid of Smith's longtime friend from North Carolina, Graham Barden, chairman of the House Committee on Education and Labor, the most conservative bill reached the floor unscathed.[80]

All sides lobbied intensively for their own version. While Halleck convinced the president to support the Landrum-Griffin bill, Smith, as usual, worked his magic "quietly by telephone and in the cloakrooms [to line] up the Southern votes which Halleck needs." Rumors abounded that the "beetle-browed" Smith had pledged southern support against unions in return for a Republican promise not to push civil rights legislation that fall. When the final vote came in August 1959, the House narrowly consented to the Republican measure. Rayburn was unable to prevent four-fifths of the southern Democrats from joining the vast majority of Republicans in approving the bill.[81]

But like Taft-Hartley, the Landrum-Griffin Act never fulfilled the aims of labor restrictionists to control internal union affairs. One scholarly account concluded that the new law "does not really disturb what goes on within unions, as a practical matter." Moreover, powerful unions such as the Teamsters were "affected very little by the statute." According to many union officers, the act resulted chiefly in increasing their operating costs. Small, local unions hiked membership dues to cover mounting legal fees, accounting fees, mailing charges, and election rerun costs. The decline in the union movement in recent years owes more to independent economic factors like the shift from industrial labor to services than to legislation. Once more, Smith's legalistic mind had put a misplaced confidence in the political arena, believing that social and economic forces could be dissipated by restrictive laws.[82]

As it became clear that southern Democrats would break with the party's leadership on the Landrum-Griffin bill, northern and western Democrats met in John Shelley's office to discuss ways of countering southern strength. James Roosevelt of Los Angeles complained, "I am tired of voting for peanut price supports and then have our Southern friends turn around and scuttle" liberal bills. Roman Pucinski of Chicago criticized the alliance between Smith and Halleck for sidetracking public housing and urban development bills.[83]

By the end of the 1959 session, a group of 130 frustrated liberal House Democrats had formed the Democratic Study Group to present a united front against conservative roadblocks. They believed their very political survival to be at stake unless certain federal aid bills passed before the 1960 election. The liberals organized their forces to press more vigorously for civil rights, housing, school construction, expanded minimum wage coverage, and assistance to economically depressed areas. In sharp contrast to Smith's informal conservative coalition, the study group assembled a staff of eighteen in the House Longworth Building, developed a whip organization, and published weekly summaries of upcoming legislation. Chairman Lee Metcalf denied the group was a revolt against Rayburn's impotent leadership, but he regretted the Speaker's failure to extract major bills from Rules. Rayburn was aware of the liberals' frustration, later admitting to a reporter that "the boys are serious this time." The positions of both southern Democratic powerhouses, Sam Rayburn and Howard Smith, were to be tested in the next session.[84]

Richard Bolling, a Democratic insurgent born and bred in Alabama, for months had been following a complementary strategy to secure passage of the five liberal measures. He realized that the public was unaware of Smith's "real perversion" of the Rules Committee's role. Hence, he "forced votes" on each controversial measure, even when he knew his cause was at least temporarily futile. He wanted to rally public opinion against Rules by clearly demonstrating its negative performance. "I think we ended up getting one, or maybe two of them. But in the process we were getting this enormous record. And what I was doing with the record—of course I knew all the lobbyists—I was making sure they all got their noses rubbed in the fact that the Rules Committee killed the bills, so that they were mad at the Rules Committee. I raised the level of consciousness, and I did it systematically."[85]

The presidential election year of 1960 saw increasing liberal momentum for civil rights legislation and Rules Committee reform. At the close of the previous session, a new civil rights bill was locked in Rules. The new measure put more teeth in the 1957 act. It set federal penalties for violently obstructing school desegregation orders and for fleeing across state lines after bombing schools and churches. The bill also required state officials to preserve election records for federal investigators of voter discrimination. Judiciary chairman Celler finally decided to dislodge the bill by filing the rarely used discharge petition. If the petition failed to attract enough signatures, Celler threatened to resort to rules suspension and Calendar Wednesday procedures. Responding to liberal demands for civil rights, a beleaguered Rayburn took the virtually unprecedented step of inviting House members to sign the petition. In early January he announced that this was the only way for the majority to "work its will." The Speaker's decision amounted to his first open break with Judge Smith.[86]

Instead of attacking the beloved Speaker, Smith lashed out at the less powerful Celler, contending the Judiciary chairman had "dillied, dallied, and delayed" the bill in his own committee for seven months and now wanted immediate Rules action. Smith dismissed the civil rights bill as a mere political ploy to arouse powerful minority groups into a "frenzy." Besides, he declared, the bill's practical effect would take the South back to the carpetbag governments of Reconstruction because federal registrars would dictate to southerners again. When the discharge petition needed only ten more signatures, the Rules Committee decided to discharge the bill in February. Because of public and administration pressure, committee Republicans sided with the northern Democrats.[87]

When the civil rights bill landed in the House, Smith continued his diatribe. In March he castigated the measure on several grounds. He noted that the *United States Code* already listed fifty-three separate civil rights laws. Surely, he suggested, another one was unnecessary. The Democrats, moreover, would reap no credit for backing a Republican proposal. To states' righters, he pointed out that federal judges would appoint the local voter referees. Finally, he solicited strict constructionist support when he argued that the bill ruled out constitutionally mandated jury trials.[88]

The following day, Smith demonstrated his parliamentary flair against the civil rights bill. When liberal Democrats attempted to strengthen the administration's referee plan, Smith held back his supporters until everyone else had filed past the voting tellers. Then, with all eyes upon him, the Virginian led his band forward, marching slowly through Celler's Democratic side. Smith and the southern Democrats inexplicably had voted for the liberal amendment, which carried. But immediately afterward, they switched sides, joining the Republicans to kill the whole section. At this point, civil rights supporters offered a new referee plan matching the old proposal. Smith instantly raised the point of order that once a provision is beaten no similar one could be introduced. The temporary Speaker pondered the motion momentarily before rejecting it. Despite southern opposition, the House passed the bill nearly three-to-one.[89]

Smith was not downcast, however, because he had helped remove some objectionable provisions. These included federal technical assistance to schools undergoing desegregation and the creation of a permanent commission to investigate racial discrimination in government contracts. In addition, the referee section had been weakened to the point of being "unworkable." Smith also suspected the Senate might dilute the bill further. His optimism proved unfounded, for the Senate approved the bill by a wide margin, and the president signed it in May. Even though the bill had passed, Senator Byrd spoke for many white Virginians when he hailed Judge Smith's role in softening the "punitive" and "unconstitutional" law.[90]

Despite the passage of this bill, Smith and like-minded Rules committeemen killed other liberal measures, including area redevelopment, common-site picketing, and federal aid to education. The education episode was typical. As a result of the "baby boom" after World War II, the nation suffered from overcrowded schools and inadequate staffing. To meet this compelling need, the House Education Committee in 1959 proposed a bill providing $1.1 billion yearly for school construction and teacher salaries, but the Rules Committee denied the request. Judge Smith later explained that the United States was already "getting along well and doing an extraordinarily good job" in education, so it made sense "not [to] rock the old boat too much with controversy." The Senate Subcommittee on Education then drew up a bill calling for $500 million per year based on matching state grants.[91]

In 1960 Smith held the House version in Rules for two months. Finally, in May the Education Committee voted to use the Calendar Wednesday procedure. Under this threat, the Rules Committee sent the bill to the floor. When the full House acted a week later, it passed the education measure over southern Democratic opposition. As a routine matter, Senate majority leader Johnson requested a joint conference to iron out differences between the two competing bills. But Smith, his conservative Rules colleagues, and Charlie Halleck ignored the request, and the bill died.[92]

In the unusual 1960 fall session, John F. Kennedy, the Democratic presidential standard-bearer, hoped to secure approval of at least part of his New Frontier program in order to benefit his campaign. But Vice-President Richard M. Nixon, the Republican candidate, made sure Senate Republicans did not vote for the Kennedy plan to provide federal medical care for the aged. The bill lost by four votes, as southern Democrats abandoned their party leader.[93]

Kennedy suffered a worse defeat in the House. Ignoring Rayburn's pleas to cooperate, Smith, who held "a very dim view" of the New Frontier's "great big gravy train," gave Kennedy Democrats an ultimatum: Either drop the short session proposals on federal aid to housing and education, as well as the bill to weaken the Taft-Hartley Act, or the Rules Committee would kill the $1.25 hourly minimum wage sought by Kennedy. When the final wage figure was cut to $1.15 per hour, one Kennedy backer commented, "This isn't Kennedy's Congress. It's Judge Smith's Congress." Customarily, Smith avoided stretching the patience of Democratic leaders too far on major bills. But his legislative conduct in this session led the *Washington Post* to predict that an effort would be made in 1961 to break the Rules Committee's veto power "no matter who is elected President in 1960."[94]

Once he became chairman of the House Rules Committee in 1955, Howard Smith had the position to sustain a valiant fight for his fundamental values of constitutional government, fiscal conservatism, and racial segregation. He believed the best way to protect southern society lay in resisting the federal government and in restoring state sovereignty. No other congressman excelled him in parliamentary skill. He employed such effective obstructionist tactics as hearing hostile witnesses, logrolling,

STICKY WICKET

Original drawing presented to Howard W. Smith, Jr., of cartoon by Bill Mauldin in the *St. Louis Post-Dispatch*, June 30, 1960 (reprinted by permission of Bill Mauldin and Wil-Jo Associates, Inc.)

"PLAY BALL!"

From the *St. Louis Post-Dispatch*, December 30, 1960
(reprinted by permission of Bill Mauldin and Wil-Jo Associates,
Inc.)

holding up a bill until late in the session, permitting open debate and unlimited amendments, and even deserting his party's leadership.

Liberal Democrats, however, desired federal aid to help solve problems in their mostly urban, industrial, and heterogeneous districts. To secure federal programs from Rules, they advocated specific procedural measures to tip the balance of power away from Smith's autocratic control. When it became clear that Speaker Rayburn was unable to assist the insurgents, the liberals formed a Democratic Study Group and turned to the methods of the discharge petition and Calendar Wednesday to obtain legislation. Finally, patience with Smith snapped as he sabotaged more federal aid bills in 1960. A congressional conflagration was inevitable in the coming year. Only one question remained: Could the anti-Smith forces outmaneuver the man organized labor called the reigning "lord high executioner" of the House?

CHAPTER 7

Chairman of the Rules Committee: The Kennedy and Johnson Years

*I am a conservative Democrat, I am a southern Dem-
ocrat, and I believe my country's welfare is more important than any political party and I further believe
that this matter of packing the Rules Committee affects
more closely our area of the country than anywhere else.*

Howard W. Smith (1963)

Just five days before Christmas, 1960, president-elect John F. Kennedy discussed his legislative program with top Democratic leaders at his parents' home in Palm Beach, Florida. Along with Lyndon Johnson, the new vice-president, and Speaker Rayburn, he recalled Smith's recent hatchet work on liberal proposals. Without some dramatic action, Kennedy maintained, "nothing controversial would come to the floor" in the upcoming Congress. Rayburn reluctantly agreed, reminding the others that the election had cost the Democrats twenty-one seats in the House, which would weaken party control over Rules. Nevertheless, he asked the president-to-be to let the House handle the problem of obstruction.[1]

Alarmed at the new administration's proposed restructuring of Rules, Smith quickly organized his southern Democratic legion. In early December he and his assistant, Bill Colmer, corresponded with their supporters, warning them that "the self-styled liberals" planned to "capture the Rules Committee." Exactly how this would be done, Colmer did not know, but he feared a diluted committee would permit such "left-wing legislative proposals" as civil rights and equal employment opportunity.[2]

When Rayburn returned to Capitol Hill, House liberals reminded him of his broken promise to bring all major bills to the floor. John Blatnik of the Democratic Study Group complained that Rules "was never intended to be the arresting officer, judge and jury of legislation" and suggested that Colmer, Smith's closest associate on Rules and its vice-chairman, be purged. But Rayburn firmly opposed this suggestion for three reasons. He believed that purging would be unfair since the Dixiecrats and Harlem congressman Adam Clayton Powell had not been punished for deserting the party's presidential nominee in 1948 and 1956, respectively. Moreover, Colmer's removal meant Rayburn would have to tamper with the congressional seniority system—the very system that had brought and kept the Speaker in power—and instill party discipline, which he was often loathe to do. Finally, Rayburn feared that the removal of a southern Democrat would only stiffen the conservative coalition's resolve against upcoming liberal measures. Alabama's Carl Elliott, already chosen for the new Rules Committee, recalled that Rayburn felt Colmer's dismissal "would have created so many bad feelings in the House, particularly in the southern branch."[3]

On New Year's Day, 1961, the House Speaker squared off against the Rules chairman in what Dick Bolling, Rayburn's "pet," described as a "straight, knock-down power struggle." The Speaker presented Smith with the choice of either having Colmer dumped or having three new members, including two Democratic loyalists, added to the Rules Committee. Rayburn, whom Smith claimed had "an iron fist, but a glove of velvet," apparently expected the Judge to accept the additional committeemen. In fact, he had been lining up candidates for an enlarged Rules Committee since the previous fall. But Rayburn underestimated his foe; Howard Smith never ceded control without a fight. Smith later counterproposed releasing to the floor five Kennedy bills on depressed areas, housing, the minimum wage, health insurance, and education. To retain his long-term base of power, the chairman would willingly release a handful of liberal legislation. But Rayburn turned down the offer because, he said, Kennedy's New Frontier "may have forty bills!"[4]

With liberals outnumbering conservatives in the Democratic

178

"What's This Ugly Talk About Applying Rules to ME?"
—Herblock in The Washington Post.

From the *Washington Post*, December 7, 1960 (reprinted with permission from *Straight Herblock* [New York: Simon & Schuster, 1964])

caucus, Rayburn knew he could remove Colmer. Instead, he chose the more dangerous path of enlarging the Rules Committee, which necessitated full House approval. If he lost the packing fight, Rayburn realized that "Smith would emerge as the undisputed dictator of the House." Aided by administration officials, the AFL-CIO, the National Farmers Union, the National Education Association, and the Americans for Democratic Action, the Speaker began to call in political debts to win votes for Rules expansion. Republican Joe Martin assisted his old friend Rayburn as a way of "repaying" Smith's partner Charlie Halleck for deposing him as minority leader in 1959. But when early indications showed the outcome still in doubt, Rayburn told the administration, "Mr. President, I don't believe we have the votes to expand the Rules Committee." Kennedy was "stunned" by this report and convinced Rayburn to postpone the crucial vote from January 26 until the last day of the month. Dick Bolling thought the Speaker appeared to be "unaccustomedly worried and unconfident."[5]

In the interim, both sides tried to determine the outcome. Amused at the delay, Smith and Halleck lined up friendly southern congressmen and conservative organizations like the National Association of Manufacturers, the American Farm Bureau Federation, the Southern States Industrial Council, the U.S. Chamber of Commerce, the American Medical Association, and the Republican House Policy Committee. To his conservative allies, the seventy-eight-year-old Virginian characterized the enlargement as a "sinister packing" not unlike Franklin Roosevelt's outrageous court-packing attempt twenty-four years earlier. Once more Judge Smith promised the liberal Democrats that he would grant Rules Committee visas for the five Kennedy bills and would refrain from leaving Congress to "milk cows." But he refused to give the written guarantee of cooperation that the Speaker demanded. At one point Halleck grabbed the lapels of Nebraskan Glenn Cunningham, a turncoat Republican congressman, shaking him until he switched his allegiance back to Smith's side. As for the administration, President Kennedy wielded patronage and dished out federal plums from the General Services Administration, Air Force, and Post Office to wavering representatives. One administration backer went so far as to send a case of bourbon to a Smith supporter who drank heavily in the vain hope of having

"MIND YOU, I'M ONLY AN INTERESTED CITIZEN."

From the *St. Louis Post-Dispatch*, January 27, 1961 (reprinted by permission of Bill Mauldin and Wil-Jo Associates, Inc.)

"IT LOOKS LIKE THE SAME OLD TRIBE AT THE PASS."

From the *Washington Post*, January 29, 1961 (reprinted with
permission from *Straight Herblock* [New York: Simon &
Schuster, 1964])

him miss the vote altogether. Rayburn also called in what Bolling described as the "incredible" number of political chips he had accumulated in nearly two decades as Speaker. Rayburn urged representatives "to give this young man in the White House a chance."[6]

To head off the committee packing, Smith made a limited pledge: "I will cooperate with the Democratic leadership just as long and just as far as my conscience will permit me to go." Liberal congressmen chuckled at Smith's promise, knowing it would destroy Kennedy's domestic program. The Judge could not resist retorting: "Some of these gentlemen who are laughing maybe do not understand what a conscience is. They are entitled to that code, and I think I am entitled to mine." At the close of the debate, Rayburn, the revered seventy-eight-year-old Speaker, received a standing ovation that included whistles and shouts as he entered the House from his rococo corner office. Smith stayed slouched in his seat. A somber Rayburn then made a rare floor speech in his "gobbler's voice": "The issue, in my mind, is a simple one. We have elected to the Presidency a new leader. He is going to have a program that he thinks will be in the interest of and for the benefit of the American people. . . . Let us be sure that we can move it. And the only way that we can be sure this program will move . . . is to adopt this resolution today." He claimed that the enlargement of the Rules Committee was a "painless" temporary increase that would "embarrass no one."[7]

Tension mounted in the chamber as the twenty-five-minute roll call slowly proceeded. The overflow crowd of congressional family members, government officials, lawyers, lobbyists, students, and fur-coated women sided with the administration and met each Smith vote with "a low, hissing gasp of disappointment." When the vote finally ended, Rayburn was rescued from a humiliating defeat, 217 to 212. Forty-seven southern Democrats and twenty-two Martin Republicans turned their backs on Smith and the conservative coalition. Only Mississippi and South Carolina cast unanimous negative votes in the biggest House fight since the revolt against autocratic Speaker Joe Cannon in 1910. Forcing a wan smile, Smith grumbled, "Well, we done our damnedest." The age of effective Rules obstruction was at last coming to an end.[8]

Bitter and resentful, Smith purposely tried to embarrass the

Democratic leadership. His committee had performed a useful service, he maintained, in waylaying measures by representatives insincerely appeasing their local constituencies. To get even with Rayburn, the Judge refused to give the three new committee members—Democrats Carl Elliott of Alabama and Bernie F. Sisk of California and Republican William H. Avery of Kansas—the same "lean-back, swivel-type, padded-leather, executive" black chairs enjoyed by the other twelve members. Instead, he provided them with the straight-back brown chairs used by spectators. Elliott's constituents "got all in an uproar" over the injustice and bought him a fancier $1,800 model, replete with a brass plate identifying the chair as his. The Alabama representative recalled that the gesture "offended Smith very greatly, just offended him something terrible," and the chairman immediately shipped the new chair to the Alabaman's congressional office. A fortnight later, as the flap continued and made its way into the press, Smith thought better of his spite and ordered the House clerk to purchase three new plush chairs.[9]

The Rules chairman also flooded the House with bills the Speaker opposed. In February, Smith commented wryly that some of these bills were "silly," and "in the past I helped sidetrack them, but the House gave me a mandate not to do it any more." The next day, proadministration Rules members tabled bills permitting television broadcasts of House proceedings—anathema to Rayburn—and banning "back-door spending" that bypassed the Appropriations Committee. The majority also killed several other resolutions, prompting Smith to remark mischievously that the newly enlarged Rules Committee was more "obstructionist" than its predecessor.[10]

Despite Smith's evident hard feelings, the administration tried to put their differences behind them. In June the White House awarded a $2.7 million naval contract to a company in the Virginian's district. It also listened sympathetically to Judge Smith's request that the president accept a liberty tree from the Loudoun County Junior Chamber of Commerce. Kennedy's paramount act of reconciliation was his appointment of Smith's longtime friend Judge Albert V. Bryan, Sr., to the Fourth Circuit Court of Appeals.[11]

The president's efforts notwithstanding, the release of administration bills from Rules remained dependent on a slender one-

"NO HARD FEELIN'S, MR. SAM—BY THE WAY, HOW *ARE* YOU FEELIN'?"

From the *St. Louis Post-Dispatch*, February 24, 1961 (reprinted by permission of Bill Mauldin and Wil-Jo Associates, Inc.)

vote margin. The new committee members, especially Elliott, who often held the balance of power, brought a liberalizing influence, but Chairman Smith retained his informal powers of obstruction, particularly that of scheduling infrequent meetings. Elliott later remembered that Smith also had lost none of his considerable powers of persuasion: "He was the most personable fellow to have as an opponent you've ever seen. It was all Virginia cavalier gentleman. He'd say, 'No,' and make you feel like he was doing you a big favor, that he was really being helpful, that he was being compassionate with you, and keeping you from getting off into the brambles where you were headed." Moreover, Democratic committee members occasionally voted against the House leadership when bills damaging to their constituents arose. For example, James Delaney, a New York representative from a heavily Catholic district, sided with the conservatives in tabling federal aid to public but not parochial schools. Similarly, liberal southerners James W. Trimble and Elliott defected on civil rights. Bolling recalled how precarious the enlarged committee was: "There was always the opportunity for a pick off and make an 8–7 win an 8–7 loss. Smith and Colmer together or separately were capable of figuring out who to approach and how; be it in terms of district or personal preference or a trade-off or whatever, they had eight targets sitting there. If they get one, it turns from a majority to a minority."[12]

These political facts of life meant Rules reported many controversial New Frontier measures, such as area redevelopment, federal housing, and increased minimum-wage and unemployment benefits; but, conversely, it took no action on at least twenty equally significant Kennedy measures, including college classroom construction, youth unemployment remedies, and funding for mass transit. House majority leader Carl Albert concluded that "we never did really have control of the Rules Committee."[13]

Ever the cunning chairman, Smith also successfully used delaying tactics to slow down committee deliberations. Elliott painfully recalled several dilatory episodes. After Smith agreed to consider a minor administration bill, his conservative colleagues debated its merits interminably: "We'd bring that up and there would be discussion all over the place about it. Smith would discuss it. Colmer would discuss it. All the other folks on the Committee there that were on his side would discuss it. The rest of us would wait for an opportunity to vote, hoping that they wouldn't discuss it to death." Smith also refused to bring up federal aid bills if the Speaker or a liberal Rules member was absent, feigning genuine interest in the absentee's health or fair play for the administration's program. Other times, to cut off a liberal colleague, he would pound his gavel and announce, "The gentleman has used up his time." Smith then would glance at his watch and remark in polite dismissal, "It's getting pretty late and I promised" another congressman a favor. The Judge, Elliott asserted, "made it appear that if he were a despot at all that he was a very enlightened despot. He had going for him all these Virginia manners, considerations, plastic considerations all the time. He went through all those motions just over and over."[14]

Though the liberals had weakened the Rules chairman's official powers, they had weakened neither Smith's determination nor his devotion to long-held principles, including fiscal conservatism. Deficit spending became a critical issue during the 1961 session when Smith and his conservative colleagues decided to eradicate what they derisively called "back-door spending." The Constitution clearly proscribed appropriations not made by law, but Congress had allowed the practice since World War I. In essence, liberal congressmen funded government agencies in unorthodox ways such as borrowing directly from the Treasury in order to bypass the conservative-dominated Appropriations Committee. What especially alarmed Smith was the Kennedy administration's willingness to rely on backdoor spending. In 1955 this financing had amounted to $3.3 billion, but the figure reached the all-time high of $19.6 billion in 1961. The committees on banking and currency, veterans, foreign relations, and agriculture allowed Kennedy to fund the Area Redevelopment Act, the Housing Act, direct home loans for veterans, the Foreign Assistance Act, and three agricultural laws.[15]

Although Smith for years had tried to forbid backdoor spending, he had never been successful. Most representatives publicly disapproved of "treasury raiding," but they would not support requiring Appropriations Committee approval of all financing measures. The Virginia congressman once tried to explain why his amendments did not reach the floor: "The trouble of it is that everybody thinks it is a bad situation, but if you ask somebody connected with the committee that happens to be doing it at the moment, he will agree with you that it is bad but 'It ought not to apply to me.' It ought to apply to the other fellow, but we have a special situation." Smith's lack of success did not deter him. Several times in 1961, he stressed the perils of backdoor spending. Pointing to the $290 billion national debt, Smith warned that backdoor financing violated the Constitution, increased the debt ceiling, and undermined the American dollar. At other times, he recognized that he was "beating my head against a stone wall." Indeed, he even voted to raise the debt limit and to extend veteran home loans because these bills were "simply a continuation of the sins we have been committing in the past." But he pleaded with his colleagues either to support his amendment on the appropriations bill or to "figure out some way to stop this thing before it breaks the country." Appropriations chairman Clarence Cannon added his voice to Smith's suggesting that the United States would succumb to communism if backdoor spending continued. But the House neither approved the Smith amendment nor stopped the transfer of Treasury funds to executive agencies.[16]

Because the Judge continued, undaunted, to block the New Frontier, President Kennedy decided in early 1962 to undercut the Virginian's clout. First, the president requested a personal meeting with the statesman nearly twice his age. Dutifully, Smith appeared at the White House at 5:30 P.M. on January 10. After an exchange of pleasantries, Kennedy outlined his forthcoming proposals. At this juncture, Smith "interrupted to say that while I would like to cooperate with him in any way that I could I had certain fixed views that I could not yield, that I had learned in the hurly burly of Congressional fights that one used such weapons that came to hand." When Kennedy then pushed for the proposed urban affairs department, Smith stubbornly "complained about our fiscal situation and the repeated measures [being sent] annually to Congress asking for an increase in the debt limit." Only after forty-five minutes of polite arm-twisting did Smith defer to the president, agreeing to let the House hear the department creation bill.[17]

The president's next move was to increase administration contact with Smith when controversial measures surfaced in Rules. In January the president curried the powerful chairman's favor for higher government employee pay. Aware that Smith opposed pay hikes, Kennedy presented an argument that differentiated between "pay raise" and "pay reform." He insisted that the current bill was based on "the principle of comparability with private industry" and explained that its provisions would be delayed for one year. In March, Kennedy personally asked Smith to report a bill permitting the Justice Department to compel the release of antitrust evidence.[18]

Since Smith usually found even personal presidential requests unpersuasive, the administration watched Rules proceedings closely. In April the Rules Committee had received administration bills on school aid, youth employment, and public reclamation projects. To find out their status, presidential assistant Lawrence O'Brien dispatched Jim G. Akin, the congressional liaison officer of the Department of Health, Education, and Welfare, to a Rules meeting. There, Akin heard Smith make "a personal appeal to the members of the Committee not to report at this time any of the major bills pending." Except for one reclamation project, Smith's allies concurred. After the meeting Akin telephoned a waiting O'Brien staff member. The liaison officer reported that Smith could rely on Mississippi Democrat John Bell Williams and Ohio Republican Samuel L. Devine, as well as others, "who will do some behind-the-scenes work for him" on legislative matters. Armed with this information, O'Brien plotted strategy with John W. McCormack, the new Speaker after Sam Rayburn had died of cancer in 1961.[19]

These steps were still insufficient. The administration next turned to the House Democratic leadership and liberal members on Rules. In the case of the White House bill on the Youth Conservation Corps, Kentucky Democrat Carl D. Perkins advised McCormack and liberal Rules member Richard Bolling to push hard because "it has been obvious . . . that Howard Smith will not raise his finger to bring it up much less out of the Rules Committee." McCormack replied that he had already done "everything I can to try to get a rule out of the Rules committee," including buttonholing Smith on two occasions. But Smith believed unskilled young people did not need public service jobs; so his colleagues' entreaties went unheeded. It was Smith who finally made a proposition to the administration. He would support the job bill when the White House secured passage of a bill beautifying the land across the river from George Washington's home,

Mount Vernon. But even after the beautification bill passed, Rules detained the youth training measure.[20]

Ultimately, the administration concluded that Judge Smith would never cease to impede the New Frontier unless drastic measures were pursued immediately. Permanent enlargement of the Rules Committee provided the solution. In December 1962, after an uncontested election, Smith laid down the gauntlet to the White House: "The Rules Committee issue is not negotiable." On the same day, President Kennedy told reporters: "I hope that the Rules Committee is kept to its present number, because we can't function if it isn't. We are through if we lose—if they try to change the Rules. Nothing controversial in that case would come to the floor of the Congress. Our whole program in my opinion would be emasculated."[21]

When the new Congress opened in January 1963, the Rules chairman naturally opposed the resolution making the enlargement permanent. He aimed his defensive strategy at other southern representatives, warning them that the continued packing of Rules would mean that his committee would act like a sieve, letting through such "unsound" measures as raising the federal debt ceiling. He did not need to remind them of the recent civil rights and anti–poll tax bills. Smith ended his remarks by reading a *Washington Star* editorial which argued that the enlargement was unnecessary because the House already had other procedures for releasing stalled bills.[22]

An acrimonious debate ensued. Longtime Smith supporter W. J. Bryan Dorn of South Carolina denounced the resolution, saying the move amounted to "another step toward a Hitler-type rubberstamp Congress." On the other side, New York Democrat William F. Ryan endorsed the enlargement as essential to the House's dual role of policy-making and problem-solving. The resolution also enjoyed the unexpected support of Georgia's Philip Landrum, who deserted Smith in order to win a seat on the powerful Ways and Means Committee. Another anti-Smith southerner, Carl Elliott, contended that the Judge opposed the Rules enlargement "to give some validity to the facade that he was presenting about the country going to hell in a handbasket because of big spenders and people of more liberal mind than he were spending it into complete bankruptcy or they were violating the

Constitution and mixing church and state." The permanent expansion measure passed by a slightly more comfortable margin than the temporary one had two years earlier. The octogenarian Smith lamented the outcome because of the southern defections and because "it reduces my responsibility very much." A resentful Bill Colmer put the defeat in a larger context, claiming the vote made the South "a whipping boy to win racial minority votes in big metropolitan centers."[23]

The enlargement vote notwithstanding, Smith resumed his obstructionism. One of the first battles of the Eighty-eighth Congress came in March 1963 when the administration recommended a medical training aid bill. The bill would establish a multiyear program of matching grants for construction or repair of medical and dental schools, as well as a student loan program. In the Rules Committee, Smith, Colmer, and five Republicans decided to hold the medical school bill hostage until they saw that the pending general education bill did not duplicate or otherwise waste government monies. When the medical training measure came to a vote, Rules deadlocked because Ray J. Madden, an administration supporter, fell ill.[24]

The day after the tie vote, President Kennedy openly criticized Smith and Colmer. When asked by a reporter why Congress was reluctant to approve the New Frontier, Kennedy replied that the two southern Democrats were not true party members. Howard Smith quickly corrected the president. After hinting that the chief executive should not attack members of a coordinate branch of government, the Judge explained that his committee was sympathetic to the medical school aid proposal. But he regarded the "whole subject of Federal Aid to Education, both as to existing programs and new programs proposed by you, [as] in a state of utter chaos." He appealed to the president to "lead the Congress out of the maze of conflicting and overlapping" education programs.[25]

In response to Smith's request, Kennedy met with the chairmen considering education bills. The president assured the Rules chairman that none of these bills conflicted or overlapped. Apparently Smith agreed, because Rules cleared the medical education bill in April. By month's end, the House passed the measure over mainly Republican opposition. Smith sided with the majority, saying, "If there is any good reason for Federal aid to education I believe medicine would be the prime field in which it might be used." With the Senate's consent, Kennedy signed the bill in September. For the first time he had swayed his diehard foe on legislation.[26]

But Smith still proved intractable on the civil rights question. The need for federal government intervention had been building since the spring of 1963, when police in Birmingham, Alabama, had brutally suppressed black demonstrations led by Martin Luther King, Jr. After Alabama governor George C. Wallace theatrically defied a federal court order admitting two black students to the state university, an enraged Kennedy directed U.S. marshals to intervene. In a landmark speech, the president stressed the urgent need for federal legislation. Encouraged by this show of support, King applied more pressure by bringing two hundred thousand sympathizers to Washington's Lincoln Memorial in August. Racial eruptions continued in the fall. Kennedy then secured bipartisan support for a revised and stronger civil rights bill.[27]

After months of deliberation, the Judiciary Committee sent the bill to Rules in November 1963. Characteristically, Smith set it aside. When asked about a hearing date, the Rules chairman replied that "the Supreme Court had laid down a law that things should be done with deliberate speed, and I'm a law-abiding citizen." By this time, the eighty-one-year-old Virginian's advancing years had rounded his shoulders and reduced his gait to a hesitant walk; but the burning desire to oppose civil rights still shone in his flinty brown eyes. Finally, 165 representatives petitioned Smith to begin committee hearings, to which he grudgingly consented on January 9, 1964. The *New York Times Magazine* predicted that Smith would "delay the bill a while and harass its backers" until they made substantial concessions.[28]

After Kennedy's assassination in late November, Lyndon Johnson of Texas picked up the civil rights banner. He told Congress and the nation, "No memorial oration or eulogy could more eloquently honor President Kennedy's memory than the earliest possible passage of the civil rights bill for which he fought." The Johnson civil rights bill contained expansive provisions to secure full citizenship for black people. It sought to ensure black access to voting booths and public accommodations, to empower the federal government to use the courts to desegregate public facilities and schools, and to endow the Civil Rights Commission with new powers. The bill also authorized the president to withdraw funds from discriminatory programs and allowed the Justice Department to submit a friend-of-the-court brief in pending civil rights cases. Among other things, the measure required employers and unions to practice equal employment opportunity or risk running afoul of the proposed watchdog agency, the Equal Employment Opportunity Commission (EEOC).[29]

As Smith had promised, the Rules Committee, took up "this nefarious bill" in mid-January 1964. But the committee delayed the bill for three more weeks. Speaking in "dirge-like tones" to the committee and the overflow crowd of fifty reporters, the chairman called the first witness, Emanuel Celler, chairman of the Judiciary Committee. Smith delivered a stern lecture to his colleague for rushing the fifty-six-page compromise measure through committee without following the usual procedure of discussing every paragraph. Before long, the Virginian painted Celler into a legal corner, where the New York Democrat contradicted himself. Smith concluded that Celler "just doesn't know what's in this bill."[30]

On January 21, as the hearings dragged on, Speaker McCormack asked Smith to release the bill by the end of the month. Aware of the upcoming recess for Lincoln's birthday, McCormack planned to limit debate by holding the recess as bait for quick action. Judge Smith promised only to complete committee hearings by January 31, which meant the House could not vote on the bill until mid-February and the Senate two weeks later. When Bolling tried to cut off debate nine days early, Smith adjourned the committee the instant the Missouri Democrat stepped out of the meeting room. On January 23, Smith announced that the committee planned to call twenty-six more witnesses. But because favorable Rules action seemed a foregone conclusion, southern Democrats used the hearings to demonstrate their segregationist leanings to their home districts.[31]

Because Smith played a critical role in civil rights legislation, the National Broadcasting Corporation's Sunday television news program "Meet the Press" invited him to appear on January 26. During the questioning, the congressman declared unconstitutional the bill's guarantee of free access to public accommodations. He recalled that the Supreme Court in 1883 had struck down a similar law passed during Reconstruction. In his view, once the Court had ruled on an issue, it could never reverse itself, a narrow interpretation that dismissed the commonly accepted idea of organic law. He also regarded as unconstitutional the section making any citizen with a sixth-grade education eligible to vote. The Constitution, he pointed out, gave the states the power to determine electoral qualifications (an argument which conveniently ignored the next provision in the Constitution, which allows Congress to "by Law make or alter such Regulations"). When one panelist prodded Smith about when long-suffering blacks would be accorded full civil rights, the Virginian replied that integration had already made substantial headway in his lifetime. Time, not law, would eventually erode segregation. Convinced that racial integration would be accomplished only gradually, he asked: "Why all this sudden rush to do it overnight? Is it because we have a national election approaching?"[32]

Back on Capitol Hill, Smith and Colmer mapped opposition strategy with sixty other southern Democrats the day before Rules released the bill. After the closed-door meeting, Colmer announced the group would no longer pursue delaying tactics to defeat or to modify the bill. He feared that obstruction would antagonize moderates who might otherwise support crippling amendments. Instead, the group proposed eliminating the bill's sections prohibiting racial discrimination in employment, public accommodations, and federally funded programs. With the southern plan established, the Rules Committee released the measure as scheduled. The civil rights bill had finally broken free, "managing to escape a plot in Judge Smith's graveyard in which so much liberal legislation had been entombed in the past."[33]

For the next ten days, Chairman Smith ably coordinated southern opposition to the bill. On February 1 he charged that the bill "infringed upon" the liberties of 90 percent of Americans, and in an allusion to miscegenation, he concluded that "this monstrosity of unknown origin and unknown parentage" was an unfit substitute for the slain president's original bill. He ridiculed the bill, saying that it was "as full of booby traps as a dog is of fleas" and citing the inconsistency of requiring barbers in hotels, but not other barbers, to accept a biracial clientele. Two days later, Smith introduced a three-word amendment confining the voting rights guarantee to federal elections. But when one of the bill's sponsors noted that the amendment could nullify the voting rights provision, the House rejected Smith's proposal.[34]

On the evening of February 4, Judge Smith offered another diversionary amendment, this time on public accommodations. Reminding the House that involuntary servitude was illegal, he tried to permit an individual to work under personally acceptable conditions. Judiciary chairman Celler attacked Smith's latest bid to weaken the bill. He rejected the Virginian's notion that the bill conflicted with the Thirteenth Amendment. In fact, Celler argued, Smith's amendment made the bill "just a paper sword," for under its protection a motel or restaurant owner could refuse black patrons. The House agreed with Celler and threw out the amendment.[35]

Smith's most surprising tactic came on February 8, when he attempted to add a ban on sex discrimination to the bill's prohibition of discrimination based on race, creed, color, and national origin. His purpose was to sink civil rights for blacks by adding a similar guarantee for women; although some congressmen would grant equal rights for men of both races, Smith was certain that they would never extend those rights to women. He knew that the Johnson administration opposed the sex amendment because it threatened to dissolve the fragile coalition supporting the civil rights bill. Michigan Democrat Martha W. Griffiths, a women's activist, later confirmed that Smith told her "the amendment was a joke." A Smith associate, Florida Democrat Sydney Herlong, agreed with Griffiths: Smith "didn't want to help the bill; I promise you that." On the contrary, Smith attached the sex amendment with "tongue in cheek." The Rules Committee counsel, T.M. Carruthers, also dismissed the suggestion that Smith was for sex equality: "The ladies gave him credit for helping them, but he had another motive. I wouldn't say he was in favor of civil rights." A fellow southerner, economic liberal Carl Elliott, put it more bluntly: "Smith didn't give a damn about women's rights, black rights, equality. He was trying to knock off votes either then or down the line because there was always a hard core of men who didn't favor women's rights."[36]

Smith may have had a secondary purpose in supporting the sex amendment. Southern industry, particularly textile mills, such as those in Virginia, relied heavily on cheap female labor toiling in sweatshop conditions to remain profitable. Recently passed protective laws for women had endangered this exploitation. A sex amendment would strike down such sex-based legislation that hurt southern companies. As a result, Smith and other southern Democrats may have adopted a chivalrous pose to assist local businesses. By adding the sex amendment, the Judge apparently hoped either to defeat the bill or, if it passed, to assist southern businessmen.[37]

On the House floor Smith insisted he was "very serious" about his amendment. But his remarks quickly passed over the unequal pay women workers received to poke fun at sex equality. Always the Virginia gentleman "operating behind a screen of Southern courtesy," Smith observed that women outnumbered men in the population and joked that the imbalance between the sexes deprived many women of their "right to a nice husband and family," as one of his female constituents had written him. The other congressmen roared with laughter. Smith urged Congress to rectify this "grave injustice . . . particularly in an election year."[38]

An irate Emanuel Celler, floor manager of the bill, resisted Smith's sex amendment, insisting it would open what another congressman later called "a Pandora's box of revolutionary changes." In Celler's view, as well as that of Assistant Labor Secretary Esther Peterson, the measure should not outlaw sex discrimination. He and Peterson believed that "discrimination based on sex . . . involves problems sufficiently different from [racial] discrimination . . . to make separate treatment preferable." If Smith's amendment passed, Celler foresaw an "upheaval" leading to the drafting of women into military service, the changing of alimony and rape laws, and the elimination of preferential laws for working women. Although the Judiciary chairman considered the sex amendment "illogical, ill timed, and improper," he nonetheless recognized Smith's astuteness.[39]

After several congresswomen spoke for "this little crumb of equality," the House approved the sex amendment. Although there was no roll call, Martha Griffiths, who served as a teller for the vote, remembered that the amendment's supporters were largely southerners and Republicans. When the vote was revealed, women in the gallery cheered. One ecstatic spectator shouted, "We've won, we've won!" Another woman cried, "We made it! God Bless America!" before guards removed her. Indeed, they had. Contrary to Smith's expectations, his scheme did not weaken the bill's support. Later, Smith humbled his liberal enemies for opposing sex equality. A shamefaced Dick Bolling recalled that Smith gleefully waved a finger in his face for voting against the sex amendment. In this remarkable turn of events, Smith had used the federal government to fortify and expand women's push for equality. Women, much more than blacks, used the EEOC to overturn job discrimination. Along with Betty Friedan, who wrote the pioneering book *The Feminine Mystique* in 1963, Smith must be credited with giving the modern feminist movement a powerful, if unanticipated, push forward.[40]

On February 10, Smith made two last-ditch attempts to undermine the civil rights measure. First, he proposed striking out language requiring employers to maintain records on job applications and employment practices. Appealing to the traditionally business-oriented Republicans, Smith pointed out that his amendment would save businesses hundreds of thousands of dollars by freeing companies from keeping costly and time-consuming records. Celler and California Democrat James Roosevelt dismissed this argument, noting that businesses already prepared related records for tax statutes and the minimum wage law. The House once more turned down the Virginian.[41]

Later that day, Smith made a second bid to dilute the civil rights bill. Nearly a week earlier, he had tried unsuccessfully to amend the public accommodations section by allowing an individual to choose the conditions under which he would work; now, he presented the same amendment to the entire bill. As he saw it, northern representatives had a chance to redeem their "sin" of not voting for the amendment the first time, but he was not sanguine about its passage: "I do not expect you to adopt this amendment. I just want to make you feel ashamed of yourselves. I know what you are going to do about it. I know you are not going to adopt this amendment, but I just want to see you squirm. I just want to see you feel ashamed of yourselves. I want to see you get up and argue against the 13th amendment which you placed on the books 100 years ago."[42]

Smith's gloomy expectations were correct, for his final proposal went down to defeat. Shortly afterward, the House overwhelmingly approved the civil rights bill, the most significant one since Reconstruction. Contrary to Smith's expectations, the inclusion of sex equality did not prevent the bill's passage. Smith, the rest of the Virginia delegation, and all but seven other southern Democrats voted against the "punitive" legislation.[43]

The Johnson administration did not rest with this major triumph. The president knew well that after the civil rights bill cleared the Senate, a revised version would come before the House Rules Committee. By June 1964 presidential assistant O'Brien was proceeding on the assumption that "Howard Smith will delay as long as possible on granting a rule, and that he can parade witnesses through for several weeks unless we move to cut him off." He informed Johnson that the best way to stop Smith was to have any three Rules members call for a committee meeting as soon as the revised bill came to the House. According to this new procedure, the chairman had seven calendar days to call a meeting, or a majority of the committee could ask the House clerk to convene Rules the following day.[44]

When the bill reached the House on June 22, administration Democrats put O'Brien's plan into action. The House had to pass the bill exactly as it came from the Senate, lest another crippling filibuster in the Senate kill the measure. Judiciary chairman Celler asked that the House consider the bill immediately. But when several southern Democrats objected, the motion was defeated. He then filed a resolution calling for a vote on the measure after one hour of debate. Because the resolution had to go to Rules, three Democrats on that committee—Ray J. Madden of Indiana, B. F. Sisk of California, and John Young of Texas—tried to compel Smith to hold a meeting. Taking no chances on another disappearing act, the party loyalists conveyed their urgent desire for a hearing in registered letters sent to the chairman at five different addresses. As in 1957, Smith agreed to a meeting on the last allowable date, June 30. On that day, Smith and Colmer took turns flaying the bill's eighty-seven Senate amendments and the one-hour floor debate limit. Desperate to delay what Colmer called this "political monstrosity," the Rules leadership called forth a stream of hostile southern congressmen and demanded Judiciary and conference committee action and a four-hour debate. But Madden led an "unprecedented" revolt to end the hearings precisely at five o'clock that same afternoon and to have Madden, not the chairman, handle the resolution on the floor.[45]

In one last gasp against the civil rights bill, Smith condemned the measure before the House on procedural and substantive grounds. On July 2 he called unfair the debate limitation permitting its opponents just fifteen minutes. He also argued that this bill, with its Senate amendments, was not the same one approved by the House in February. Smith and a succession of other southern Democrats assailed the bill for recreating the conditions of Reconstruction. "Already the second invasion of carpetbaggers of the Southland has begun. Hordes of beatniks, misfits, and agitators from the North, with the admitted aid of the Communists, are streaming into the Southland on mischief bent, backed and defended by other hordes of Federal marshals, Federal agents, and Federal power." Hopeful that the country might be saved from impending disaster, the Judge closed his speech with the brief prayer, "God save the United States of America." But the vote was a foregone conclusion; the House passed it by better than a two-to-one margin. The southern president called the act "a proud triumph" and signed it into law that night.[46]

In practice, the 1964 Civil Rights Act had several significant weaknesses. The law prevented registrars from applying different voting requirements based on race; yet, it did not abolish literacy tests, which had been widely used to disfranchise blacks and poor whites. Second, the law exempted "private clubs" from provisions regarding equal access to facilities. Third, the act authorized but did not mandate the withdrawal of federal funds from discriminatory programs. Finally, the law's enforcement placed primary responsibility on aggrieved individuals, most of whom could not afford expensive legal action. On the other hand, the law represented a major victory for civil rights activists. For the first time, segregation in most areas of society was illegal. Civil rights groups such as the NAACP now had another weapon in attacking racial discrimination. The act also had an immediate effect. In southern cities blacks crossed "white only" sections to eat, to watch movies, to swim, and to sleep. Although compliance was not universal, the barriers to integration were beginning to crumble. Indeed, the vehement resistance of such reactionary southerners as Howard Smith testified to the bill's importance.[47]

Having lost on civil rights, Smith turned to the related issue of equal representation in legislative bodies. The issue had arisen in 1962 in the path-breaking *Baker* v. *Carr* case, when the U.S. Supreme Court first "entered the political thicket" to consider malapportionment of state legislatures. The next year the Court went further, promulgating the principle of "one man, one vote," which required legislative districts to be apportioned as equally as possible. Many state legislatures had grossly unequal districts that underrepresented growing urban areas with large minority populations. For example, six million Angelenos in one state senate district had the same voting power as 14,000 other Californians—a ratio of 420 to 1. In 1964 the Court ruled that the populations in congressional districts had to be roughly equal and that both houses in a bicameral legislature should be based only on population, not geography or other factors.[48]

Virginia's method of legislative apportionment violated the Court's dictum of equal representation. The disparity between the largest and smallest state senate districts was two-to-one, and it was four-to-one in the House of Delegates districts. As for congressional districts, the state had discriminated against the heavily black city of Norfolk, whose district was 36 percent above average, and against the federal government workers near Washington, D.C., whose district was 24.6 percent above average. Smith's Eighth District, by contrast, was nearly 10 percent below average. In 1964 the U.S. Supreme Court ordered the Virginia assembly to reach a more equitable population division among congressional districts by the following year. The directive meant that the Eighth District would be enlarged, probably by including some of the government employees in Alexandria, Arlington, and Fairfax whom Smith had escaped in the last redistricting.[49]

As always, Smith posed as a statesman, couching his objections to the Court's apportionment decisions in constitutional terms. He saw the doctrine as the most harmful in a long series of judge-made laws because the Court usurped congressional prerogatives under the Constitution: "This decision of the Supreme Court in this legislative apportionment matter is the first case that I have ever been able to discover where the Federal courts of the United States have just set out deliberately and with malice aforethought to invade the province of the Congress and to themselves actually write legislation that is to be inscribed in the books of the States," a danger he had recognized when the New Deal was upheld in 1935.[50]

To forestall a judicial dictatorship, Smith backed a bill stripping jurisdiction over state reapportionment from the federal courts.

The bill, though presented by his fellow Virginian Bill Tuck, probably was written by Smith, given Smith's long-standing interest in similar legislation and his practice of letting others introduce controversial measures. The Tuck bill languished in Celler's Judiciary Committee through the summer of 1964. In August, Smith asked the House to let the Rules Committee pry the bill from Judiciary, a move the Democratic leadership opposed. The bill's opponents strongly objected to Smith's unorthodox suggestion that Rules, a procedural committee, be allowed to supersede Judiciary, a legislative committee. Chairman Celler understandably complained the loudest: "I feel that the Rules Committee has usurped power, and we can well say it is using its tyrannous power like a giant in a cavalier manner." The Speaker, however, overruled Celler, noting that Rules possessed the seldom-used right to report any bill it chose. The House passed the bill only to see the Senate let it die without debate.[51]

Smith's 1964 reelection campaign became a referendum on his efforts to block civil rights and Johnson's other Great Society programs. Although Eighth District Republicans declined to field a candidate, local Democrats divided in their support of the incumbent. Prominent area Democrats George C. Rawlings, Jr., of Fredericksburg and John F. Barrett of Stafford County refused to endorse Smith's nomination until the Judge publicly declared for the national Democratic ticket of Lyndon Johnson and Hubert H. Humphrey. In July, Smith ignored these nascent signs of discontent. At the state Democratic convention in Richmond, he attempted to prevent party endorsement of President Johnson, whom he regarded as a regional turncoat. But the convention backed Johnson anyway.[52]

Disgusted by Smith's party disloyalty, Virginia attorney Floyd C. Bagley of Dumfries ran as a Democrat-turned-independent for the Eighth District congressional seat. Bagley repeatedly endorsed the Great Society, but his campaign was plagued by poor organization and insufficient support. As a result, Smith worried more about record increases in black voter registration. Under the recently ratified anti–poll tax amendment, Orange County blacks comprised 75 percent of the five hundred new county voters who had registered since June 1. Despite increased black registration, Smith still captured every county and city in the district, but his voting percentage was the lowest he had received in a contested election in a dozen years.[53]

In December Smith expressed private fears about the requests the Johnson administration might make of the next Congress. He had, after all, just witnessed enactment of historic measures on civil rights, antipoverty, and mass transit. With the administration's landslide victory in November, Johnson would undoubtedly have an even greater measure of support in the upcoming session: The Democratic party had picked up thirty-nine House seats for a total of 295, more than double the Republican total of 140; worse, most of the new Democratic representatives were northerners. Johnson would have the largest majority in the House of any president since Franklin D. Roosevelt. Writing to his daughter, Smith admitted: "I am not looking forward with any pleasure to the coming session of Congress. I think it will be pretty wild and LBJ may have some trouble restraining his wild horse or the other animals."[54]

Smith's fears were realized when the administration pushed a legislative avalanche through Congress. Two of the most important bills dealt with federal aid to education and voting rights. In March 1965 the House Education Committee reported a bill that would set up a three-year program of federal grants to school districts with many low-income families. It also provided grants to purchase books, to create supplemental educational centers in local communities, to conduct educational research, and to strengthen state education departments. To avoid the parochial school question that had defeated earlier education bills, this one gave aid for individual, rather than institutional, benefit. With Smith and Colmer opposed, Rules barely cleared the bill.[55]

On the House floor, Judge Smith voiced his displeasure. Calling this "the end of the road" for local control of education, Smith singled out "several basic defects" in the legislation. He blamed "the hysteria that is going on now relative to the minority race" for providing the impetus for the bill. He especially criticized preachers who championed civil rights by deserting their flocks and "tramping through the mud on the second Sherman march through the South." Clearly, Smith regarded the bill as antisouthern. The chief fault he found with it was the unfair formula for distributing education funds. The bill offered lesser amounts to states currently spending a proportionately smaller sum per pupil. Since southern states like Virginia were reluctant and often unable to appropriate additional monies for black students, they stood to be hurt most by the aid distribution formula. The Rules chairman urged his colleagues to reject this "great wrong."[56]

At the end of March, Smith presented an amendment to the education bill requesting judicial review of its constitutionality. His announced purpose was to "at least recognize that we do have a Constitution which is supposed to govern this country." As was often the case in the Johnson years, Emanuel Celler led the fight against Smith's rearguard action. He found it "rather anomalous" that his Virginia colleague wanted to have recourse to the courts in this instance, while seeking to strip the federal judiciary's jurisdiction elsewhere. More significantly, Smith's amendment was completely unnecessary because judicial review was already implied. Persuaded by Celler's argument, the House rejected the amendment and voted for the bill. In April the president signed the measure outside the Texas schoolhouse he had attended as a child, making this the first general law for federal school aid.[57]

The voting rights bill was Smith's other principal concern in the 1965 session. The measure was a response to the white southern backlash against Martin Luther King's efforts in early 1965 to dramatize black difficulties in voter registration. In Selma, Alabama, a black voter applicant had to register on the two days allotted each month, to complete a complex form with fifty blanks, and to sign a loyalty oath to Alabama and to the United States. This complicated procedure kept the number of black registrants to a minimum. In Dallas County surrounding Selma, blacks made up 57.6 percent of the population but just 2.1 percent of the registered voters.[58]

On January 18, King led hundreds of blacks to the Dallas County Courthouse to register. Within weeks, Sheriff Jim Clark and his deputies, armed with electric cattle prods, had arrested more than two thousand marchers for "parading without a permit." To resolve the heated situation, a federal judge ordered the County Board of Registrants to speed its voter registration process. Because previous court orders had been ignored, frustrated blacks planned a peaceful march from Selma to the state capital in Montgomery. King then met with President Johnson to discuss the provisions of a federal voting rights law. When King returned to Selma to lead the Freedom March, Governor Wallace commanded the demonstrators to disband.[59]

The marchers defied the edict. In early March television audiences across the nation saw bloody, screaming demonstrators fleeing from state troopers and mounted deputies brandishing whips, nightsticks, tear gas, and firearms. Horrified citizens flooded the White House with telephone calls and letters, demanding presidential action. On March 15 Johnson appeared before a joint session of Congress to push for rapid approval of voting rights legislation. In a moving passage, he declared, "It is not just Negroes, but it is all of us, who must overcome the crippling legacy of bigotry and injustice. And we *shall* overcome."[60]

The administration's measure went beyond the judicial system to solve voting registration inequities. It specifically voided the use of literacy and similar tests as qualifications for voting in federal elections. The bill also empowered the U.S. attorney general to send federal examiners to supervise voter registration in localities in which qualifying tests had been required and in which fewer than 50 percent of voting-age residents either had registered or had voted in the 1964 election. This provision meant that Virginia and five other southern states faced the prospect of federal voting examiners. Only 38.3 percent of Virginia's eligible blacks were registered, and nearly half of these had come since the 1962 federal anti–poll tax resolution. In addition, the measure set forth criminal penalties for those interfering with would-be voters and ordered the Justice Department to sue those states that continued to use the now unconstitutional poll tax.[61]

Judge Smith viewed the administration's request for minority voting rights as another example of the telling effect that well-organized and well-financed groups could have. Speaking to the House on Jefferson's birthday, Smith allowed that the civil rights movement "may have been well meaning" in the beginning, but its underlying motive was subversion. As a self-proclaimed expert on disloyalty, he blasted the protestors: "There can be no doubt that many Communists, subversives, fellow travelers, and others of doubtful loyalty to their country, have attached themselves to this movement." Their revolutionary intent, he suggested, could easily be seen in their dangerous slogan, "We shall overcome." In his opinion, normally prudent people were blinded to the movement's true character by the participation of "many good, well-meaning Christian people," who had "served to clothe the mobs with an air of respectability."[62]

Once the bill cleared Celler's Judiciary Committee in June, Smith locked it in "the cooler." Celler waited three weeks for Rules to act. Finally, he resorted to the new twenty-one-day rule, which prodded the Rules chairman to spring the bill. Before the House, Smith angrily attacked the measure as "dripping venom" from every sentence and as an "open and flagrant violation of the Constitution for punishing deeds of previous generations." As Smith expected, these sentiments had no impact. In July the House approved the bill over the resistance of Smith and just fifty-nine other southern Democrats. Several southerners who voted for the voting rights measure received standing ovations. After the Senate adopted the conference report, the president signed the momentous bill into law in August.[63]

The Voting Rights Act had an immediate impact on registration. To enroll voters, the federal government assigned registrars to Alabama, Georgia, Louisiana, Mississippi, North Carolina, South Carolina, and Virginia. In August 1965, 381 Selma blacks signed up to vote, more than had registered in all the years since 1900. In the next primary, Dallas County blacks helped defeat their nemesis, Sheriff Clark. Within five months, black registration in the Deep South increased 40 percent. From 1964 to 1969 registered blacks in Mississippi went from 7 percent to 67 percent of the eligible black voters, and similar increases occurred in Alabama and Georgia. Over this same period, Virginia blacks boosted their registration from 38.3 to 59.8 percent of potential black voters.[64]

The 1965 session had proved enormously successful for the administration. The institution of the twenty-one-day rule in January had enabled the House Democratic leadership to bypass the Rules Committee six times. Of the six bills reported under this rule, five passed the House. These included repeal of the Taft-Hartley section allowing states to ban union shops, amendment of the Bank Holding Act of 1956 to bring two holding companies—Du Pont and Financial General—within its scope, federal aid for school construction in areas hit by natural disasters, establishment of a National Foundation on the Arts and Humanities, and a salary increase for government employees. The last three bills passed the Senate and were enacted into law. At year's end,

Smith's committee had before it only five lesser administration bills.[65]

The president's success reflected the weakening of the conservative coalition. According to the *Congressional Quarterly Almanac*, the coalition managed to beat northern Democrats in the Congress just one-third of the time in 1965, the coalition's worst performance since the *Almanac* began keeping records in 1957. In the House, the coalition won only a quarter of all votes, a drop-off of nearly 50 percent since the epic 1961 Rules fight. In large measure, this shift occurred because so many liberal Democrats replaced conservative Republicans, who had been handicapped by their unpopular 1964 presidential candidate, Barry M. Goldwater of Arizona. The change in the House's political complexion prevented the coalition from defeating or emasculating voting rights, Medicare, aid to education, a housing bill, the creation of the Department of Housing and Urban Development, and sharply increased monies for the antipoverty program.[66]

In the Kennedy and Johnson years, liberal Democrats systematically weakened Howard Smith's institutional powers. As a result, he was no longer as effective as he had been in the forties and fifties in holding back social welfare legislation. The process had begun in the first month of Kennedy's administration with the expansion of the Rules Committee. This process continued in 1963 and 1965, when liberal Democrats made permanent procedural changes that reduced Smith's ability as Rules chairman to withhold or modify measures he opposed. Other changes, including two activist presidents, public acceptance of federal programs, and liberal Democratic control of Congress, also accounted for liberal triumphs. Judge Smith, the once mighty kingpin of Rules, eventually could do little more than join with other southern Democrats in denouncing and delaying briefly these "iniquitous" federal aid programs and civil rights bills. He had become little more than the legislative traffic cop that he had always despised.

CHAPTER 8

Electoral Upset

I regard it as the most dangerous campaign I have had since the purge campaign of 1938. It is going to be necessary to get every voter of our persuasion to the polls.

Howard W. Smith (April 1966)

In the early 1960s political developments that would pose serious threats to Smith's service in the House slowly began to coalesce. Those unfavorable trends included local Democratic impatience with Smith's refusal to support this party's presidential nominee and his failure to secure federal benefits for the district. Sharp increases in black voter registration, congressional redistricting, and the emergence of a vocal and tireless liberal Democratic challenger further intensified the aging politician's problems.

Long accustomed to large electoral majorities, Smith typically made only a few perfunctory campaign appearances. Ensconced in distant Alexandria, he relied primarily on courthouse politicians and personal friends to finance and direct his campaigns and to keep him abreast of potential trouble in the district. In 1960, for instance, he asked his friend Edmund T. Dejarnette of Richmond County to "organize some type of campaign in my behalf. . . . Any advertising that my friends would care to run in their local papers would be most helpful." Although Smith cited his heavy work load in Washington as the reason for his absence from the hustings, he simply did not need to mount aggressive campaigns. The traditional lack of intraparty competition, the near moribundity of the Republican party, the large size and conservative character of the district, and the restricted electorate due to poll tax assessments virtually eliminated powerful challengers. Having always merely stood for office, the Judge would prove ill equipped to handle an attractive and energetic opponent.[1]

A second source of trouble for Smith lay in his alienation of two significant local Democratic groups. Diehard party loyalists resented Smith's—not to mention Byrd's—refusal to endorse Kennedy in 1960 and Johnson in 1964 for the presidency. In the past, Smith rarely had been challenged over his political positions, but in October 1960 the Spotsylvania County Democratic Committee unanimously passed a resolution calling on Smith "to publicly announce his support of the Democratic ticket." Prominent citizens in Charlottesville and Fredericksburg bombarded Smith with letters requesting him to break his silence on Kennedy's presidential bid. These Democrats did not accept Smith's argument that the national party platform supporting civil rights made endorsement impossible. A small liberal wing of the party also was disturbed by Smith's unwillingness to back expansive federal government programs. In 1964 Fredericksburg liberals led by Delegate George C. Rawlings, Jr., asked city Democrats not to endorse any party candidate except President Johnson. Although Smith weathered these challenges to his leadership to win reelection in the early sixties, progressive Democrats had become increasingly restive under his reluctance to back social welfare proposals.[2]

Most Eighth District blacks, even more than white liberals, chafed under Smith's opposition to civil rights, federal aid to education, and the antipoverty program. But black voting had long been depressed by the $1.50 state poll tax. Black farmers were deterred from voting by the deliberate timing of the tax, which came in the middle of the planting season, and by the tax's cumulative assessment of up to three years. While most blacks were disfranchised by the tax, Judge Smith admitted that the Byrd organization "did pay poll taxes" for poor white supporters. Moreover, whites intimidated the few blacks who voted. A Smith aide described a composite case: "In the old days, [blacks] didn't bother much about voting at all, and half the time they were afraid to go to the polls, not that anybody would probably harm them. But I'd see John Doe at the polls come out there and say, 'Mister, lend me some money.' And I'd say, 'You went down to the polls and voted for Joe Smith, didn't you? Well then, I won't be able to help you any!' There's a little scare campaign going on here, you see."[3]

After the *Brown* decision, there were signs of increasing black political involvement. Between 1957 and 1966 the percentage of blacks who had registered more than doubled, from 21.5 percent to 48 percent, while white voter registration remained fairly constant at about 50 percent. By the 1966 Democratic primary, blacks comprised an estimated 20 percent of the 133,000 registered voters in the Eighth District. Blacks accounted for at least 40 percent of the registrants in nearly half of the twenty counties, including Caroline, Charles City, Essex, Goochland, King and Queen, King William, Lancaster, Louisa, and New Kent. And four of these counties had been brought into the district in the previous year's redistricting. With Smith neglecting their needs, blacks were looking elsewhere to place their political allegiance.[4]

The 1965 redrawing of Virginia's congressional districts also sapped Smith's political strength. The 1960 census revealed that the state's suburban north and black Tidewater were seriously underrepresented in the Byrd-dominated General Assembly. But because Virginia did not lose a congressional seat, Attorney General Robert Y. Button, Smith's ally in the 1952 redistricting fight, argued that no change in district lines was required. The Virginia Supreme Court of Appeals rejected this argument in order to comply with the U.S. Supreme Court's historic one-man, one-vote principle. The Old Dominion was ordered to redistrict or institute at-large elections, the remedy that had been employed in 1932 when Smith first ran for reelection. Judge Smith responded to the ruling with a terse, "I expected it." In late August 1965 Governor Albertis S. Harrison, Jr., convened the Assembly, which itself had been reapportioned under court decree the previous year, to obey the judicial decision.[5]

Having survived two earlier redistricting battles, Congressman Smith let his guard down this time. He later recalled that he "didn't like it, but I didn't do anything about it"; he was too preoccupied on the House Rules Committee holding back the liberal onslaught. One delegate remembered that the veteran representative "was not alert to the danger enough." Liberal Fredericksburg attorney George C. Rawlings, Jr., and the charismatic delegate from Norfolk Henry E. Howell, Jr., persuaded Harry Byrd's son,

state senator Harry F. Byrd, Jr., to put part of populous Fairfax
County in the Eighth District, which was 10 percent below the
state's average district population, rather than leaving it in the
Seventh where the Byrds lived. The younger Byrd assumed that
Smith could withstand the federal government workers in the suburban county, which Smith had managed to get rid of in 1952.
In addition, Smith accepted the heavily black counties of Charles
City, Essex, King and Queen, and New Kent because the poll tax
had long disfranchised black citizens, thus keeping local offices
in conservative white hands. The legislature also removed from
his district areas that had traditionally supported Smith, including the city of Charlottesville and the predominantly conservative counties of Albemarle, Culpeper, Fluvanna, Greene, and
Orange. The redrawn district contained more blacks, more urban
areas, and more people overall; it also added greater numbers of
better educated and more affluent residents. Many whites and
blacks in the new district wanted the federal programs and civil
rights guarantees that Smith had long fought.[6]

George Rawlings capitalized on these trends. A native Virginian thirty-nine years Smith's junior, Rawlings had earned degrees
at Randolph-Macon College and the University of Virginia
School of Law. After presiding over several local organizations,
he successfully challenged a Byrd organization politician, Francis
B. Gouldman, for the General Assembly in 1963. Styling himself
the candidate of "hope and progress," Rawlings promoted the progressive federal programs of the New Frontier, as well as local
projects, and campaigned ceaselessly. His political philosophy,
extroverted personality, and colorful politicking stimulated a renewed interest in local politics among liberals, union workers,
and blacks. Representing the Sixty-first District of Fredericksburg, Spotsylvania, and Stafford in the House of Delegates, Rawlings energetically worked for a boost in the state minimum wage,
expansion of educational facilities, and improved health services.
But his efforts counted for little in the conservative-dominated
Assembly. Nevertheless, he retained his seat in 1965 as he with-
stood attacks on his liberal record.[7]

Shortly after his reelection, Rawlings began to assess his
chances of challenging Smith for the 1966 Democratic nomination to Congress. He studied the 1964 district voting patterns and
considered possible campaign issues that would find chinks in

Smith's political armor. He noted that Smith's 1964 opponent, Floyd Bagley, had managed to get 30 percent of the vote in spite of a poorly organized campaign. Bagley raised issues that Rawlings supported, namely, minimum wage extension, federal aid to education, higher pay for federal employees, and federal assistance for low-income families. He also emphasized Smith's advanced age of eighty-one, arguing that it was time for a new, younger congressman. Despite the handicap of running as an independent, Bagley had attracted considerable support.[8]

Rawlings weighed other changes in the composition and political climate of the Eighth District. The removal of the poll tax in federal elections in 1964 opened a floodgate for new voters. More people cast ballots in the Smith-Bagley race than in any previous district election. Also, Bagley received the second highest number of opposition votes in the eighteen elections in which Smith had run for Congress. In addition to the end of the poll tax, congressional redistricting changed the district's political character overnight. Smith lost thousands of conservative voters and picked up thousands of new, liberal constituents. A liberal politician would benefit not only from these liberal voters but also from the new voters who would not vote for Smith out of habit.[9]

The decisive change, in Rawlings's view, was to a party primary from the Democratic convention that traditionally nominated Smith by acclamation. As Smith's Rules counsel, T. M. Carruthers, recalled, the whole procedure at the convention ordinarily took Smith's forces just minutes to complete. "After the opening ceremony at the convention, somebody would rise very quickly and put your name up—'Howard W. Smith'—in nomination to represent the Eighth District of Virginia. And somebody would jump up real quick and second it. And somebody would jump up real quick and make a motion for the nominations to be closed. And somebody else jumped up and seconded the motion and that's it. He's nominated." No other Democrat in that closed arena stood a chance at the nomination. Several of Smith's lieutenants urged him not to switch to a primary "because the other way was so easy." Carruthers, especially, warned Smith that his duties as Rules chairman had isolated him from the district: "Judge, it's been a long time since you've been kissing babies and shaking hands with people—campaigning." But out of a sense of fair play; a desire to attract the new constituency of Fairfax County, which had historically shunned the convention system; and misguided overconfidence, Smith urged his party to select the nominee by a primary. He told Mississippi Democrat Thomas Abernethy, a longtime supporter, "Well, I think this is the time that the people ought to have an opportunity to vote on us, to either endorse or reject my record and I'm going to take it to a Democratic primary election. . . . If they don't like Judge Smith, well, I'll go back to my dairy." In 1966, then, candidates for the Democratic nomination would have to curry popular favor for the first time in sixteen years. Rawlings believed the primary could offer a clear choice in age and political philosophy: Smith was old and reactionary, while he was young and progressive. These opportunities persuaded Rawlings to run for Congress.[10]

Smith filed his petition for reelection in mid-March 1966. In accordance with state law, he submitted a $600 filing fee, pledged not to run in the general election if defeated in the primary, and turned in a petition with more than the minimum 250 qualified voter signatures. He immediately expressed fears to long-term supporters that turmoil was brewing. He pointed to a number of disturbing signs, including the removal of the poll tax that allowed anyone who was "alive and twenty-one years of age" to vote, greater numbers of "our colored friends" registering at the polls, and the presence of liberal state senator Henry Howell, who was raising money and making speeches for Rawlings in the district. When Rawlings entered the race later that month, Smith's fears were confirmed.[11]

Smith campaigned more actively than usual, according to most local newspapers. He hired a full-time public relations agent for the first time and began to visit areas that had not seen him for years. His campaign staff sent thousands of political circulars to registered voters and previous supporters. Smith loyalists distributed the usual campaign fare of specially made buttons, posters, and autographed pictures of their grimly sober candidate. The Judge, meanwhile, blanketed the district with thousands of letters written on House Rules Committee stationery:

> I am writing you in the hope that I may have your vote and support in the primary election. . . . As you may know, I have served in the Congress for many years and due to my long service, I am Dean of the Virginia Delegation in the House of Represent-

atives. I have been Chairman of the House Committee on Rules
for the past ten years, which Committee considers all important
legislation before it goes to the Floor of the House for debate. I
am fifth ranking Member in point of service in the House of Representatives, and the Chairmanship of the Committee on Rules is
a position of prestige and importance in the House that has never
heretofore been enjoyed by any Member from Virginia. I believe
that my experience and knowledge of the operations of the Congress is of value to my District and my country.

   I have consistently supported sound fiscal policies and a decent
respect for the limited powers granted to the Federal Government
under our Constitution. My record in the Congress is well known
and on that record I stand.

These circulars elicited widespread expressions of support from
longtime Smith backers who were "outraged" to learn of opposition to such a fine man and dedicated public servant.[12]

   Most of Smith's campaigning was aimed at rekindling interest
among known supporters because he identified apathy as his worst
enemy. He sent his personal secretary, Calvin Haley, to take the
district's political temperature and to rouse the faithful, especially
attorneys, doctors, state Democratic party officials, dairy farmers,
businessmen, and newspaper editors. Smith solicited their endorsement through form letters and telephone calls. To stimulate
local interest, he and his wife mingled with old acquaintances
and party regulars at small receptions held in their honor. The
informal gatherings preserved the eighty-three-year-old Smith's
physical strength and minimized his forgetfulness of faces and
poor hearing. Smith also advertised widely in local newspapers
and ran taped advertisements on more than a dozen radio stations. In all of these efforts, Smith's managers concentrated on
striking a positive response among conservative friends.[13]

   In stark contrast to Smith's campaign style, Rawlings criss-
crossed the district, pumping as many hands as he could find. A
tall man known for his colorful bow ties, Rawlings organized
"Rawlings for Congress" committees in nearly every district city
and county. These committees constructed potential voter lists
and distributed leaflets informing residents that the poll tax had
been repealed. Further, they offered to answer questions on voter
registration and to drive citizens to polling stations. The indefa-

tigable Rawlings, who was heavily backed by organized labor, campaigned actively at rallies and especially in front of super-markets, believing women were more easily reached than men.[14]

Through circulars and speeches, Rawlings stressed Smith's "negative record" and accentuated his own support of federal ben-efits for labor, education, health, and transportation. At a local reception he charged that it was "impossible for a congressman who favors the status quo . . . to give enthusiastic backing to projects which will make for change and will bring development and new people to the district." He scored Smith's votes against federal aid to housing and education, the civil rights acts of the 1950s and 1960s, Medicare, and the antipoverty program. "The fact is," he said, "that the present Congressman can show no con-structive record of help to the many of us. What about help for the mentally ill, better education, minimum wages, Federal pay raises, new Government installations, the Salem Dam and many other proposals which could help the majority of our people?" If elected, Rawlings promised to vote for these progressive mea-sures.[15]

Smith countered these attacks by asserting that he had "the courage to vote no" to the giveaway programs of President John-son's Great Society. In a meeting with his constituents, Smith recalled that he was accused of voting against two-thirds of John-son's proposals: "I don't keep count, but if I voted for 'em one-third of the time, I may just owe you folks an apology." The Judge decried the "nit-picking" of his record and suggested that voters should select the party nominee on the basis of "performance, not promises." As for Rawlings, Smith labeled him as a "yes-man" who "has no business being in the Congress." He lamented his limited schedule of campaigning only at night and on weekends. But, he insisted, "someone has to stay at the Capitol and tend the store and get in a few licks for the taxpayer."[16]

Many of Smith's supporters expressed great confidence in the outcome. A Prince William County resident wrote, "I see you have an opponent from Fredericksburg but from what I hear in conversation with others you will not have much to worry about from that source." Smith doubted this prognosis. He feared the efforts of "the left-wing of the party to eliminate me from Con-gress." In fact, he regarded his 1966 campaign as the "most dan-gerous" since the 1938 purge attempt. Favorable voter turnout in large numbers, he believed, held the key to reelection. "The outcome is going to depend on how much of the Negro vote [Rawlings's campaign workers] can arouse and how much appeal they make to the youth of the State," he speculated. Upon learning that most counties had experienced massive black registration, Smith sent an alarm to his friends to help however they could.[17]

Smith took several specific steps to appeal to the new liberal constituency of the Northern Neck. Within a two-month span, he announced progress on five federal programs beneficial to the district. In late April he informed reporters that a proposed road and bridge project in King George County had been approved by federal agencies. Smith then rescued the largest antipoverty program in northern Virginia. Working closely with Sargent Shriver, director of the Office of Economic Opportunity, Smith secured an extension of the Fairfax Head Start program to permit five hundred children to continue their schooling at least through the summer. Just a few days later, local newspapers showed Smith proudly approving a bill authorizing the construction of a $30 million federal office building in Reston. Following this report, Smith's staff released a favorable Army Corps of Engineers study on the Salem Dam project north of Fredericksburg that Rawlings had long advocated. Then, one week before the election, the Judge capped off his liberal vote-getting crusade. He declared success in winning a $300,000 grant from the Interior Department for a pilot sewage treatment program in Prince William, a pivotal county. A family friend wrote Smith's son-in-law, "You would think the Judge was 'a screaming liberal.'"[18]

All these projects, designed to aid the Eighth District, contrasted sharply with Smith's earlier legislative performance. Recalling Smith's long-standing opposition to federal assistance, Rawlings asked the voters to "not be fooled" by the sudden passage of measures aiding the district. Smith had accomplished only a handful of things as a representative, Rawlings claimed, "and a majority of them have been done since we started this campaign." One disgruntled citizen complained: "All of a sudden we've got a Congressman. It's pretty cynical of 'Judge Smith' to offer us a small barrel of pork just now."[19]

Rawlings had problems of his own. His advocacy of liberal programs made him popular with academicians, professionals, and government employees, but he also had to appeal to blue-collar workers. Rawlings saw the need to allay fears that he would be, as *Richmond News Leader* editor James J. Kilpatrick suggested, "one more rubber stamp for Lyndon Johnson, Martin Luther King and the knee-jerk Liberals of the far-out left." On the contrary, Rawlings insisted, his staunch support for progressive measures would aid laborers. He spoke out loudly for higher wages for the workingman. He charged that the real threat to the lower and middle classes came from Smith. He called Smith "the No. 1 enemy of the working man in the Eighth" because as a congressman he "has done nothing to put meat on the working-man's table," to create more jobs, to provide a better education, or to help establish equal opportunity for all citizens. He accused Smith of having blocked federal aid because the Judge and his wealthy friends had no need of it themselves.[20]

These accusations packed a powerful punch in northern Virginia, for many of the new constituents were acutely sensitive to bread-and-butter issues. Most blacks strongly supported President Johnson's civil rights bills eliminating employment discrimination. Fairfax County residents who worked for the federal government wanted pay comparable to that in private business. Both white liberals and many blacks had experienced extreme anguish under the state's massive resistance program of the late 1950s that had closed public schools rather than integrate them. Rawlings's public opposition to this regressive policy and his support of Johnson's civil rights laws had endeared him to many black and liberal voters. Rawlings also gained support among suburban voters when he took a commuter bus in 90° weather from Washington to McLean and committed himself to improved rapid transit service.[21]

Rawlings complemented his public appeals for black support with a high-powered organization which registered them to vote. In the Northern Neck, he had six black students from Norfolk State University spread the Rawlings's gospel to every black farm. He also relied on local black leaders to canvass their areas. Dr. James Bowles personally controlled several hundred black voters in Goochland County, and J. Allan Ball, a black teacher, worked Tappahannock and Kilmarnock. The black registration drive enrolled six thousand voters for the first time. One white Democrat for Rawlings testified indirectly to the success of this effort in Westmoreland County: "I'm for you, George, but I'm the only one. All the rest are *darkies!*"[22]

Besides blacks, professionals, government employees, and blue-collar workers, Rawlings attracted other groups as well. As a member of the Fredericksburg Jaycees and the Spotsylvania County Planning Commission, he had known and worked with many local businessmen for years. The younger ones backed Rawlings over Smith. Moreover, Rawlings had ingratiated himself with a number of poor whites by offering free or low-cost legal advice to indigent clients in the Fredericksburg area who sought personal injury settlements, divorces, and release from jail. As Rawlings helped these troubled whites out of their predicaments, they, in turn, praised him to their neighbors.[23]

While building bridges to long unrecognized district groups, Rawlings also launched devastating attacks on the incumbent late in the campaign. He accused Smith of questionable ethics in two cases. First, Rawlings claimed that Smith had pocketed large contributions from coal-mining executives for his obstruction of mine safety bills. Second, he dropped a political bombshell when he charged the incumbent with a financial conflict of interest. He alleged that Smith, while chairman of the Alexandria National Bank, had repeatedly blocked legislation indirectly affecting the bank. Smith had opposed divesting Financial General, which had a controlling interest in his bank, of its nonbanking holdings and had opposed placing the corporation under the Federal Reserve Board's supervision. Because Smith could not gut the divestiture bill himself, he persuaded fellow Virginian A. Willis Robertson to have the Senate give Financial General a twelve-year exemption. Rawlings concluded that Smith was "in effect an employee of Financial General" who "used his position, influence and authority to benefit a private concern in which he had a direct and important interest." He called for a full House investigation and spread columnist Jack Anderson's account of the purported misconduct throughout the district. Despite Smith's denial, many people were deeply disturbed by the story.[24]

By late June most political analysts rated the election a toss-up. Recognizing the precarious situation, Smith's campaign staff searched for any advantage over the challenger. They eventually persuaded Governor Mills E. Godwin, Jr., a Byrd organization stalwart, to declare publicly his support for Smith. In a letter released to newspapers, Godwin wrote Smith campaign director Tom Frost that "Judge Smith has my every good wish for an overwhelming victory." Since political custom in Virginia ordinarily required the governor's neutrality in intraparty struggles, Godwin's endorsement demonstrated the Byrd organization's anxiety over the election.[25]

Two last-minute events further clouded Smith's hopes for reelection. Reid T. Putney, chairman of the minor Conservative party, issued an appeal to all Conservatives to abstain from voting in the Eighth District Democratic primary because to do so was illegal and seemed to sanction that party's "foul and filthy" practices. Since Smith was popular among conservative-thinking Virginians, the call for Conservative party supporters to absent themselves from the polls would hurt him, not Rawlings. Smith's campaign also suffered when he had to quash a story of his alleged indifference toward the election. A rumor in a Washington newspaper quoted Smith as saying that "the election was not my fight. If you defeat me you'll proably be doing me a favor." Smith categorically denied the statement, attributing it to a misunderstanding.[26]

To salvage Smith's sinking campaign, district and state newspapers printed thought-provoking editorials in a last-ditch effort "to get out the white vote." The *Richmond News Leader*, a strong Smith supporter, expressed outrage at Rawlings's statements:

> For the past three months, residents of the Eighth have had their ears offended by one of the most insulting campaigns ever waged in Virginia. Delegate George C. Rawlings has insulted not only Judge Smith. More to the point, he has insulted and reviled the entire electorate of the Eighth. The voters are so stupid, so blind, and so lacking in judgment, Mr. Rawlings avows, that for 36 years they have voted for a man who is an enemy of labor, an enemy of education, an enemy of the Negro, an enemy of social advancement. In the last couple of weeks, Mr. Rawlings has enlarged the insult: The voters of the Eighth for 36 years have supported a crook who would use the office for his own personal profit.
>
> Now, those who know Judge Smith will have nothing but contempt for the source. Mr. Rawlings is all mouth. He is all foam

without one solid ounce of substance. He has less influence in the
Virginia House of Delegates than the third assistant doorman. If
some wild mischance of fate sent him to the House of Representatives, he would be one more rubber stamp for Lyndon Johnson.
Is this what the voters of the Eighth District want? We cannot
believe it.

Smith supporters quickly copied the editorial and mailed it
around the district.[27]

On July 12, 1966, a hot, muggy day, fifty thousand district
voters, including a record number of blacks, cast their ballots.
The next day, newspapers reported that Rawlings had defeated
Smith by 364 votes in one of the most stunning defeats ever sustained by a Byrd organization candidate. This election marked
Smith's first defeat in sixty years of public life. Although he had
rarely lost a county in earlier elections, this time seven counties
and one city slipped from his grasp. He lost the heavily black
counties of Caroline, Charles City, King and Queen, and New
Kent, suburban Fairfax, and Rawlings's political base of Fredericksburg, Spotsylvania, and Stafford. Even in four counties that
Smith won—Fauquier, Goochland, Loudoun, and Prince William—Rawlings reduced Smith's traditional victory margin by
more than 20 percent. The tide of opposition to Smith had finally
reached floodstage.[28]

In a press release the next day, Judge Smith refused to concede
before the official canvass was made. Under state law, he could
request a recount because the difference between the candidates
did not exceed five hundred votes. But Smith's possible challenge
became academic when the canvass showed Rawlings ahead by
645 votes, 27,115 to 26,470. Smith soon sent a letter to his constituents thanking them for allowing him to serve so long. In sum-
ming up his career, Smith believed that he had fought to preserve
Virginia's heritage of "personal liberty, order under law, Constitutional government, [and] respect for the God-given dignity of
man." Embittered by his defeat, Smith urged Eighth District voters to defend their "magnificent heritage" against erosion by "apathy and indifference."[29]

Smith's stunning defeat can be explained by the complex events
that occurred in the years preceding the election. Smith himself
must shoulder much of the blame. In the first place, he had

grown used to weak challenges and had permitted his political connections to erode. On one occasion, Smith admitted as much: "What went wrong was I was very much engrossed in Washington. . . . I didn't have time to fool with the campaign and Calvin Haley, my secretary, used to be very active in my campaigns. He was better at it than I was. His wife had taken ill and he had to quit. And I didn't get around. But I did caution my friends that I was in trouble. I knew I was in trouble. But they said, 'Judge always hollers wolf, wolf at every election. Nobody can beat him.'" Second, Smith had followed Byrd's lead in keeping silent on the Democratic presidential nominees of 1960 and 1964, which angered die-hard party loyalists. Third, his rigid political philosophy did not bend with the times, even though large numbers of northern Virginians clearly supported some federal laws and programs. Fourth, unlike the redistricting of 1952, he was unable or too confident to influence the drawing of district lines in 1965. In part, he simply believed that defeat was unimaginable. Smith also had lost many valuable supporters in business and politics to retirement and death, not the least of whom was Harry Byrd, Sr., who was on his deathbed. As a result, the Assembly gave Smith a revised district that encompassed more urban, liberal, and black voters than he could handle. Fifth, when he instituted the primary process, he provided his opposition the slim chance it needed to triumph. No one could have beaten Smith in a convention.[30]

Two other factors beyond Smith's control contributed to his defeat. The anti–poll tax amendment of 1964 encouraged many blacks to vote. In the Eighth District 159 percent more blacks had registered in 1966 than in 1960, while only 43.4 percent more whites had done so. Although black registration was still a small part of all enrolled voters, blacks tended to vote as a bloc for liberal candidates who supported civil rights and federal aid programs. For example, Charles City County, with a black population of 74.2 percent, enrolled 70.8 percent black voters and cast 78 percent of its votes for Rawlings. Black registration and subsequent voting were effective for Rawlings partly because he minimized racial fears among Smith's backers by coordinating election drivers and black voters so that they arrived late in the day.[31]

Smith's defeat also came about because of Rawlings's brilliant campaign strategy and execution. After closely examining the recent changes in the district, Rawlings tailored his appeal to the new voters who wanted the programs Smith blocked. More than this, he organized the most vigorous campaign in district history and tirelessly promoted his liberal message. With money donated largely by organized labor, Rawlings could afford to wage a vigorous campaign. In fact, he spent nearly $42,000, the largest amount ever spent in a Virginia congressional primary up to that time. It was Rawlings who made the difference, for without his skillful, well-financed campaign, these developments might have gone untapped.[32]

Strangely enough, age was probably not an important factor in Smith's defeat. In the campaign Rawlings had repeatedly emphasized the incumbent's age, and indeed Smith was highly sensitive to the suggestion that advancing years had diminished his legislative ability. As Smith explained several years later: "Those newspaper boys. They couldn't write my name without putting an 83 after it. It was like I had a Ph.D. degree." But a close look at precinct voting in the Eighth District indicates that Smith did not lose for this reason. Of the three major Byrd organization candidates in the Democratic primary—eighty-three-year-old Smith, seventy-nine-year-old Senator A. Willis Robertson, and Senator Harry F. Byrd, Jr., who was in his mid-forties—all received very similar numbers of votes in Smith's district. Organization regulars ignored their candidates' ages but were able only to elect the younger Byrd. In short, Smith did not lose many votes over the age question. Rawlings simply brought out voters who had not voted against Smith previously.[33]

In the November general election, Rawlings faced fifty-year-old Republican William L. Scott, a conservative Fairfax attorney who worked for the Justice Department. Scott enjoyed several advantages over Rawlings. Unlike the Democrat, Scott began his campaign with a united though inexperienced party, sufficient funds, and the assistance of the Republican National Committee. The key to the campaign was Scott's ability to entice disaffected conservative Democrats into Republican ranks. Scott downplayed his party label and echoed Smith's support of Virginia's right-to-work law and opposition to such federal programs as Medicare and antipoverty. Moreover, since he was from Fairfax and worked in Washington, he seemed better suited than Rawlings to appeal to commuter voters.[34]

Publicly, Smith remained tight-lipped about the race to succeed him. But in September he wrote a damaging letter that was
leaked to the *Fredericksburg Free Lance-Star* shortly before the
election. Without mentioning Rawlings by name, Smith said he
had been the victim of "a mud-slinging, character assassinating
campaign of libel and abuse," which he could "never forgive or
forget." He hoped the voters would see that this "gutter-type of
campaign" had no future in Virginia. Scott's forces circulated
thousands of copies throughout the district to show Smith's obvious distaste for Rawlings.[35]

On election eve, a self-employed Fairfax grocer gave a common assessment of the contest: "I wanted Judge Smith to win, but
a lot of people let him down. Now I think they've seen the light
and they're going to keep Rawlings out of office. We don't want
any more left-wingers up there than we've already got." In an
extremely heavy vote, Scott unexpectedly and decisively defeated
Rawlings, 53,190 to 37,929. Scott's vote nearly equaled the combined Democratic primary figure for the Smith-Rawlings race
and almost doubled the conservative votes that Smith had received. Scott also captured four counties—Caroline, Fairfax,
New Kent, and Stafford—that Smith had lost. Although Rawlings improved his primary showing by nearly 40 percent, much
of his additional support came in conservative counties like Essex
and Louisa, which he nevertheless lost again. Rawlings also lost
Stafford County and barely held on to the other two areas of his
Assembly district.[36]

Scott probably won the election for four reasons. First, many
district conservatives deeply resented Rawlings for having defeated Smith. The best proof of conservative Democratic reluctance to back Rawlings can be found in the fact that Rawlings
received only 70.8 percent of the total Democratic primary vote
in the general election. Given the tremendous turnout and the
traditional weakness of the Republican party, it seems clear that
Rawlings suffered many defections. Second, the Republicans
conducted an active, opportunistic, and well-financed campaign,
outspending Rawlings by nearly 10 percent. Third, Rawlings mis-
calculated when he believed that he could hold together his coalition of liberals, blacks, and union workers and still win over
Smith supporters. By praising social welfare programs, he kept his
coalition in line, but at the same time, he alienated conservatives

he needed to win. His heavy-handed attempt to force loyalty oaths on conservative Democratic politicians went over badly. Finally, a national reaction had developed by 1966 against President Johnson's domestic policies. Republicans across the country rode the issues of inflation, race riots in seven major cities, staggering levels of federal spending, and the Vietnam War to record an "above-average" gain for the minority party in an off-year election. In part, Rawlings lost because 1966 was a Republican year. To Howard Smith, Rawlings's defeat was a vindication, but small comfort for having to leave Capitol Hill after nearly four decades.[37]

CHAPTER 9

Retirement

Always the judge was determined to do what he thought right and fair and he had the courage of his convictions. . . . He is truly one of the greatest Americans I have ever known.

Republican Leslie C. Arends (October 1966)

In late September 1966 state delegate Tom Frost of Warrenton organized a huge testimonial dinner in honor of the defeated incumbent, Judge Smith. Eight hundred people attended the event in the Fauquier County National Guard Armory and heard a number of speakers praise the honored guest. The evening began with the irrepressible Frost handing Speaker McCormack a crushed piece of paper that was identified as a bill on which Smith had been sitting for years; Frost jokingly invited McCormack to press for its passage in the new Congress. McCormack then delivered the night's longest address, calling Smith "this great man, this good man, this great Virginian, but over and above that this great American." In an unusual display of humor, and perhaps confession, McCormack told the appreciative audience that during a close legislative fight, he would offer "a little prayer that Howard would be on my side." When Smith's turn came, he thanked the other speakers for their kind words, even though "a lot of 'em made me feel like a durn fool." Smith admitted that his primary defeat had been painful: "I'd been around a long time and got to feel like I owned that job. Nobody enjoys being beaten. I'm not going to tell you any story—I didn't enjoy the sensation. But I've gotten over the acute pain. I've been thinking—36 years in Congress, the friends, the memories, the kindness from the people. It's been a wonderful time to live. I have nothing more to deserve or want." Although he did not recommend electoral defeat ordinarily, he thought that the dinner made his loss "well worth taking."[1]

The tributes continued in October, when his colleagues gathered in the House just before the end of Smith's thirty-six-year congressional career. The conservative Virginia delegation led the plaudits. David Satterfield, a Richmond Democrat, acknowledged his gratitude for having known Smith. It was a privilege, Satterfield said, "to share the pleasure of his company" and "to observe his abiding loyalty, his impeccable honesty and integrity, his keen intellect and above all, his unswerving dedication to principle." Smith's close ally former governor Bill Tuck joined the chorus, stating that Smith's congressional record would "cause him to be recognized as one of the greatest men who has ever lived in this body from any state." Representatives from outside the Old Dominion used such words as "father," "courageous," "Herculean," and "irreplaceable" to describe the departing Rules chairman. Mississippi's Bill Colmer, a like-minded reactionary and the apparent successor to Smith's chairmanship, asserted that Smith had not been outdone by Virginia's other great sons, Washington, Jefferson, and Lee, in dedication to duty.[2]

At first, Smith's retirement affected him profoundly. His cousin the Reverend Samuel Chilton recalled that Smith "missed [Congress] like the dickens. What he really missed was the contact he had with the people and dealing with legislative matters rather than a particular legislative matter that he wanted to push through." Despite his advanced age and a nearly forty-year absence from legal practice, Smith began setting up his old law office in Alexandria, although he saw few clients. Writing to his daughter, he candidly admitted the strain of reverting to private life:

> I have just not felt like I was able to make a trip anywhere and had sort of gone into my hole and tried to recuperate my nerves and my physical and mental situation that I found that I had gotten into only after I had completed the matter of moving my office and my papers and all and settled down and decided I would relax and regain my physical strength because I really felt when I did

relax and sit down that I was pretty close to the point of collapse, which I had never admitted outside the family.[3]

Now that Smith had no public responsibilities, he wanted to restore his farm to prime condition. On average, he spent four days a week there, occasionally riding his horse. Smith decided to have the house repainted and, because of the five-year drought, to dig a three-hundred-foot well. One of his principal problems was finding a suitable tenant to operate the farm. He complained that the "good, hard, conscientious workmen, whom we had in the past" had been replaced by a generation of men preferring unemployment checks to hard farm labor. Eventually, however, he found someone he could trust.[4]

Although Smith was occupied with personal matters, he kept an eye on national affairs. He especially followed the spreading black riots, one of which occurred in Cambridge, Maryland, in the summer of 1967. To his irritation, the leader of the riot, H. Rap Brown of the Student Nonviolent Coordinating Committee, fled to Alexandria, where the Federal Bureau of Investigation promptly arrested him. Smith thought the media acted irresponsibly in giving Brown "as much publicity and advertisement as they would any foreign potentate or the President of the United States." But he put most of the responsibility on his former congressional colleagues for resorting to "the same old pussyfooting and blame-shifting from one to another" that had led to the riots in the first place. Because the Supreme Court, in his view, had "repealed" the Smith Act, he thought that the only hope of ending black rioting, or "monkey business," rested with distraught constituents who pressured their representatives. He did not know how the "extremely dangerous situation" would turn out.[5]

During the first years of his retirement, Smith discussed his career with interviewers from the American Enterprise Institute, a conservative think tank in Washington. He hoped the institute would use his papers "to write a sort of one volume history of (what I call) erosion of constitutional government from the beginning of Roosevelt's New Deal through the whole period that I served." Smith believed that the proposed study would be valuable for historical reasons, as well as for an antidote to popular acceptance of the "unconstitutional departures in our system of government." But as far as he was concerned, the periodic interviews with the institute were "a little too slow to suit my fancy." By the early 1970s the project was abandoned altogether.[6]

In 1968 the civil rights movement struck closer to Smith's door than ever before. When his priest at Grace Episcopal Church in The Plains integrated the church, held a memorial service for the slain Martin Luther King, Jr., and collected monies for "the Negro revolution," Smith stopped attending, just as he had in Alexandria thirteen years earlier when his clergyman there embraced integration. He regarded these actions as leading ultimately to an unacceptable "mixture of the races" that would "mongrelize America." One Sunday in October, when the regular priest was away, Smith's wife talked him into returning, but then he had to endure what he called the new "mumbo jumbo" communion service adopted by the Episcopal church.[7]

As the years passed, Smith's family was his chief concern. At one point in July 1970, he reassured his daughter that "my main interest in life is my family, collectively and individually." He decided to encourage his thirteen grandchildren to live life as productively as he had. Repeatedly, he tried to steer one grandson into law because no other grandchild had entered that profession. But he reminded him that law required diligent work. Later, the Judge began writing homiletic stories of his early life, thinking his grandchildren would benefit from the lessons he had learned.[8]

Smith also continued to watch national political matters. In 1972 he looked at the tumult over the presidential candidacy of liberal Democratic senator George S. McGovern of South Dakota and described the "ridiculous" campaign as "a burlesque show." He particularly rued McGovern's triumph at the Virginia Democratic convention.

> The whole McGovern "miracle" has been brought about by capable organization of students and negroes. To the students it is just another exciting contest like a football game, the negroes— because it promises bigger and better freedom and welfare. Neither group having any knowledge of the American system of government. I wonder if some of these wealthy students know that amongst McGovern's wild programs is to confiscate, through inheritance taxes, one hundred percent of the fortunes of the wealthy.

The McGovern candidacy so disturbed Smith—perhaps because he feared his nearly $2 million estate would not be passed on to his heirs—that he became chairman of the Fauquier County Independents for the Reelection of President Nixon. For the first time, the lifelong Democrat openly backed a Republican candidate. But then Judge Smith always had regarded the Democratic party as a mere instrument to protect his reactionary ideology. When the Democratic party categorically rejected his ideas, he threw the party overboard, a move not without precedent in the South.[9]

When the Watergate crisis erupted in 1973, Smith did not immediately blame Nixon. Indeed, he believed the president provided a convenient scapegoat for American social ills, including rising energy costs. In his view, "the drive by the politicians and the press and television, the effort to crucify [Nixon] for everything bad that has happened or threatens to happen is disgusting." By August 1974, when Nixon resigned, Smith had come to regard "Nixon's fatal mistake" as poor staff selection. Assessing the new Republican president, Gerald R. Ford, Jr., of Michigan, Smith admitted that he "never thought much" of him when they served together in the House because Ford had been too partisan. But Ford's first statements and demeanor served to reassure the Judge.[10]

At the very end, old age enfeebled Judge Smith, and he thought about entering an Episcopal center for the aged in Alexandria. His wife opposed the move, however, and Smith died of congestive heart failure in his home on October 3, 1976. Expressions of sympathy poured in from friends and opponents alike. House Speaker Carl Albert of Oklahoma, a former Rhodes scholar, sent a telegram to Smith's widow calling Smith "the brightest man with whom I ever served." A former Rules colleague, B. F. Sisk of California, wrote that "Congress lost one of its truly great legislators when he left." President Ford also sent his condolences. Three days after Smith's death, a funeral service was held at Alexandria's venerable Christ Episcopal Church, which he had attended for years. Members of Virginia's "dwindling old guard of political warriors," including former governors Darden and Tuck, Governor Godwin, and Senator Harry F. Byrd, Jr., gathered to pay tribute to their colleague. A favorite Old Testament verse read during the ceremony summed up Smith's predilection for hard work instead of government welfare: "Whatever thy hand findeth to do, doeth it with all thy might." Prayers were said and hymns sung before Mrs. Smith patted her husband's casket for one last time. Smith's remains were interred in a family plot beside an old, abandoned church near Cedar Hill. The *Richmond News Leader* printed an epitaph that Howard Smith would have liked: "He was a giant among giants, one of the last of an endangered breed. . . . Now the legendary fox of Fauquier is gone. His achievements were many, but the celebrations of them too few. He was one of the last men of principle among legislators too often driven not by motives of what is right, but rather by motives of what will least offend. . . . He was a supremely principled Virginian. That says it all."[11]

Retrospective

*Let historians of tomorrow say who best served God
and man today.*

Howard W. Smith, 1939

A generation has passed since Howard W. Smith left Congress in
1966. Since then, Smith's importance to modern American history has been overlooked. This neglect can be traced largely to
his political style and aversion to publicity. One congressman who
knew him well recalled that Smith "wasn't a headline man";
rather, the Virginian was a homebody who studied legislation
endlessly for potential defects. Nor was Smith an eloquent speaker
in the grand southern tradition. He performed his legislative leg-
erdemain away from the camera's glare. Moreover, Smith has not
received his due because the chief causes for which he spent his
career, namely, silencing radicals, weakening labor unions, halt-
ing civil rights, and preventing government deficits, were rearguard actions in what turned out to be losing causes. Historians
generally prefer to write their accounts from the perspective of the
"victors," who in this case were John F. Kennedy and Lyndon B.
Johnson, one witty and charismatic, the other powerful and dy-
namic. But these presidents never forgot Howard Smith's influence over liberal bills.

Such omissions must not be allowed to assign Smith to obscu-
rity. The fact remains that he was one of the most powerful legislators in this century. Few other representatives, if any, have
held as much power. Certainly, Smith's peers recognized his importance. His congressional colleagues from Virginia especially
applauded his service. Senator Harry F. Byrd, Sr., often remarked

that Smith was "the greatest living Virginian." And former Old Dominion governor Bill Tuck called him "the finest and best that there is in our State and in the Nation." House Speaker Carl Albert of Oklahoma claimed that "Judge Smith was one of the main forces slowing down the liberalization process of legislation—one of the very main forces in Congress" since 1937. Even Smith's unremitting enemies admired his ability. Missouri Democrat Dick Bolling, a member of Smith's Rules Committee, found him to be "the second best legislator I ever worked with. Rayburn was the best. Smith was very nearly a genius. He was terribly bright. His application was unbelievable. I never saw a man work that hard."

Smith was motivated to work hard principally to defend the South in which he was reared after the Civil War. In most respects, he mirrored white southern attitudes about society, politics, and the economy. A product of his time and place, he embraced such widely accepted concepts as states' rights; a small, frugal government; and racial separation and nativism. He believed in a fixed, hierarchical society in which certain groups and institutions took priority over other groups and institutions. This meant specifically that individual states outranked the national government, that employers were more important than their employees, and that native-born white Americans mattered more and were more qualified to exercise political rights than black Americans and immigrants. These lesser groups, in Smith's opinion, could never equal or dislodge their social superiors. Smith found justification for this political faith in the Constitution, which contained the unchanging (to him) truths handed down by such founding fathers as George Washington and James Madison. Above all, Smith regarded himself as a disciple of Thomas Jefferson. More than once, Smith reminded his audiences that these Virginians had lived in his district, implying that he had inherited their mantle. Over his life span of ninety-three years, he clung tenaciously to the nineteenth-century ideas that he had learned as a Virginia farm boy.

As Smith looked around him, the South he knew had been under serious attack since the 1930s when he had entered the House of Representatives. The federal government represented the greatest danger. He believed that it had expanded its powers illegally at the expense of the states in order to address what he saw as short-term problems. Smith thought that Congress had erected a massive welfare state which borrowed billions of dollars to provide unemployment relief and old-age pensions. Because the government financed its benefit programs by direct taxation and depreciated currency, business appeared to bear the brunt of such safeguards. Southern businessmen, traditionally antiunion, also faced organized workers whose position had been bolstered by national laws that mandated collective bargaining. In the fifties and sixties, the federal government took aim at the heart of southern society, overturning de jure racial segregation. Once the U.S. Supreme Court dictated racial integration, northern representatives rushed to approve pathbreaking laws and to set up federal agencies in order to protect black workers from discrimination and to enroll black voters Smith deemed unqualified. In brief, Smith believed that the federal government had swallowed the states and arrogated to itself control over the poor, the workers, and race relations. As far as he was concerned, these twentieth-century innovations overturned the Constitution and therefore were intolerable.

Smith's essential importance lies not in his beliefs, which were shared by most of the other conservative southern Democrats, but in his brilliant parliamentary ability to frustrate socioeconomic change. Alabama Democrat Carl Elliott concluded that Smith "felt it was his bounded duty to keep this nation, as nearly as possible, in the era of the long, long ago. And he had more ability doing that than nearly anybody." He understood that the lengthy and sometimes torturous legislative procedure for approving any measure invariably favored its opponents. As gatekeeper of the Rules Committee, Smith decided which bills would reach the House floor for deliberation. At his direction, other committees were compelled to weaken bills on such diverse subjects as public housing, absentee voting, polio vaccine inoculation, TVA financing, and area redevelopment. Smith opposed many of these measures because they required increased federal government spending, which would be paid for by higher taxes or additional borrowing. He also attacked minimum wage hikes, arguing that the states, not the federal government, were responsible for regulating their own economies. He once claimed that unions should realize that if the federal government had the right to increase wages, it also had the implicit right to lower them. Unsurprisingly, union leaders found Smith's thinking specious, and they funneled money and votes to his political opponents in northern Virginia. Smith's chief supporters, who included employers and large farmers, realized at once that their representative helped to preserve their economic self-interest by keeping wages low.

Always, Smith defended his performance, asserting that "the Rules Committee did not commit [legislative] murder or mayhem or even assault and battery." He pointed out that his committee did nothing illegal or improper and that Congress could remove any bill that was stuck in a Rules' logjam. Smith's arguments were technically true. In practice, however, Rules Committee action dictated a bill's fate. Only on the most exceptional occasions did even a single bill emerge from Rules against Smith's will. To spring waylaid reform bills from Rules, liberal representatives had to resort to inordinately difficult procedures, such as a discharge petition that required 218 signatures in the House. Even if liberal bills leapfrogged Smith and the Rules Committee, they faced an uncertain future as conservatives resorted to other methods to attack them.

Not only did Smith chair the most important committee in the House, he also headed the most important bloc of representatives, the conservative coalition of southern Democrats and Republicans. All told, Smith often controlled nearly one-fourth of the representatives on controversial issues. On the Democratic side of the coalition, the inner circle of fifteen or so southerners plotted strategy in their offices or on the floor itself to sink hated bills that had escaped Smith's clutches in Rules. Customarily, the coalition turned to two devices to kill liberal measures. In one method, various coalition members tacked on a host of amendments, many of which were at cross-purposes with the bill's original intent. The other method involved repeated quorum calls. Coalition supporters hid in adjoining cloakrooms while forty-five-minute roll calls ensued. One insider compared the quorum call to the Senate's practice of allowing members an unlimited time to speak: "That was our way of filibustering."

So vast were Smith's institutional powers that key liberal bills remained stranded in Rules for months or even years. Northern Democrats, such as Lee Metcalf of Montana and John Blatnik of Minnesota, felt so powerless against Smith that they formed a parallel organization to the conservative coalition, called the

Democratic Study Group. Among other things, the group care-fully tracked pet bills as they entered Smith's legislative cove. By the end of the 1950s, the liberals pressured Speaker Sam Ray-burn, a Texas Democrat and New Dealer, to guarantee Rules Committee cooperation in releasing federal aid bills beneficial to their constituents. Rayburn's assurances proved ineffective. After John F. Kennedy was elected president in 1960, he quickly gath-ered his top advisers to discuss ways to pry New Frontier programs from Smith's committee. At stake was nothing less than the con-trol of Congress. Kennedy promoted Rayburn's reluctant plan to add two administration backers and another Republican to the Rules Committee in order to tilt it to the administration's will. A titanic struggle erupted at the end of January 1961. Smith lost by a mere five votes out of 429. In the words of one congressman, the committee's packing marked "the end of the beginning." Even so, the Kennedy administration felt obliged in the coming years to monitor legislation in Rules and to curry Smith's favor through appointments and bills aiding his district.

Although Smith is best remembered as a superbly skilled ob-structionist, he occasionally seized the initiative to push his own significant legislation. He sought to limit radical, labor, and black influences in American life, as well as in southern society. His first substantive law came in 1940, when Congress selected his alien registration bill from dozens of similar antiradical proposals. The law weakened the American Communist party still further. Today, the Smith Act is used primarily to register aliens each January. During World War II, Smith tackled organized labor with the Smith-Connally Act of 1943. This law had the un-intended effects of encouraging unions to abandon their no-strike pledge during the war and of mobilizing labor political action committees. After the war, Smith teamed with Republicans to dilute labor's strength. He wrote the open-shop section of the Taft-Hartley Act of 1947, permitting laborers to work without having to join unions. In this instance as in many others, Smith let less prominent legislators get the credit. In the 1950s Smith tried to give state laws, especially those relating to sedition, precedence over comparable federal laws and to forbid easy access to the na-tional treasury by federal agencies. Off the record many repre-sentatives agreed with Smith that federal spending was out of control, but they feared reprisals by their constituents if they axed popular social programs. As a result, federal spending sky-rocketed, and tax receipts failed to keep pace. Smith's final legis-lative contribution came in the middle of the civil rights fight. In the summer of 1964 he presented an amendment which prohib-ited sex discrimination. This tongue-in-cheek suggestion was in-tended to defeat civil rights for blacks. President Lyndon Johnson saw through Smith's ploy and urged liberals to delay sexual equal-ity in favor of racial equality. The great irony of Smith's public life is that Congress followed his lead in banning both sex and race discrimination, making him a midwife of the modern femi-nist movement.

Smith exercised a profound influence on the twentieth century, even though his obstruction and laws could not prevent the liberal tide from enveloping him. For thirty-six years he held the reform-ers at bay. In human terms, this meant that those who needed public assistance in the form of low-cost housing, subsidized medical care, job training, or hot school lunches had to go with-out. Unskilled workers earned small wages that consistently trailed inflation. Smith and other opponents of the welfare state had first opposed any minimum wage established by the federal government and subsequently fought increases in it. Blacks who had for so long been on the fringe of American society saw Smith rail against the very idea of racial equality. Millions of blacks were denied quality education, professional careers, and even their ba-sic right to vote until Congress passed civil rights acts in the mid-sixties. To Smith, human problems were a transient matter when compared to the holy trinity of states' rights, free enterprise, and a small and balanced budget. Smith was convinced that to stretch the Constitution even once to help those in hardship was to place the federal government and his beloved southern society in per-manent jeopardy. It was a risk that Smith, for one, was unwilling to take.

NOTES
BIBLIOGRAPHY
INDEX

Notes

Chapter 1   *Growing Up at Cedar Hill*

1   William A. Link, "Public Schooling and Social Change in Rural Virginia, 1870–1920" (Ph.D. diss., University of Virginia, 1981), pp. 25–54.

2   Allen W. Moger, "Industrial and Urban Progress in Virginia from 1880 to 1900," *Virginia Magazine of History and Biography* 66 (1951): 307–36.

3   Joseph Robert, *The Tobacco Kingdom: Plantation, Market, and Factory in Virginia and North Carolina, 1800–1860* (Durham, N.C., 1938), pp. 15–17, 55–64; *Richmond Dispatch*, July 29, 1871; *Richmond Exchange Reporter*, Jan. 28, 1892; Edward A. Pollard, *The Virginia Tourist: Sketches of the Springs and Mountains of Virginia* (Philadelphia, 1870), pp. 264–65.

4   John F. Stover, *The Railroads of the South, 1865–1900* (Chapel Hill, N.C., 1959), pp. 61, 193, 204, 233–56; Allen W. Moger, *Virginia: Bourbonism to Byrd, 1870–1925* (Charlottesville, 1968), p. 81; Link, "Public Schooling and Social Change," p. 34.

5   Link, "Public Schooling and Social Change," p. 33; Thomas Nelson Page, *The Old Dominion: Her Making and Her Manners* (New York, 1908), pp. 332–33, 335.

6   Link, "Public Schooling and Social Change," pp. 34, 39.

7   Charles E. Wynes, *Race Relations in Virginia, 1870–1902* (Charlottesville, 1961); C. Vann Woodward, *The Strange Career of Jim Crow*, 3d rev. ed. (New York, 1974), pp. 67–109; J. Morgan Kousser, *The Shaping of Southern Politics: Suffrage Restriction and the Establishment of the One-Party South, 1880–1910* (New Haven, 1974) pp. 59, 241; Moger, *Virginia: From Bourbonism to Byrd*, p. 217; James E. Cutler, *Lynch-law: An Investigation into the History of Lynching in the United States* (Montclair, N.J., 1969), p. 179; *Lynchburg News*, Sept. 8, 1892.

8   Moger, *Virginia: Bourbonism to Byrd*, pp. 181–202.

9   Bernard Bailyn, "Politics and Social Structure in Virginia," in James M. Smith, ed., *Seventeenth-Century America: Essays in Colonial History* (Chapel Hill, N.C., 1959), pp. 90–115; Mary Allan-Olney, *The New Virginians*, 2 (London, 1880): 172–73.

10   William B. Crawley, Jr., *Bill Tuck: A Political Life in Harry Byrd's*

Virginia (Charlottesville, 1978), p. 11; J. Harvie Wilkinson III, *Harry Byrd and the Changing Face of Virginia Politics, 1945–1966* (Charlottesville, 1968), pp. 14–22.

11   *Richmond Whig*, Feb. 14, 1873; *Richmond Dispatch*, Jan. 20, 1871.

12   Virginius Dabney, *Virginia: The New Dominion* (Garden City, N.Y., 1971), pp. 411–58; James A. Bear, Jr., "Thomas Staples Martin: A Study in Virginia Politics, 1883–1896" (M.A. thesis, Univ. of Va., 1952); Crawley, *Bill Tuck*, pp. 3–16; V. O. Key, Jr., *Southern Politics in State and Nation* (New York, 1949), pp. 19–22.

13   Page, *Old Dominion*, p. 198; U.S. Department of Commerce, Bureau of the Census, *Report on Statistics of Churches in the United States at the Eleventh Census: 1890* (Washington, D.C., 1894), p. 40; Garnett Ryland, *The Baptists of Virginia, 1699–1926* (Richmond, 1955).

14   Howard W. Smith, *Our Paternal Hearth* (privately printed, 1976), pp. x, 14–15, 17–21, 39–42, 47.

15   Ibid., pp. 8–13, 18–20.

16   *Warrenton Virginian*, Jan. 5, 1893.

17   Annie G. Day, *Sketches and Illustrations of Warrenton and Fauquier County, Virginia* (n.p., 1908); A. Di Zerega, Jr., et al., *Fauquier County Geography Supplement* (Warrenton, Va., 1927), pp. 3–4, 8–21, 29; Harry Connelly Groome, *Fauquier County, Virginia: Historical Notes* (Warrenton, 1914); *Warrenton Virginian*, Jan. 5, 1893.

18   *Warrenton Virginian*, Oct. 19, 1893.

19   Ibid., Jan. 16, March 13, 1897, April 29, 1899, March 10, April 14, 1904.

20   *True Index* (Warrenton), July 25, 1896; *Warrenton Virginian*, March 3, 1904.

21   Ibid.

22   W. Worth Smith, Jr., to Lucy Smith, probably November 1902, Violett Smith Tonahill collection, Jasper, Tex.

23   Lucy Price, *The Sydney-Smith and Clagett-Price Genealogy* (Strasburg, Va., 1927), pp. 15–28, 35–81; Smith, *Our Paternal Hearth*, pp. 30–31; Will Smith to Lucy Smith, May 1, Oct. 25, 1901, Tonahill collection; Violett Smith Tonahill, interview, Jasper, Tex., Dec. 30, 1978; Gordon Lewis, interview, The Plains, Va., April 26, 1979; Moger, *Virginia: Bourbonism to Byrd*, p. 80.

24   Interviews with Lewis and Tonahill; Smith, *Our Paternal Hearth*, pp. 48, 64.

25   Interviews with Lewis and Tonahill; Smith, *Our Paternal Hearth*, pp. 5, 56–57.

26   P. Alex Smith to Will Smith, Sept. 22, 1886, Tonahill collection; John G. Tyler, ed., *Men of Mark in Virginia*, 2 (Washington, D.C., 1907): 332–33;

Henry C. Ferrell, Jr., *Claude A. Swanson of Virginia: A Political Biography* (Lexington, Ky., 1985), p. 32; Jean S. Doptis, "Presley Marion Rixey," *Arlington Historical Magazine* 6 (Oct. 1977): 27–38; William C. Braisted and William H. Bell, *The Life Story of Presley Marion Rixey: Surgeon General, U.S. Navy, 1902–1910* (Strasburg, Va., 1930).

27   Smith, *Our Paternal Hearth*, pp. 17–21, 44–45.

28   Interview with Lewis.

29   Link, "Public Schooling and Social Change," p. 108.

30   Ibid., pp. 95–148.

31   Will Smith to Lucy Smith, Jan. 12, 1902, Tonahill collection.

32   Smith, *Our Paternal Hearth*, pp. 52–53; *True Index*, May 28, 1887, Sept. 2, 1899, June 14, 1902; *Warrenton Virginian*, Jan. 5, 1893; *Annual Announcement for 1892–93 and Catalogue of Bethel Military Academy, Fauquier County, Va.* (Warrenton, 1892), pp. 3–7, 10–18; Howard W. Smith (hereafter HWS) to A. C. Gochnauer, May 2, 1933, Howard W. Smith Papers, University of Virginia Library, Charlottesville; Raymond P. G. Bowman, "Secondary Education in Virginia, 1870–1886" (Ph.D. diss., Univ. of Va., 1938), pp. 336–39.

33   *True Index*, June 16, 1900; interview with Tonahill; Howard W. Smith, Jr., interview, Alexandria, Va., Oct. 20, 1978; HWS certificates of excellence, Tonahill collection.

34   Smith, *Our Paternal Hearth*, pp. 59–61; interview with Smith, Jr.

35   *True Index*, April 1, 1899; Rt. Rev. Samuel B. Chilton, interview, Alexandria, Va., Nov. 11, 1978; interview with Tonahill; Carl Elliott, Sr., interview, Jasper, Ala., Jan. 12, 1984; Virginia Waller Davis, "Star Performer on 'The Hill,'" *Virginia Record* 79 (May 1957): 14.

36   Smith, *Our Paternal Hearth*, pp. 48–49.

37   Philip A. Bruce, *History of the University of Virginia, 1819–1919*, 4 (New York, 1921): 287–92; W. Hamilton Bryson, "The History of Legal Education in Virginia," *University of Richmond Law Review* 14 (Fall 1979): 193–203; Holly Beth Fitzsimmons, "The Law and the Reason Thereof: John B. Minor and Legal Education at the University of Virginia, 1845–1895" (M.A. thesis, Univ. of Va., 1976).

38   John Ritchie, *The First Hundred Years: A Short History of the School of Law of the University of Virginia for the Period 1826–1926* (Charlottesville, 1978), pp. 54–63.

39   *Bulletin of the University of Virginia* 1, no. 1 (1901): 132–45.

40   W. Hamilton Bryson, *Legal Education in Virginia, 1779–1979: A Biographical Approach* (Charlottesville, 1982), pp. 252–63.

41   Edward J. Woodhouse, "Raleigh Colston Minor: Scholar, Teacher, Jurist, Leader of American International Thinking," *Virginia Law Review* 12

(Feb. 1926): 1–24; Raleigh C. Minor, *Notes on the Science of Government and the Relations of the States to the United States* (Charlottesville, 1913), pp. 112–90.

42   Minor, *Notes on Government*, pp. 96–104, 110–22, 124–25, 128–35; Frank Tariello, Jr., *The Reconstruction of American Political Ideology, 1865–1917* (Charlottesville, 1982), pp. 11–31; Leslie Wharton, *Polity and the Public Good: Conflicting Theories of Republican Government in the New Nation* (Ann Arbor, Mich., 1980), pp. 13–31.

43   Minor, *Notes on Government*, pp. 191–92.

44   "Editorial," *Virginia Law Register* 4 (Oct. 1898): 390–91.

45   Thomas M. Cooley, *The General Principles of Constitutional Law in the United States of America* (Boston, 1891), pp. 28–30, 32–35, 100, 237.

46   National Education Television transcript, Oct. 5, 1966, Smith Papers; HWS to F. D. G. Ribble, Sept. 27, 1957, F. D. G. Ribble Papers, Arthur J. Morris Law Library, University of Virginia; *Fauquier Democrat* (Warrenton), Sept. 22, 1966.

47   William H. Harbaugh, *The Life and Times of Theodore Roosevelt* (New York, 1961), pp. 149–423.

48   HWS to L. A. Lewis, Oct. 3, 1902, HWS to Lucy Smith, Oct. 3, 1902, Jan. 25, 1903, Tonahill collection; Smith, *Our Paternal Hearth*, pp. 63–65, 92.

49   HWS to Lucy Smith, Oct. 3, 1902, Will Smith to Lucy Smith, Feb. 12, 1903, HWS to L. A. Lewis, Oct. 3, 1902, Tonahill collection; Smith, *Our Paternal Hearth*, pp. 66–67.

50   Smith, *Our Paternal Hearth*, p. 67; *Journal of the House of Delegates of the State of Virginia* (Richmond, 1902), pp. 1054, 1080, 1085, 1115, 1266, 1275.

Chapter 2   *Law and Politics in Alexandria*

1   W. Andrew Boyd, *Boyd's Directory of Alexandria, Va.* (Washington, D.C., 1917), preface; Writers' Program of the Works Projects Administration in the State of Virginia, *Alexandria* (Alexandria, 1939), pp. 4–11; *Alexandria Gazette*, May 20, 1908; Betty Carter Smoot, *Days in an Old Town* (Washington, D.C., 1934).

2   Writers' Program, *Alexandria*, pp. 3–4.

3   Luther H. Dudley interview, Alexandria, Va., Nov. 11, 1978; Albert V. Bryan, Sr., interview, Alexandria, Nov. 24, 1978; *Alexandria Gazette*, May 30, 1916. *The Directory of Alumni of the Law School: The University of Virginia* (Charlottesville, 1963) pp. 196, 215, 226, 228, 240, lists among its graduates such political worthies of Alexandria as attorney Gardner S. Boothe, Congressman John F. Rixey, Judge James R. Caton, Judge Robinson Moncure, and Judge Albert V. Bryan, Sr.

4 *Alexandria Gazette,* May 20, 1908; Smith, *Our Paternal Hearth,* pp. 86, 93; interviews with Dudley and Chilton.

5 Smith, *Our Paternal Hearth,* pp. 98–100.

6 Interview with Bryan; *Alexandria Gazette,* July 19, 1904; General Index to Deeds, no. 10, 1904–10, pp. 45, 49, 57, 136, 138, 211, 213, 341, 450–51, 475, Corporation Court, Clerk of Court's Office, Alexandria; HWS to Lucy Smith, Oct. 11, 1904, Smith Papers.

7 *Alexandria Gazette,* May 20, Sept. 10, 1908; interview with Dudley; Ferrell, *Swanson,* p. 88.

8 *Alexandria Gazette,* June 8, 10, 11, Sept. 1, 14, 23, 1908.

9 Moger, *Virginia: Bourbonism to Byrd,* pp. 203–30; Bear, "Thomas Staples Martin," pp. 90–210; *Alexandria Gazette,* June 12, 13, Sept. 23, 1908, Sept. 1, 1910, June 11, 12, Aug. 31, Sept. 3, 1912, Sept. 1, 1914, June 14, 1916 (these are accurate and complete reports of the proceedings recorded by hand in the Alexandria City Council Minutes, City Hall).

10 Smith, *Our Paternal Hearth,* pp. 86–91; interview with Tonahill; *Alexandria Gazette,* May 1, 1911, June 18,1921, Feb. 5, 1984, Feb. 5, 1985; Lewis A. Stearman to author, Nov. 23, 1985.

11 Interviews with Dudley and Tonahill. See, for example, Alexandria Deeds, Book 58, Feb. 13, 1909, pp. 211–15, Book 61, Jan. 12, 1912, pp. 476–77, Book 62, Nov. 9, 1912, pp. 333–34, Book 76, April 12, 1923, pp. 160–62, Book 86, May 27, 1926, pp. 479–80.

12 Interviews with Lewis and Dudley; Alexandria Deeds, Book 61, Jan. 12, March 12, 1912, pp. 476–77, 562, Book 62, Oct. 5, 11, 25, Nov. 9, 1912, pp. 269–70, 278, 280–81, 301, 333–34, Book 65, Oct. 18, 1916, p. 463, Book 69, Nov. 5, 1919, p. 321.

13 Interview with Lewis; Alexandria Deeds, Book 107, June 10, 1931, pp. 154–55.

14 Alexandria Deeds, Book 65, Nov. 14, 1916, p. 502, Book 66, Sept. 17, 1917, pp. 280–81, Book 75, Feb. 21, 1923, pp. 481–82, 484–86.

15 Ibid., Book 62, May 12, 1913, p. 572, Book 64, June 8, 1915, pp. 373–74, Book 65, Oct. 18, Nov. 14, 1916, pp. 463, 502, Book 69, Nov. 22, 1919, p. 416, Book 75, Feb. 21, 1923, pp. 481–82, 484–86, Book 107, June 10, 1931, pp. 154–55.

16 *Alexandria Gazette,* Nov. 4, 1913; *Richmond's Directory of Alexandria, Va.,* 1900 (Washington, D.C., 1900), p. 178; Boyd, *Boyd's Directory,* p. 217.

17 *Alexandria Gazette,* Nov. 4, 1913; Smith, *A Supplemental List of the Descendants of Henry Marrs Lewis and Presley Lycurgus Smith to Include Those Born Subsequent to the Publication in 1927 of the Book by Lucy Montgomery Smith Price* (privately printed, 1970), p. 11. See also Richard B. Dow, *A History of the Second Presbyterian Church, Alexandria, Virginia, 1817–1950* (Richmond, 1952), pp. 47–61.

18   *Alexandria Gazette*, Sept. 8, 1914.

19   Ibid., June 5, 14, 1916.

20   Ibid., June 4, 5, Sept. 2, 1918.

21   Smith, *Our Paternal Hearth*, pp. 70–82; interview with Dudley.

22   *Alexandria Gazette*, Sept. 4, 1918; *Annual Report of the Secretary of the Commonwealth to the Governor and General Assembly of Virginia* (Richmond, 1920), p. 35; Corporation Court of Alexandria, Minutes, Sept. 4, 1918, p. 446, Sept. 11, 1918, p. 452, May 12, 1919, pp. 111–12, Sept. 13, 1920, p. 406, clerk of court's office; interview with Bryan; Corporation Court, Criminal Policy Files, nos. 442½, 535, ibid.; Robert N. Pollard, ed., *Pollard's Code Biennial, 1918, Containing All Statutes of a General and Permanent Nature Passed by the General Assembly of Virginia* (Richmond, 1918), pp. 348–90.

23   *Alexandria Gazette*, Jan. 20, 1919; interview with Chilton.

24   HWS to Annie Corcoran, July 1, 1920, Smith Papers.

25   Claude A. Swanson to HWS, Aug. 30, Sept. 9, 1921, HWS to Swanson, Aug. 31, 1921, Claude A. Swanson Papers, University of Virginia Library; *Alexandria Gazette*, July 7, 20, 22, 25, 26, 29, 31, Aug. 1, 2, 1921; Jack T. Kirby, *Westmoreland Davis: Virginia Planter-Politician, 1859–1942* (Charlottesville, 1968), pp. 145–57; Henry C. Ferrell, Jr., "Claude A. Swanson of Virginia" (Ph.D. diss., Univ. of Va., 1964), pp. 287–95; Ferrell, *Swanson*, p. 128. See also the shorter essays on Davis and Swanson by Kirby and Ferrell, respectively, in Edward Younger and James T. Moore, eds., *The Governors of Virginia, 1860–1978* (Charlottesville, 1982).

26   *Alexandria Gazette*, Oct. 18, 20, 21, 26, 1922; L. Stanley Willis, "E. Lee Trinkle: Prelude to Byrd," in Younger and Moore, eds., *The Governors of Virginia, 1860–1978*, pp. 221–32; J. K. M. Norton to Claude A. Swanson, May 15, 1922, Swanson Papers; Corporation Court, Minutes, Nov. 10, 1922, p. 409; interview with Bryan.

27   Corporation Court, Minutes, Nov. 21, 1922, Feb. 25, March 9, April 30, June 9, Oct. 21, Nov. 9, 1925, Feb. 25, April 6, 1926, pp. 7–8, 12–13, 44, 73–75, 119, 127, 171, 189; Corporation Court, Criminal Policy Files, no. 1158; interviews with Tonahill and Bryan.

28   Key, *Southern Politics*, pp. 21–22.

29   Marriage license, June 27, 1923, Marriage register no. 8, p. 91, Fauquier County Circuit Court, Warrenton, Va.; Smith, *List of Descendants*, p. 11; *Alexandria Gazette*, June 27, 1923; interviews with Dudley, Tonahill, Smith, Jr., and Lewis.

30   *Alexandria Gazette*, July 20, 25, 1928; interview with Bryan; Corporation Court, Minutes, July 25, 1928, p. 26.

31   Sixteenth Circuit Court of Virginia, Chancery Order Book, Sept. 13, 1928, p. 381, clerk of court's office, Alexandria; *Alexandria Gazette*, March 17, April 9, 11, 1930; interview with Bryan.

32 Interview with Dudley.

33 *Alexandria Gazette*, March 8, 1930.

34 Ibid.; Smith, *Our Paternal Hearth*, p. 86; *Congressional Record*, Feb. 26, 1902, pp. 2293–95.

35 *Alexandria Gazette*, March 17, 18, 1930; U.S. Department of Commerce, Bureau of the Census, *Fifteenth Census of the United States: 1930*, 3, pt. 2 (Washington, D.C., 1932): 1141–96.

36 *Alexandria Gazette*, March 8, 1930.

37 *Fauquier Democrat*, Jan. 18, April 5, Oct. 1, 1930; interview with Smith, Jr.

38 Interview with Dudley; *Alexandria Gazette*, March 17, 28, April 1, 1930; *Fairfax Herald*, Jan. 25, Feb. 1, April 12, May 24, Nov. 1929, April 4, 11, 1930.

39 *Alexandria Gazette*, June 7, July 19, 1930; *Fairfax Herald*, March 21, June 6, July 18, 25, 1930; *Fauquier Democrat*, June 7, 11, 1930; *Central Virginian* (Louisa), April 3, 1930; *Fredericksburg Free Lance-Star*, July 18, 1930; Smith, *Our Paternal Hearth*, p. 99.

40 Ferrell, *Swanson*, pp. 46, 194–95; *Fairfax Herald*, July 11, 1930; *Fredericksburg Free Lance-Star*, July 28, Aug. 4, 1930; Francis Pickens Miller, *Man from the Valley: Memoirs of a 20th-Century Virginian* (Chapel Hill, N.C., 1971), pp. 142–43; Smith, *Our Paternal Hearth*, p. 99; Kenneth G. Crawford, *The Pressure Boys: The Inside Story of Lobbying in America* (New York, 1939), p. 232.

41 *Central Virginian*, May 1, 1930; *Fauquier Democrat*, July 26, 1930.

42 *Central Virginian*, March 13, 1930.

43 *Fauquier Democrat*, July 19, 26, 1930; *Fredericksburg Free Lance-Star*, July 7, Aug. 4, 1930; Smith, *Our Paternal Hearth*, pp. 86–87.

44 *Fauquier Democrat*, July 19, 26, 1930.

45 *Fredericksburg Free Lance-Star*, July 7, 1930; interview with Dudley; Alexandria Deeds, Book 62, Oct. 5, 1912, pp. 269–70.

46 *Fauquier Democrat*, July 19, 1930; *Fairfax Herald*, July 11, 1930.

47 *Fauquier Democrat*, July 5, 1930; *Central Virginian*, July 31, 1930.

48 *Central Virginian*, April 3, May 8, July 10, 1930; *Fairfax Herald*, March 28, July 25, 1930; *Alexandria Gazette*, July 19, 1930; *Fredericksburg Free Lance-Star*, July 28, 29, 1930.

49 *Fauquier Democrat*, July 16, 1930; *Central Virginian*, June 26, July 10, 31, 1930.

50 *Washington Post*, Feb. 6, 1955.

51 *Alexandria Gazette*, July 28, 1930; *Fauquier Democrat*, July 30, 1930; interview with Bryan.

52   *Alexandria Gazette,* July 28, 1930; *Fauquier Democrat,* July 30, 1930.

53   Ibid. For Ball's rebuttal, see *Alexandria Gazette,* Aug. 2, 1930.

54   *Alexandria Gazette,* July 28, 1930; *Fauquier Democrat,* July 30, 1930.

55   Ibid.; interview with Smith, Jr.

56   *Alexandria Gazette,* Aug. 6, 1930; *Fairfax Herald,* Aug. 8, 1930.

57   *Fredericskburg Free Lance-Star,* Aug. 6, 1930; *Central Virginian,* Aug. 14, 1930; *Alexandria Gazette,* Aug. 6, 1930; interview with Bryan.

58   Interview with Bryan.

59   *Fredericksburg Free Lance-Star,* Sept. 10, 13, 1930; *Richmond News Leader,* Sept. 12, 17, 1930.

60   Alexandria Gazette, Aug. 6, Nov. 5, 6, 1930; State Board of Elections, *Statement of the Vote, 1920[–1930] Election* (Richmond, 1920–30).

Chapter 3   *An Anti–New Dealer*

1   *Congressional Record,* Dec. 8, 15, 1931, Feb. 11, 1932, pp. 131, 169, 551–52, 3792; *Virginia Star* (Culpeper), Dec. 17, 1931, July 16, 21, 1932; *Alexandria Gazette,* Jan. 15, 1932. Smith kept neither a diary nor a detailed record of his activities in Congress; see HWS Remarks, Dec. 21, 1968, Smith Papers.

2   David Burner, *Herbert Hoover: A Public Life* (New York, 1979), pp. 245–83; Murray N. Rothbard, *America's Great Depression* (Los Angeles, 1972), pp. 261–65; *Congressional Record,* Jan. 15, 1932, pp. 2054, 2072, 2081; HWS interview with Sam Crutchfield, June 13, 1968, Smith Papers.

3   *Richmond News Leader,* Nov. 9, 1932; Robert L. Peabody, *Leadership in Congress: Stability, Succession, and Change* (Boston, 1976), p. 46.

4   *Congressional Directory* (Washington, D.C., 1933), p. 220; Tom Wicker, *JFK and LBJ: The Influence of Personality upon Politics* (New York, 1968), pp. 70–71; HWS interview with Sam Crutchfield, May 29, 1968, Smith Papers; George Goodwin, Jr., *The Little Legislatures: Committees of Congress* (Amherst, Mass., 1970), p. 73; Richard D. Bolling, interview, Washington, D.C., May 31, 1983.

5   Christopher Van Hollen, "The House Committee on Rules (1933–1951): Agent of Party and Agent of Opposition" (Ph.D. diss., Johns Hopkins University, 1951), pp. 23–32. See also James A. Robinson, *The House Rules Committee* (Indianapolis, 1963), pp. 57–63; George B. Galloway, *History of the House of Representatives* (New York, 1961), pp. 49–57; Neil MacNeil, *Forge of Democracy: The House of Representatives* (New York, 1963), pp. 39–60.

6   Van Hollen, "House Committee on Rules," pp. 135–39.

7   *Congressional Record,* March 11, 1933, p. 214; Richard Bolling, *Power in the House: A History of the Leadership of the House of Representatives* (New

York, 1968), pp. 126, 128; James T. Patterson, *Congressional Conservatism and the New Deal: The Growth of the Conservative Coalition in Congress, 1933–1939* (Lexington, Ky., 1967), pp. 1–31; James M. Burns, *Roosevelt: The Lion and the Fox* (New York, 1956), p. 267.

8 *Central Virginian*, Feb. 19, 1931; Smith, *Our Paternal Hearth*, p. 85; Crawley, *Bill Tuck*, pp. 32–34.

9 *Central Virginian*, July 27, 1933; *Fredericksburg Free Lance-Star*, July 25, 1933.

10 *Central Virginian*, July 27, 1933.

11 Ibid., April 20, Aug. 3, 1933; *Fredericksburg Free Lance-Star*, July 25, 1930; Joseph A. Fry, "George Campbell Peery: Conservative of Old Virginia" (M.A. thesis, Univ. of Va., 1970), pp. 39–52.

12 F. Frazier McCall to Carter Glass, May 6, 1933, Carter Glass Papers, University of Virginia Library.

13 HWS to Mr. Chew, July 3, 1933, Smith Papers.

14 Harry F. Byrd to Carter Glass, July 10, 1933, Glass Papers; *Fauquier Democrat*, Sept. 22, 1966.

15 *Central Virginian*, Aug. 10, 1933; Key, *Southern Politics*, p. 28. Worth Smith ran once more for state office four years later, this time for attorney general. But when John Galleher, another nonorganization candidate, refused to step aside, Smith withdrew shortly before the party primary. See Alvin L. Hall, "James H. Price and Virginia Politics, 1878 to 1943" (Ph.D. diss., Univ. of Va., 1970), pp. 139–41.

16 Patterson, *Congressional Conservatism*, pp. 29–30; *Congressional Record*, May 26, 1933, pp. 4368–69; Arthur M. Schlesinger, Jr., *The Coming of the New Deal* (Boston, 1958), pp. 87–118; William E. Leuchtenburg, *Franklin D. Roosevelt and the New Deal, 1932–1940* (New York, 1963), pp. 57–58.

17 *Congressional Record*, May 26, 1933, pp. 4326–28, 4374–75; "An Elder Statesman Looks at U.S. Today," *U.S. News and World Report* 61 (Oct. 31, 1966): 53. See also Frank Friedel, *F.D.R. and the South* (Baton Rouge, La., 1965), esp. pp. 59–102.

18 Patterson, *Congressional Conservatism*, pp. 19–20.

19 Ronald L. Heinemann, *Depression and New Deal in Virginia: The Enduring Dominion* (Charlottesville, 1983), pp. 172–91.

20 HWS Recollections, March 15, 1970, Smith Papers; Leuchtenburg, *Roosevelt and the New Deal*, pp. 124–25.

21 *Congressional Record*, Jan. 23, 1935, pp. 850–51; Gerald Gunther and Noel T. Dowling, *Cases and Materials on Constitutional Law*, 8th ed. (Mineola, N.Y., 1970), pp. 268–69, 574.

22 *Congressional Record*, Jan. 24, 1935, p. 942; *Richmond News Leader*, Feb. 27, 1935; Leuchtenburg, *Roosevelt and the New Deal*, pp. 124–30.

23   U.S. Department of Health, Education, and Welfare, Social Security Administration, *Social Security Programs in the United States* (Washington, D.C., 1968), pp. 3–6.

24   Arthur J. Altmeyer, *The Formative Years of Social Security* (Madison, Wis., 1966), pp. 3–42; Roy Lubove, *The Struggle for Social Security, 1900–1935* (Cambridge, Mass., 1968); Charles McKinley and Robert W. Frase, *Launching Social Security: A Capture-and-Record Account, 1935–1937* (Madison, Wis., 1970), pp. 3–17.

25   Rita Riccardo Campbell, *Social Security: Promise and Reality* (Stanford, Calif., 1977), pp. 3–5.

26   *Congressional Record*, April 11, 18, 19, 1935, pp. 5467–70, 5475–77, 5983, 6069–70; Philip Booth, *Social Security in America* (Ann Arbor, Mich., 1973), pp. 3–14; McKinley and Frase, *Launching Social Security*, pp. 3–17.

27   Hall, "James H. Price and Virginia Politics," pp. 169–75.

28   Leuchtenburg, *Roosevelt and the New Deal*, pp. 150–52; *Congressional Record*, June 19, 1935, pp. 9692–95.

29   *Congressional Record*, June 19, 1935, pp. 9692–95.

30   Ibid., pp. 9713–17; Leuchtenburg, *Roosevelt and the New Deal*, p. 236.

31   Leuchtenburg, *Roosevelt and the New Deal*, pp. 155–57; Patterson, *Congressional Conservatism*, pp. 52–56.

32   Van Hollen, "House Committee on Rules," pp. 172–75; HWS Remarks, Dec. 21, 1968, Smith Papers; Patterson, *Congressional Conservatism*, pp. 38–39, 52–53, 54–57; Bolling, *Power in the House*, pp. 129–31; Leuchtenburg, *Roosevelt and the New Deal*, p. 155.

33   *Congressional Record*, July 2, 1935, p. 10637; Patterson, *Congressional Conservatism*, pp. 54–57; George B. Galloway, *Congress at the Crossroads* (New York, 1946), pp. 302–3. See also Mack C. Shelley II, *The Permanent Majority: The Conservative Coalition in the United States Congress* (University, Ala., 1983).

34   *Congressional Record*, March 27, 1936, pp. 4525–26, 4536.

35   See, for example, John C. Gall to HWS, Aug. 24, 1940, Smith Papers.

36   *Congressional Record*, March 27, June 17, 1936, pp. 4514–41, 9743–53, April 29, 1940, p. 5233.

37   "Silicosis," *Time* 27 (Feb. 3, 1936): 54; *Charlottesville Daily Progress*, Jan. 14–16, 20, 28, Feb. 6, 7, 1936; Crawford, *The Pressure Boys*, pp. 234–40.

38   *Congressional Record*, Feb. 7, 24, April 1, 1936, pp. 1674, 2725, 4751–53; Alicia Tyler, "Dust to Dust," *Washington Monthly* 6 (Jan. 1975): 49–51; *New York Times*, Jan. 15, 23, 25, 28, Feb. 7, 8, 16, 23, 1936; "Silicosis Village," *Nation* 142 (Feb. 5, 1936): 162; Vito Marcantonio, "Dusty Death," *New Republic* 86 (March 4, 1936): 105–6; Crawford, *The Pressure Boys*, pp. 234–40; *Daily Worker* (New York), Jan. 15, 1961.

39   *Buffalo News*, Sept. 28, 1986; Tyler, "Dust to Dust," pp. 53–55; Marcantonio, "Dusty Death," pp. 105–6. For a definitive account, see the report of Marcantonio's nine-day House investigation reprinted in Jim Comstock, ed., *West Virginia Heritage* 7 (1972): 1–193; *Congressional Record*, Jan. 13, 1936, p. 367.

40   *Charlottesville Daily Progress*, Jan. 16, 28, Feb. 6, 1936; Tyler, "Dust to Dust," pp. 55–57; Crawford, *The Pressure Boys*, pp. 239–42; *Congressional Record*, Feb. 7, 24, April 1, 1936, pp. 1674, 2725, 4751–53.

41   *Congressional Record*, June 18, 1936, p. 9973.

42   Ibid., pp. 9975, 9986–87.

43   Ibid., pp. 9985–86, Jan. 5, 1937, p. 30.

44   *Charlottesville Daily Progress*, Jan. 7, 9, July 6, 1936; *Virginia Star*, June 18, Sept. 17, 24, Oct. 1, 8, 29, 1936; interview with Tonahill; HWS to Franklin D. Roosevelt, Oct. 31, 1935, FDR Papers, FDR Library, Hyde Park, N.Y.

45   State Board of Elections, *Statement of the Vote, 1936 Election*.

46   Patterson, *Congressional Conservatism*, pp. 134–35, 167–68; *Congressional Record*, April 8, 1937, pp. 3296–3301; Alvin M. Josephy, Jr., *On the Hill: A History of the American Congress* (New York, 1979), p. 344.

47   *Virginia Star*, April 22, 1937; *Cases Adjudged in the Supreme Court at October Term, 1936*, 299 (Washington, D.C., 1937): 334–53; *Congressional Record*, Feb. 15, 1937, p. 1227.

48   James MacGregor Burns, *Congress on Trial: The Legislative Process and the Administrative State* (New York, 1949), pp. 68–82; Van Hollen, "House Committee on Rules," pp. 190–98; O. R. Altman, "First Session of the Seventy-fifth Congress," *American Political Science Review* 31 (Dec. 1937): 1081–82; Frances Perkins, *The Roosevelt I Knew* (New York, 1946), pp. 246–67.

49   Patterson, *Congressional Conservatism*, pp. 86–97, 165–66; Leuchtenburg, *Roosevelt and the New Deal*, pp. 231–38; HWS interview with Sam Crutchfield, June 13, 1968, Smith Papers.

50   Leuchtenburg, *Roosevelt and the New Deal*, pp. 236–39; Alfred H. Kelly and Winfred A. Harbison, *The American Constitution: Its Origins and Development* (New York, 1976), pp. 712–50.

51   Patterson, *Congressional Conservatism*, pp. 149–50; Burns, *Congress on Trial*, pp. 69–72; Leuchtenburg, *Roosevelt and the New Deal*, p. 261.

52   Patterson, *Congressional Conservatism*, p. 178; *New York Times*, Aug. 1, 1937.

53   Burns, *Congress on Trial*, pp. 73–74; "Roast Chicken," *Time* 30 (Aug. 23, 1937): 11–12; Van Hollen, "House Committee on Rules," pp. 190–98; *New York Times*, Aug. 22, 1937.

54   *Congressional Record*, Aug. 16, 1937, pp. A2445–48.

55   Ibid.

56   Thomas L. Stokes, *Chip off My Shoulder* (Princeton, N.J., 1940), pp. 505–6; interview with Elliott.

57   Burns, *Congress on Trial*, pp. 74–76; *Congressional Record*, Dec. 2, 17, 1937, pp. 759–60, 1834–35.

58   Burns, *Congress on Trial*, pp. 76–82; Patterson, *Congressional Conservatism*, pp. 243–45; Leuchtenburg, *Roosevelt and the New Deal*, p. 262.

59   *Congressional Record*, June 14, 1938, pp. 9246–55, 9266–67.

60   Morton J. Frisch, *Franklin D. Roosevelt: The Contribution of the New Deal to American Political Thought and Practice* (Boston, 1975), pp. 74–82; James A. Farley, *Jim Farley's Story: The Roosevelt Years* (New York, 1948), pp. 120–39; Burns, *Roosevelt: The Lion and the Fox*, pp. 358–80; Robert Dallek, *Democrat and Diplomat: The Life of William E. Dodd* (New York, 1968), pp. 322, 326. A. Cash Koeniger, "The New Deal and the States: Roosevelt versus the Byrd Organization in Virginia," *Journal of American History* 68 (March 1982): 876–96; *Washington Star*, June 24, 1938; *Washington Daily News*, June 24, 1938; *New York Times*, June 30, 1938; *Arlington Sun*, July 8, 1938; Harold L. Ickes, *The Secret Diary of Harold L. Ickes: The Inside Struggle, 1936–1939* 2 (New York, 1954): 416, 420–21; *Washington Post*, June 25, 1938; HWS interview with Sam Crutchfield, Aug. 29, 1968, Smith Papers; Columbia Broadcasting System, *CBS Reports*, "The Keeper of the Rules: Congressman Smith and the New Frontier," Jan. 19, 1961, p. 2 (© CBS Inc. All Rights Reserved).

61   *Richmond News Leader*, July 16, 1938; *Washington Star*, July 16, 1938.

62   William E. Dodd, Jr., press releases, April 18, 27, May 3, 5, 10, June 13, 1938, Smith Papers; *Washington Times*, July 22, 1938; *Ashland Herald*, March 9, 1938; *Congressional Record*, June 9, 1938, pp. A2510–11. See also Bruce J. Dierenfield, "A New Deal Backlash: The Attempted Purge of Representative Howard W. Smith," *Magazine of Albermarle County History* 37–38 (1979–80): 187–229.

63   *Arlington Courier*, July 14, 21, 1938.

64   HWS campaign announcement, no date, 1938, Smith Papers.

65   *Charlottesville Daily Progress*, July 29, 1938; *Washington Post*, July 29, 1938.

66   HWS interview with Sam Crutchfield, Aug. 29, 1968, Smith Papers; *Washington Post*, July 30, 31, 1938; *Washington Star*, July 30, 1938; *Richmond News Leader*, July 29, 1938.

67   Virginia did not compile election results for party primaries in the 1930s; consequently, these county and precinct returns were obtained from not always reliable newspaper reports. See *Washington Herald*, Aug. 3, 1938; *Orange County News* (Gordonsville), Aug. 4, 1938; *Charlottesville Daily Progress*, Aug. 3, 1938; *Manassas Journal*, Aug. 4, 1938; *Fauquier Democrat*, Aug. 4, 1938; *Virginia Star*, Aug. 4, 1938.

68 *Midland Virginian* (Palmyra), Aug. 4, 1938; *Fauquier Democrat*, Aug. 4, 1938; *Washington Post*, Aug. 4, 1938; *Washington Times*, Aug. 3, 1938.

69 Joseph W. Martin, Jr., *My First Fifty Years in Politics* (New York, 1960), pp. 82–85; Shelley, *The Permanent Majority*, pp. 44–48.

Chapter 4 *The War Years: Anticommunist and Labor-Baiter*

1 Michal R. Belknap, *Cold War Political Justice: The Smith Act, the Community Party, and American Civil Liberties* (Westport, Conn., 1977), pp. 1– 25; Robert J. Donovan, *Conflict and Crisis: The Presidency of Harry S Truman, 1945–1948* (New York, 1977), p. 232; J. H. Pollack, "America Registers Her Aliens," *American Scholar* 10 (April 1941): 196; Alan Schaffer, *Vito Marcantonio: Radical in Congress* (New York, 1966), pp. 78–79; Geoffrey Perrett, *Days of Sadness, Years of Triumph: The American People, 1939–1945* (New York, 1973), pp. 87–103; American Enterprise Institute, "Events Leading to Passage of the Smith Act," Smith Papers.

2 *Congressional Record*, March 20, 1939, p. 3013; *Virginia Star*, May 4, 1939; *Washington News*, March 20, 1939; *Washington Post*, Feb. 6, 1955.

3 *Congressional Record*, July 19, 1939, p. 9537.

4 Ibid., p. 10452; Zechariah Chafee, Jr., *Free Speech in the United States* (Cambridge, Mass., 1941), pp. 446–48.

5 *Congressional Record*, July 19, 1939, p. 9537.

6 Ibid., July 19, 29, 1939, pp. 9537, 10449; *Virginia Star*, Aug. 3, 1939; American Enterprise Institute, "Events Leading to Smith Act," p. 22.

7 Chafee, *Free Speech*, p. 444.

8 *Congressional Record*, July 29, 1939, pp. 10445–48, 10452–56.

9 Chafee, *Free Speech*, pp. 449–59.

10 Ibid., pp. 462–84; A. L. Wirin and Sam Rosenwein, "The Smith Act Score," *Nation* 10 (Feb. 26, 1955): 177–80.

11 Kenneth Crawford, "Open Season on Reds," *Nation* 148 (May 6, 1939): 519–20.

12 *Congressional Record*, July 29, 1939, pp. 10445–56; Pollack, "America Registers Her Aliens," pp. 207–8.

13 Belknap, *Cold War Political Justice*, pp. 17–27; Donovan, *Conflict and Crisis*, p. 232; Pollack, "America Registers Her Aliens," p. 203; Perrett, *Days of Sadness*, pp. 87–90; Frank J. Donner, "The Smith Act—Baltimore Version," *Nation* 175 (Nov. 8, 1952): 426.

14 Pollack, "America Registers Her Aliens," pp. 200, 202.

15 Ibid., pp. 202–3; Beulah Amidon, "Aliens in America," *Survey Graphic* 30 (Feb. 1941): 58–59.

16 Beulah Amidon, "Can We Afford Martyrs?" *Survey Graphic* 29 (Sept. 1940): 457–58; Amidon, "Aliens in America," pp. 59–61.

17   HWS letter summaries to the FBI, May 31, June 24, 1940, June 10, 1941, March 9, 1942, Department of Justice, Washington, D.C.

18   Amidon, "Aliens in America," p. 58; Pollack, "America Registers Her Aliens," p. 205.

19   *Congressional Record*, June 26, 1939, pp. 7907–28.

20   Ibid.; *Washington Post*, June 29, 1939.

21   Howard W. Smith, Sr., interview, Alexandria, Va., Oct. 10, 1975.

22   Thomas G. Abernethy, interview, Jackson, Miss., Jan. 11, 1984; Carl Albert, telephone interview, Aug. 3, 1983.

23   *Congressional Record*, July 13, 20, 1939, pp. 9070, 9582–91; *New York Times*, June 4, 23, 1939; Earl Latham, *The Communist Controversy in Washington: From the New Deal to McCarthy* (Cambridge, Mass., 1966), p. 133; *Washington Daily News*, July 20, 1939; *Virginia Star*, July 27, 1939.

24   "Friendless NLRB," *Newsweek* 14 (Oct. 23, 1939): 50–52; *Proceedings of the Fifty-ninth Annual Convention of the American Federation of Labor* (Washington, D.C., 1939); James A. Gross, *The Reshaping of the National Labor Relations Board: National Labor Policy in Transition* (Albany, N.Y., 1981), p. 155.

25   Robert B. Greer to HWS, July 21, 1939, S. H. Roth to HWS, July 21, 1939, Thomas Atkinson to HWS, July 29, 1939, Smith Papers.

26   *Congressional Record*, July 20, 1939, pp. 9582–84, 9591–93; interview with Elliott; Rudolf Engelbarts, *Women in the United States Congress, 1917–1972: Their Accomplishments with Bibliographies* (Littleton, Colo., 1974), pp. 30–33; Howard W. Smith, oral history interview, Jan. 30, 1969, p. 8, Labor-Management Documentation Center, Martin P. Catherwood Library, New York State School of Industrial and Labor Relations, Cornell University, Ithaca, N.Y.; Herbert Harris, "Politics and the C.I.O.," *Nation* 149 (Nov. 18, 1939): 545–46.

27   *Congressional Record*, July 27, 1939, pp. 10235–36; *Virginia Star*, Aug. 10, 1939; "Collapse in the Capitol," *Time* 34 (July 31, 1939): 8–10.

28   Gross, *Reshaping the National Labor Relations Board*, p. 151.

29   Ibid., pp. 151–53.

30   Harry F. Byrd to HWS, July 27, 1939, Edmund M. Toland to HWS, Feb. 13, 1940, William A. Stuart to Byrd, Aug. 8, 1939, Smith Papers; *Virginia Star*, Aug. 10, 1939; HWS oral history interview, p. 9; "Labor Inquiry," *Newsweek* 14 (Aug. 14, 1939): 40; Harris, "Politics and the C.I.O.," p. 546; Gross, *Reshaping the National Labor Relations Board*, 153–60.

31   *Virginia Star*, Sept. 7, 14, Oct. 26, Dec. 14, 1939; *New York Times*, Dec. 8, 10, 1939; *Washington Star*, Dec. 12, 1939; Gross, *Reshaping the National Labor Relations Board*, pp. 89–91, 159–65; "NLRB Bats for the Wagner Act," *Business Week* 521 (Aug. 26, 1939): 45–46; HWS oral history interview, pp. 53–54; "Smith of Virginia," *Newsweek* 19 (March 30, 1942): 32; HWS news

release, Dec. 1, 13, 1939, Smith Papers; Latham, *The Communist Controversy in Washington*, pp. 142–43; *Washington Post*, Dec. 12, 1939; "Labor's Safeguardians," *Time* 34 (Dec. 25, 1939): 8; Irving Bernstein, *Turbulent Years: A History of the American Worker, 1933–1941* (Boston, 1970), pp. 668–70; "Fix NLRB, Not Law?" *Business Week* 541 (Jan. 13, 1940): 39–40; "Tale of Plots and Pressure Unveiled in NLRB Inquiry," *Newsweek* 14 (Dec. 25, 1939): 40–42.

32   HWS speech, Dec. 18, 1939, Smith Papers.

33   Ibid.

34   Edwin Watson to FDR, Dec. 21, 1939, and the President's Appointment Diaries, 1939–44, p. 363, Franklin D. Roosevelt Library; HWS memorandum, Dec. 28, 1939, Smith Papers; HWS oral history, pp. 18–19; Gross, *Reshaping the National Labor Relations Board*, pp. 179–81; interview with Smith, Jr.; T. M. Carruthers, interview, Charlottesville, Va., Sept. 8, 1982.

35   *New York Times*, Jan. 17, 1940; Gross, *Reshaping the National Labor Relations Board*, pp. 182, 187; Russ Stone, "Blitzkrieg against the Labor Board," *New Republic* 102 (Jan. 22, 1940): 106–7. In 1957 the Supreme Court finally curbed the investigative powers of congressional committees when it dismissed contempt charges against labor leader John Watkins. See "The Court, Congress, Chaos," *Newsweek* 50 (July 1, 1957): 19–20, and "Supreme Court Challenges Usurpation by Congress," *Christian Century* 74 (July 10, 1957): 836.

36   *Washington Daily News*, March 13, 1940; Charles A. Halleck, interview, Rensselaer, Ind., June 15, 1983.

37   HWS memorandum, Feb. 12, 1940, and HWS interview with Sam Crutchfield, Sept. 12, 1968, Smith Papers; HWS oral history interview, pp. 19–20; Gross, *Reshaping the National Labor Relations Board*, pp. 192–93.

38   HWS memorandum, March 6, 1940, Smith Papers; *New York Times*, March 7, 1940; Gross, *Reshaping the National Labor Relations Board*, pp. 194–95.

39   U.S. Congress, House of Representatives, *Intermediate Report on the Investigation of the National Labor Relations Board* (Washington, D.C., 1940); *Virginia Star*, March 14, April 4, 1940; Crawford, *The Pressure Boys*, p. 232; Gross, *Reshaping the National Labor Board*, pp. 196–99; HWS press release, March 7, 1940, and Confidential Committee Print No. 2 (Smith's proposed bill), March 7, 1940, Smith Papers. See also Howard W. Smith, "NLRA—Abuses in Administrative Procedure," *Virginia Law Review* (March 1941): 615–32.

40   House of Representatives, *Intermediate Report*, pp. 88–89; Gross, *Reshaping the National Labor Relations Board*, pp. 198–99.

41   "Deal to Change Labor Law," *United States News* 8 (April 12, 1940): 35; *Congressional Record*, March 13, 1940, pp. 2774–82; *Detroit Free Press*, April 22, 1940; *Washington Star*, April 29, 1940; J. Joseph Huthmacher, *Sen-*

ator Robert Wagner and the Rise of Urban Liberalism (New York, 1968), pp.
259–60; "Wagner on the Wagner Act," *Time* 35 (March 25, 1940): 21–22.

42   *Congressional Record,* June 6, 7, 1940, pp. 7712–16, 7776–77, 7785,
7791, 7796, 7800; William Green to HWS, June 5, 1940, Smith Papers; *Washington Post,* June 7, 14, 140; *New York Times,* June 7, 1940; *Baltimore Daily
Record,* July 1, 1940; Huthmacher, *Wagner,* p. 260; Gross, *Reshaping the National Labor Relations Board,* pp. 206–10; Harry A. Millis and Emily Clark
Brown, *From the Wagner Act to Taft-Hartley: A Study of National Labor Policy
and Labor Relations* (Chicago, 1950), pp. 352–53.

43   *Congressional Record,* June 7, 10, 1940, pp. 7805, 7820; HWS interview with Sam Crutchfield, Sept. 12, 1968, Smith Papers.

44   "Labor Board Belabored," *Time* 35 (April 1, 1940): 14; Gross *Reshaping
the National Labor Relations Board,* pp. 213–24.

45   U.S. Congress, House of Representatives, *Final Report on the Investigation of the National Labor Relations Board* (Washington, D.C., 1941); Latham, *The Communist Controversy in Washington,* p. 133; *Chicago Tribune,*
Dec. 29, 1940; *Los Angeles Times,* Dec. 30, 1940; *New York Times,* Dec.
30,1940; "Report on NLRB," *Newsweek* 17 (Jan. 6, 1941): 39.

46   *New York Evening Post,* Dec. 31, 1940; Gross, *Reshaping the National
Labor Relations Board,* pp. 203, 224; Latham, *The Communist Controversy in
Washington,* p. 131; Alan K. McAdams, *Power and Politics in Labor Legislation* (New York, 1964), pp. 25–26; Hugh Miller, chairman, Washington Committee for Democratic Action, to HWS, Jan. 7, 1941, Smith Papers.

47   *New York Times,* Oct. 2, 10, 31, Nov. 16, 21, 28, Dec. 2, 1940; "New
Style NLRB," *Business Week* 586 (Nov. 23, 1940): 55–56; "Reformed NLRB,"
ibid., 598 (Feb. 15, 1941): 52; "NLRB's Purge," ibid., 605 (April 5, 1941): 53;
"Herzog Brings Stabilizing Influence to NLRB," ibid., 824 (June 16, 1945): 94;
Gross, *Reshaping of the National Labor Relations Board,* pp. 108, 226–51;
Emily Clark Brown, "The Employer Unit for Collective Bargaining in National Labor Relations Board Decisions," *Journal of Political Economy* 50 (June
1942): 331–40; "The New Personnel and Policies of the National Labor Relations Board," *Harvard Law Review* 55 (1941): 269–79; Julius Cohen and Lillian
Cohen, "The National Labor Relations Board in Retrospect," *Industrial and
Labor Relations Review* 1 (July 1948): 648–56.

48   McAdams, *Power and Politics,* p. 26; *Congressional Record,* Nov. 25,
1940, pp. 13733, 13740, Jan. 24, Feb. 27, 1941, pp. 304, 1499–1500.

49   *Congressional Record,* March 19, 21, April 2, June 6, 9, 1941, pp.
2381, 2459, 2472–73, 2906–7, 4826, 4890–92.

50   Ibid., Dec. 2, 3, 4, 8, 1941, pp. 9318–21, 9396–97, 9411, 9514–18;
Virginia Star, Dec. 4, 11, 1941. The other House antistrike bills were introduced by Congressmen Carl Vinson and Robert Ramspeck of Georgia, Everett
M. Dirksen of Illinois, Leland M. Ford of California, and Francis E. Walter
of Pennsylvania.

51 *Congressional Record*, Feb. 25, 26, 1942, pp. 1650–51, 1699, 1707–9, 1712.

52 Ibid., Feb. 27, 1942, pp. 1749–50; *Daily Worker*, March 19, 20, 24, 27, 30, April 6, 1942.

53 *Daily Worker*, May 22, 1942.

54 *Virginia Star*, July 16, 23, 1942; *Daily Worker*, Feb. 26, March 5, 27, May 22, 1942.

55 *Virginia Star*, July 30, Aug. 6, 13, 1942.

56 Ibid., Aug. 27, Sept. 3, 1942; State Board of Elections, *Statement of the Vote, 1942 Election*.

57 Huthmacher, *Wagner*, pp. 289–90; Millis and Brown, *Wagner Act to Taft-Hartley*, p. 299; Richard Polenberg, *War and Society: The United States, 1941–1945* (Philadelphia, 1972), pp. 159–67; Smith, *Our Paternal Hearth*, pp. 101–2; Hatton W. Sumners to Karl Hoblitzelle, June 12, 1943, Hatton W. Sumners Papers, Dallas Historical Society, Dallas; Roland Young, *Congressional Politics and the Second World War* (New York, 1956), p. 63.

58 *Congressional Record*, March 3, May 5, 1943, pp. 1771, 3993; Ralph V. Harlow, "Why the Anti-Labor Drive?" *Current History*, new ser., 2 (May 1942): 198–204; Tom Connally, *My Name Is Tom Connally* (New York, 1954), 252–54; Polenberg, *War and Society*, pp. 159–67; Young, *Congressional Politics*, pp. 64–67.

59 *Congressional Record*, June 2, 3, 4, 11, 14, 25, 1943, pp. 5221–35, 5304–5, 5335–36, 5387–92, 5726–37, 5798, 6487–89, 6548–49; *Washington Post*, June 12, 14, 26, 1943; "Something to Veto: Connally-Smith Bill," *Nation* 156 (June 19, 1943): 851–52; "Strike Curbs: Highlights of the War Labor Disputes Act," *Newsweek* 21 (June 21, 1943): 70, 72; "Angry Congress Deals Labor Biggest Setback in 10 Years," ibid., 22 (July 5, 1943): 64, 66, 69; Carl Elliott to author, Jan. 23, 1984. Elliott recalled that Luther Patrick of Alabama originally pinned the sobriquet on Smith.

60 Huthmacher, *Wagner*, pp. 289–90; Millis and Brown, *Wagner Act to Taft-Hartley*, p. 298; "Uprising," *Time* 42 (July 5, 1943): 17–18.

61 Perrett, *Days of Sadness*, pp. 306–9; Polenberg, *War and Society*, pp. 168–69; *New York Times*, March 14, 1945.

62 James MacGregor Burns, *Roosevelt: The Soldier of Freedom, 1940–1945* (New York, 1970), pp. 454–55; *Congressional Record*, May 5, 1944, pp. 4047–70; Galloway, *Congress at the Crossroads*, p. 9.

63 Polenberg, *War and Society*, pp. 170–75, 204–14; Young, *Congressional Politics*, pp. 65–66, 86; Alonzo L. Hamby, *Beyond the New Deal: Harry S. Truman and American Liberalism* (New York, 1973), pp. 34, 37.

64 Josephy, *On the Hill*, p. 335; Frank McNaughton to Bill Johnson, Feb. 5, 1943, Frank McNaughton Papers, Harry S Truman Library, Independence, Mo.

65   Josephy, *On the Hill*, pp. 335–37.

66   Ibid.; Frank McNaughton to Johnson, Feb. 5, 1943, McNaughton Papers; *Richmond Times-Dispatch*, Feb. 7, 1943; *Congressional Record*, Jan. 22, 25, Feb. 2, 5, 11, March 12, 1943, pp. 328, 533, 663, 882–83, 1953–55, 1968; *Washington Post*, Feb. 11, 1943; *Congressional Directory*, May 1943, p. 210; Alfred Steinberg, *Sam Rayburn: A Biography* (New York, 1975), p. 192; Polenberg, *War and Society*, pp. 192–94.

67   Colston E. Warne, "Pulling the OPA's Teeth," *Current History* 6 (May 1944): 410–16; "Congress and the Cost of Living," *New Republic* 109 (Aug. 2, 1943): 167–68; *Congressional Record*, Feb. 18, 19, 1943, pp. 1127, 1169.

68   Warne, "Pulling the OPA's Teeth," p. 412; *Congressional Record*, Nov. 15, 29, 1943, pp. 9557, 10106; *Virginia Star*, Dec. 2, 1943.

69   *Congressional Record*, June 7, 1944, pp. 5461–72; *Washington Post*, June 7, 1944; Van Hollen, "House Committee on Rules," pp. 209–10.

70   *Congressional Record*, Nov. 20, 1944, pp. 8202–4, 8215; *Washington Post*, June 7, 1944; *Alexandria Gazette*, Nov. 2, 3, 6, 8, 1944; *Virginia Star*, Nov. 9, 1944; Robert K. Carr, *The House Committee on Un-American Activities, 1945–1950* (Ithaca, N.Y., 1952), p. 18; William Gellerman, *Martin Dies* (New York, 1972), pp. 107, 173, 205, 225–43, 254–59.

71   Helen Fuller, "Reform, Howard Smith Style," *New Republic* 111 (Dec. 11, 1944): 791–93.

72   *Congressional Record*, Oct. 25, 1945, pp. 10056–63; "Rest in Peace," *Time* 48 (Nov. 11, 1946): 28; Hamby, *Beyond the New Deal*, pp. 79–80; Donovan, *Conflict and Crisis*, pp. 121–24, 198–99, 229, 235; Huthmacher, *Wagner*, pp. 326–27; HWS file memorandum, Oct. 26, 1945, Truman Library.

Chapter 5   *Defending the South:*
Labor-Baiter and Segregationist

1   Donovan, *Conflict and Crisis*, pp. 110–11; *Washington Post*, Jan. 4, 1946; *Congressional Record*, Jan. 15, 17, 1946, pp. 23–26, 100–103; *Virginia Star*, Feb. 21, March 14, April 4, 1946.

2   *Congressional Record*, Jan. 31, May 25, 1946, pp. 661–69, 5754–64; *New York Times*, Jan. 30, 1946; *Congressional Quarterly Almanac*, 1946, p. 86.

3   Van Hollen, "House Committee on Rules," pp. 212–14; interview with Abernethy; *Congressional Record*, May 25, June 11, 1946, pp. 5739, 6674–78.

4   *Congressional Record*, April 30, 1946, pp. 4257–58.

5   *Staunton News-Leader*, May 19, 1945, Jan. 4, 1946; *Fauquier Democrat*, May 30, June 6, 1946; *Norfolk Ledger-Dispatch*, June 3, 1946; Herman L. Horn, "The Growth and Development of the Democratic Party in Virginia since 1900" (Ph.D. diss., Duke University, 1949), pp. 446–50.

6 *Loudoun Times-Mirror* (Leesburg), June 6, 1946; *Norfolk Ledger-Dispatch*, June 1, 17, 1946; *Fauquier Democrat*, June 6, 1946; Cynthia A. Boatwright to Harry F. Byrd, May 29, 1946, Byrd to J. M. Peck, June 4, 1946, Byrd to Colgate W. Darden, Jr., June 27, 1958, Harry F. Byrd Papers, University of Virginia Library; A. Willis Robertson to Beverley W. Stras, Jr., Sept. 10, 1946, Robertson to Carter E. Talman, Sept. 28, 1946, A. Willis Robertson Papers, Earl Gregg Swem Library, College of William and Mary, Williamsburg, Va.

7 *Roanoke Times*, May 1, 5, 6, 7, 1946; *Fauquier Democrat*, April 4, 1946.

8 *Loudoun Times-Mirror*, Sept. 12, 1946; *Roanoke Times*, Aug. 26, Sept. 8, 1946.

9 J. Frank Wysor to HWS, Aug. 18, 1946, Wysor to Harry F. Byrd, Aug. 18, 1946, E. R. Combs Papers, University of Virginia Library; *Roanoke Times*, Sept. 5, 1946; *Norfolk Ledger-Dispatch*, July 16, 1946.

10 J. Frank Wysor to HWS, Aug. 18, 1946, E. R. Combs Papers.

11 *Roanoke Times*, Sept. 8, 1946.

12 *Alexandria Gazette*, Sept. 6, 1946; *Virginia Star*, Sept. 12, 1946; *Richmond Afro-American*, Sept. 14, 1946.

13 *Roanoke Times*, Sept. 7, 8, 1946; *Norfolk Ledger-Dispatch*, Sept. 6, 1946.

14 J. Frank Wysor to HWS, Sept. 8, 1946, Wysor to A. Willis Robertson, Sept. 8, 1946, Wysor to G. Fred Switzer, Aug. 24, 1946, Wysor to Harry F. Byrd, Aug. 18, 1946, E. R. Combs Papers; interview with Dudley; HWS to William M. Tuck, Sept. 12, 1946, William M. Tuck Papers, Earl Gregg Swem Library, College of William and Mary.

15 *Alexandria Gazette*, Nov. 2, 4, 6, 1946; State Board of Elections, *Statement of the Vote, 1946 Election*.

16 Watkins M. Abbitt, interview, Appomattox, Va., Oct. 31, 1980.

17 *Congressional Record*, Jan. 3, 1947, p. 42; "Smith Proposals to Modify the NLRA," Jan. 3, 1947, Smith Papers; HWS oral history interview, pp. 25–26.

18 Gross, *Reshaping the National Labor Relations Board*, p. 253; Fred A. Hartley, *Our New National Labor Policy: The Taft-Hartley Act and the Next Steps* (New York, 1948), pp. 14–15, 49–61; Gerard Reilly, "The Legislative History of the Taft-Hartley Act," *George Washington Law Review* 29 (1960): 285–300.

19 Interview with Abbitt; Abbitt to author, Nov. 15, 1980; Ed Gossett, telephone interview, June 18, 1984; W. R. Poage, interview, Waco, Tex., Oct. 14, 1983, and telephone interview, Oct. 1, 1984; interview with Halleck.

20 John F. Manley, "The Conservative Coalition in Congress," *American Behavioral Scientist* 17 (Nov./Dec. 1973): 231–32; Gross, *Reshaping the National Labor Relations Board*, p. 253.

21 Manley, "The Conservative Coalition in Congress," p. 233; David W. Brady and Charles S. Bullock III, "Coalition Politics in the House of Representatives," in *Congress Reconsidered*, ed. Lawrence C. Dodd and Bruce I. Oppenheimer (Washington, D.C., 1981), pp. 186–203.

22 *Congressional Record*, April 15, 16, 17, 1947, pp. 3412–55, 3512–75, 3616–71; *Congressional Quarterly Almanac*, 1947, p. 281.

23 *Congressional Record*, April 17, May 13, 1947, pp. 3613–14, 5108–18; *Congressional Quarterly Almanac*, 1947, pp. 284–86; Gross, *Reshaping the National Labor Relations Board*, p. 253.

24 *Congressional Record*, June 4, 6, 20, 1947, pp. 6384–93, 6495–536, 7485–89; *Congressional Quarterly Almanac*, 1947, pp. 291–97.

25 James T. Patterson, *Mr. Republican: A Biography of Robert A. Taft* (Boston, 1972), pp. 364–65; Sumner H. Slichter, "Revision of the Taft-Hartley Act," *Quarterly Journal of Economics* 67 (May 1953): 149–80; Sumner H. Slichter, "The Taft-Hartley Act," ibid., 63 (Feb. 1949): 1–31; Benjamin Aaron, "Amending the Taft-Hartley Act: A Decade of Frustration," *Industrial and Labor Relations Review* 11 (April 1958): 327–38; Joseph Shister, "The Impact of the Taft-Hartley Act on Union Strength and Collective Bargaining," ibid., pp. 339–51; Clyde W. Summers, "A Summary Evaluation of the Taft-Hartley Act," ibid., pp. 405–12.

26 Donovan, *Conflict and Crisis*, pp. 279–91; Thomas G. Paterson et al., *American Foreign Policy: A History since 1900* (Lexington, Mass., 1983), pp. 449–52.

27 *Congressional Record*, May 6, 9, 1947, pp. 4610–11, 4975.

28 Donovan, *Conflict and Crisis*, pp. 284–85.

29 Ibid., pp. 222, 287–91; *Congressional Record*, March 23, 1948, pp. 3313–20.

30 Donovan, *Conflict and Crisis*, pp. 290–91, 311, 387.

31 Belknap, *Cold War Political Justice*, pp. 6, 35–122, 152–57, 185–206.

32 Ibid.; American Enterprise Institute, "Major Legal Developments," Smith Papers; "Court Upholds Conviction of Communist Leaders," *Christian Century* 68 (June 20, 1951): 733; "Second Thoughts on the Communist Decision," ibid., July 11, 1951, p. 812; "The Week," *New Republic* 124 (June 18, 1951): 7; ibid., 125 (July 2, 1951): 7; A. L. Wirin and Sam Rosenwein, "The Smith Act Prosecutions," *Nation* 177 (Dec. 12, 1953): 485–86; Sidney Hook, "Does the Smith Act Threaten Our Liberties?" *Commentary* 15 (Jan. 1953): 63–73; Michal R. Belknap, ed., *American Political Trials* (Westport, Conn., 1981), pp. 233–62.

33 *Alexandria Gazette*, July 31, Aug. 2, Nov. 1, 3, 1948; *Virginia Star*, July 29, Aug. 5, Oct. 28, Nov. 4, 1948; HWS to William M. Tuck, Aug. 4, 1948, Tuck Papers; *Virginia Star*, Oct. 14, 1948.

34 State Board of Elections, *Statement of the Vote, 1944 Election*; ibid., *1946 Election*.

35   John W. McCormack to Sam Rayburn, Nov. 7, 1948, Rayburn to Jere Cooper, Nov. 15, Nov. 22, 1948, Rayburn to John D. Dingell, Nov. 15, 1948, Wright Patman to Rayburn, Nov. 17, 1948, Cooper to Rayburn, Nov. 19, 1948, Adolph J. Sabath to Rayburn, Nov. 29, 1948, Sam Rayburn Library, Bonham, Tex.; *Congressional Quarterly Almanac*, 1948, p. 31; Van Hollen, "House Committee on Rules," pp. 247–54.

36   HWS to Rayburn, Nov. 29, 1948, William M. Colmer to Rayburn, Nov. 30, 1948, Rayburn Library; *New York Times*, Dec. 30, 1948; Van Hollen, "House Committee on Rules," p. 248.

37   Van Hollen, "House Committee on Rules," pp. 254–67; *Congressional Record*, Jan. 5, 1949, pp. A41–42, Jan. 2, 1951, pp. A8012–14; *Washington Post*, Jan. 5, 1949; interview with Abernethy.

38   *St. Louis Post-Dispatch*, Jan. 4, 1949; *Washington Post*, Jan. 4, 1949; *New York Times*, Jan. 4, 1949; *Chicago Sun-Times*, Jan. 4, 1949.

39   *Congressional Record*, Jan. 6, 1950, p. 84.

40   Ibid.

41   Ibid., Feb. 1, 1950, pp. 1322–23.

42   Interview with Abbitt.

43   William C. Berman, *The Politics of Civil Rights in the Truman Administration* (Columbus, Ohio, 1970), pp. 6–7, 24–28, 32–33, 35–37, 158, 161, 168–71; Louis C. Kesselman, "The Fair Employment Practice Movement in Perspective," *Journal of Negro History* 31 (Jan. 1946): 30–46; *Congressional Quarterly Almanac*, 1949, p. 455; Truman to A. Philip Randolph, Feb. 6, 1946, Truman Library.

44   *Congressional Record*, Feb. 22, 1950, pp. 2165–2254; Van Hollen, "House Committee on Rules," pp. 269–79; *Congressional Quarterly Almanac*, 1950, p. 31.

45   *Congressional Record*, May 2, 1951, pp. 4734–35; interview with Abernethy; *Washington Post*, Aug. 19, 1958.

46   *Richmond Times-Dispatch*, Nov. 20, 1951; *Christian Science Monitor*, Dec. 14, 1951; interview with Tonahill; CBS, "Keeper of the Rules," pp. 27–28; HWS to Mrs. Robert H. Smith, Dec. 28, 1951, HWS to Lois Van Arsdel, Jan. 30, 1952, Smith Papers.

47   *Charlottesville Daily Progress*, Dec. 5, 1951; John W. Williams to HWS, Dec. 5, 1951, Smith Papers; *Lynchburg News*, Dec. 8, 1951.

48   HWS to Blake T. Newton, March 21, 1952, and HWS press release, March 27, 1952, Smith Papers; *Congressional Record*, May 16, 1952, pp. A3022–23. See also Peter Ros Henriques, "John S. Battle and Virginia Politics: 1948–1953" (Ph.D. diss., Univ. of Va., 1971), pp. 170–74.

49   HWS to D. M. Chichester, March 1, 1952, HWS to Hugh B. Marsh, March 17, 1952, HWS to B. C. Garrett, Jr., March 18, 1952, Smith Papers;

Charlottesville Daily Progress, April 2, 1952; *Richmond Times-Dispatch*, May 11, 1952; *Congressional Record*, May 16, 1952, p. A3155.

50   HWS to Agnes McGee, Sept. 23, 1952, HWS to Charles M. Waite, Sept. 23, 1952, A. Willis Robertson to HWS, Oct. 8, 1952, HWS to Robertson, Oct. 14, 1952, HWS to E. B. Pendleton, Jr., Oct. 23, 1952, Smith Papers.

51   Homer G. Richey broadcast no. 87, Richey collection, Charlottesville, Va.; Calvin H. Haley to Conway Clarke, Oct. 29, Nov. 28, 1952, Smith Papers.

52   State Board of Elections, *Statement of the Vote, 1952 Election;* Calvin H. Haley to HWS, Nov. 7, 1952, Smith Papers; *Congressional Record*, Jan. 3, 1953, p. 12.

53   *Congressional Record*, March 9, 1953, pp. 1760–62.

54   Ibid., pp. 1764–90, March 10, 1953, pp. 1829–30, March 11–12, 18, 1959, pp. 3890, 4038–39, 4393; *Congressional Quarterly Almanac*, 1953, pp. 301–4.

Chapter 6   *Chairman of the Rules Committee:*
The Eisenhower Years

1   *Fredericksburg Free Lance-Star*, Oct. 9, 13, 14, 21, 23, 27, 29, 30, Nov. 3, 1954; State Board of Elections, *Statement of the Vote, 1954 Election.*

2   *Washington Post*, Feb. 6, 1955; Virginia Waller Davis, "Howard W. Smith of Virginia," *Commonwealth* 22 (Aug. 1955): 11–14, 17; James L. Sundquist, *Politics and Policy: The Eisenhower, Kennedy, and Johnson Years* (Washington, D.C., 1968), pp. 169, 172, 183–87, 229–30.

3   Wicker, *JFK and LBJ*, pp. 44, 55, 57.

4   Anthony Champagne, *Congressman Sam Rayburn* (New Brunswick, N.J., 1984), esp. pp. 35–39, 52–56, 137–67.

5   "Who Rules the House?" *New Republic* 139 (Dec. 15, 1958): 5; *Washington Post*, Feb. 6, 1955; Robert Bendiner, *Obstacle Course in Capitol Hill* (New York, 1964), pp. 147–48; Norman C. Thomas and Karl A. Lamb, *Congress: Politics and Practice* (New York, 1964), p. 113; Roger H. Davidson et al., *Congress in Crisis: Politics and Congressional Reform* (Belmont, Calif., 1966), p. 127; Richard Bolling, *House Out of Order* (New York, 1965), pp. 195–200; Robinson, *House Rules Committee*, pp. 1–50; Galloway, *History of the House of Representatives*, pp. 52–55, 58–62.

6   Robinson, *House Rules Committee*, pp. 84–88; U.S. Congress, House of Representatives, *A History of the Committee on Rules, 1789–1981* (Washington, D.C., 1983), p. 167.

7   Robinson, *House Rules Committee*, pp. 1–21; "Darkened Victory," *Time* 77 (Feb. 10, 1961): 13; Joseph S. Clark, *Congress: The Sapless Branch* (New York, 1964), p. 134.

8 U.S. Congress, House of Representatives, *Committee on Rules*, pp. 133–77; Mark Green, *Who Runs Congress?* (New York, 1979), p. 68.

9 U.S. Congress, House of Representatives, *Committee on Rules*, pp. 168–69.

10 Ibid., p. 168; interviews with Elliott and Bolling; *Congressional Record*, June 20, 1945; CBS, "Keeper of the Rules," p. 5.

11 *Washington Post*, July 6, 1966; Virginia and Landon Mitchell, interview, Fort Lauderdale, Fla., Jan. 13, 1979; interviews with Carruthers, Poage, Albert, and Bolling.

12 Interview with Albert; *Washington Post*, Aug. 19,1958.

13 Interviews with Tonahill and Virginia Mitchell; Davis, "Howard W. Smith of Virginia," pp. 11–14.

14 Interviews with Carruthers, the Mitchells, and Abbitt; Hanno W. Kirk, interview, Denton, Tex., Sept. 22, 1983; David M. Olson, interview, Charleston, S.C., March 30, 1984; *We, the People: The Story of the United States Capitol* (Washington, D.C., 1965), pp. 130–31; T. M. Carruthers to William M. Colmer, Jan. 20, March 12, 1956, William M. Colmer Papers, William D. McCain Graduate Library, University of Southern Mississippi, Hattiesburg.

15 Interviews with Tonahill, Carruthers, Abbitt, and the Mitchells.

16 Interviews with Carruthers, Albert, Tonahill, and Dudley; Elliott to author, Jan. 23, 1984; Roger Mudd, telephone interview, April 18, 1984.

17 Interviews with Carruthers and Bolling.

18 Interview with Carruthers; Paul Muse, interview, Dumfries, Va., Nov. 21, 1975.

19 *Washington Post*, Feb. 6,1955.

20 HWS speech, Feb. 22, 1955, Smith Papers; *Washington Report*, March 4, 1955; Davis, "Star Performer," p. 13.

21 *Congressional Record*, Jan. 6, 1955, p. 31; *Washington Bulletin*, Feb. 15, 1955; *Rappahannock Times* (Tappahannock), April 28, 1955; *Washington Post*, April 9, 1956.

22 Belknap, *Cold War Political Justice*, pp. 214–82.

23 *Washington Post*, Jan. 7, 1955; *Congressional Quarterly Almanac*, 1955, p. 254.

24 HWS to F. E. Paulett, June 15, 1955, Byrd to HWS, July 6, 1955, Smith Papers; *Washington Post*, July 5, 1955; *Congressional Record*, July 29, 1955, pp. 12104–45.

25 *Congressional Record*, July 29, 1955, pp. 12105–6; *Congressional Quarterly Almanac*, 1955, p. 257.

26 Benjamin Muse, *Virginia's Massive Resistance* (Gloucester, Mass., 1969), pp. 11–15.

27   Ibid., pp. 1–5.

28   Robbins L. Gates, *The Making of Massive Resistance: Virginia's Politics of Public School Desegregation, 1954–1956* (Chapel Hill, N.C., 1964), pp. 28–61; Kathleen A. Murphy, "Sarah Patton Boyle and the Crusade against Virginia's Massive Resistance" (M.A. thesis, Univ. of Va., 1983); Colgate W. Darden, Jr., to Marian Gattermann, Sept. 6, 1956, Ernest W. Goodrich to Darden, June 13, 1957, Darden to Goodrich, June 17, 1957, Darden to Walter C. Rawls, Aug. 6, 1958, President's Papers, University Archives, University of Virginia.

29   James W. Ely, Jr., *The Crisis of Conservative Virginia: The Byrd Organization and the Politics of Massive Resistance* (Knoxville, Tenn., 1976), pp. 43–44; Gates, *Massive Resistance*, p. 37.

30   HWS to Joseph A. Downing, Feb. 5, 1957, Smith Papers.

31   Smith, *Our Paternal Hearth*, pp. 71–81.

32   Ibid., p. 70; CBS, "Keeper of the Rules," pp. 19–21; interviews with Dudley, Tonahill, and Chilton.

33   *Washington Post*, April 9, 1956; *Newport News Daily Press*, April 26, 1956; *Baltimore Sun*, May 11, 1956; *Lynchburg News*, May 12, 1956; *Roanoke Times*, May 14, 1956; HWS to A. Willis Robertson, Feb. 7, 1956, Robertson to HWS, Feb. 14, 1956, Robertson Papers.

34   *Washington Post*, April 3, 9, 1956; *Labor* (New York), April 28, 1956; *Congressional Quarterly Almanac*, 1956, pp. 586–87; *Congressional Record*, July 3, 1956, p. 11787.

35   A. Willis Robertson to Thomas B. Stanley, Feb. 13, 1956, Thomas B. Stanley Papers, Virginia State Library, Richmond; interview with Elliott; William Colmer to H. L. Hunnicut, March 5, 1956, Colmer Papers.

36   *Congressional Record*, March 12, 1956, pp. 4459–64, 4514–16; *Congressional Quarterly Almanac*, 1956, pp. 416–17; Muse, *Virginia's Massive Resistance*, p. 27. See also Numan V. Bartley, *The Rise of Massive Resistance: Race and Politics in the South during the 1950s* (Baton Rouge, 1969).

37   Champagne, *Sam Rayburn*, pp. 148–51; Bolling, *House Out of Order*, pp. 174–94.

38   *Washington Post*, March 13, 1956; *New York Times*, March 13, 1956.

39   Harvard Sitkoff, *The Struggle for Black Equality, 1954–1980* (New York, 1981), pp. 3–68; J. Mills Thornton III, "Challenge and Response in the Montgomery Bus Boycott of 1955–1956," *Alabama Review* 33 (July 1980): 163–235.

40   *Congressional Quarterly Almanac*, 1956, pp. 459–60; Steven F. Lawson, *Black Ballots: Voting Rights in the South, 1944–1969* (New York, 1976), pp. 140–71.

41   *Congressional Quarterly Almanac*, 1956, pp. 459–60.

42   *Congressional Quarterly Almanac*, 1956, p. 462; interview with Bolling; Crawley, *Bill Tuck*, pp. 250–54.

43   Interview with Bolling; A. Sydney Herlong, Jr., telephone interview, Sept. 11, 1983.

44   Interviews with Herlong, Bolling, Halleck, and Elliott; Peabody, *Leadership in Congress*, pp. 104–8; Elliott to author, Jan. 23, 1984.

45   Interviews with Herlong, Elliott, and Bolling; *Congressional Quarterly Almanac*, 1956, p. 461.

46   Interviews with Virginia Mitchell and Abernethy.

47   *Congressional Quarterly Almanac*, 1956, pp. 461, 463–64.

48   J. Segar Gravatt to HWS, Aug. 9, 1956, HWS to Thomas B. Stanley, Aug. 21, 1956, Stanley Papers; Muse, *Virginia's Massive Resistance*, pp. 58–62; Ely, *Crisis of Conservative Virginia*, p. 175; Bob Smith, *They Closed Their Schools: Prince Edward County, 1951–1964* (Chapel Hill, N.C., 1965).

49   Ely, *Crisis of Conservative Virginia*, pp. 38–39, 45–46, 56–58, 88, 113–16, 130–31, 157–59, 166–67, 199–200; HWS to Thomas B. Stanley, Aug. 22, 1956, Stanley Papers.

50   HWS to Harry F. Byrd, Oct. 2, 1956, Byrd to HWS, Oct. 4, 1956, Byrd Papers, University of Virginia Library.

51   *Northern Neck News* (Warsaw), July 12, 1956; *Loudoun Times-Mirror*, Aug. 23, Oct. 4, 1956; *Richmond Times-Dispatch*, Sept. 27, 1956; *Fredericksburg Free Lance-Star*, Oct. 29, 1956; *Charlottesville Daily Progress*, Nov. 6, 1956; HWS to W. Tayloe Murphy, July 7, 1956, HWS campaign circular, Sept. 15, 1956, HWS to Horace B. Clay, Sept. 25, 1956, HWS to Lee Paschall, Oct. 10, 1956, HWS to Hobert E. Doyle, Oct. 22, 1956, Smith Papers; State Board of Elections, *Statement of the Vote, 1956 Election*.

52   *Congressional Quarterly Almanac*, 1957, pp. 143, 554–55, 808.

53   Ibid., 553–69; interviews with Abbitt, Albert, and Carruthers; HWS to Karlton L. Monroe, March 13, 1957, HWS to Thomas B. Stanley, Jan. 22, 1957, J. Lindsay Almond, Jr., to Sam Rayburn, Jan. 24, 1957, HWS to C. O'Conor Goolrick, June 24, 1957, Smith Papers; Clark, *Congress: The Sapless Branch*, p. 133; Crawley, *Bill Tuck*, p. 232.

54   *Washington Post*, June 7, 1957; Lawson, *Black Ballots*, pp. 171–202; Sundquist, *Politics and Policy*, pp. 229n, 230n; Steinberg, *Rayburn*, pp. 312–13; Bolling, *House Out of Order*, p. 193; *Congressional Quarterly Almanac*, 1957, pp. 556–57.

55   *Washington Post*, June 20, 1957; *Congressional Quarterly Almanac*, 1957, pp. 558–59; *Congressional Record*, June 18, 1957, p. 9518; interview with Bolling; HWS to Burton A. Prince, June 18, 1957, HWS to William H. White, June 18, 1957, HWS to John A. Jamison, Aug. 21, 1957, Smith Papers; HWS to A. Willis Robertson, June 18, 1957, Robertson to HWS, June 19, 1957, Robertson Papers.

56   *Washington Post*, Aug. 18, 1957; Steinberg, *Rayburn*, p. 313; Bolling, *House Out of Order*, p. 197. Allen's remark is often attributed to Speaker Rayburn.

57   Interview with Carruthers; CBS, "Keeper of the Rules," pp. 12–13.

58   Interview with Carruthers.

59   *Congressional Quarterly Almanac*, 1957, pp. 553, 568–69; interview with Bolling.

60   HWS to F. D. G. Ribble, Sept. 27, 1957, Ribble to HWS, Sept. 30, 1957, Smith Papers.

61   HWS address, Jan. 25, 1958, Smith Papers.

62   Interview with Bolling; Gates, *Massive Resistance*, pp. 50, 151.

63   *Richmond Times-Dispatch*, Feb. 7, 1959; *Loudoun Times-Mirror*, Feb. 19, 1959; *Orange Review*, Feb. 19, 1959; *Washington Star*, March 6, 1959; HWS to Mrs. James P. Pollard, Feb. 12, 1959, HWS to Louise T. Campbell, Feb. 20, 1959, HWS to Conrad Harrison Goodwin, March 26, 1959, D. B. Marshall to HWS, May 8, 1959, HWS to D. B. Marshall, May 13, 1959, Smith Papers.

64   Ely, *Crisis of Conservative Virginia*, pp. 30–164; U.S. Department of Commerce, Bureau of the Census, *United States Census of Population: 1970*, 1, pt. 48, "Characteristics of the Population" (Washington, D.C., 1973), pp. 48–207.

65   "Down with the Dole," *Time* 71 (May 12, 1958): 18–19; *Washington Star*, May 2, 1958; *Congressional Quarterly Almanac*, 1958, pp. 153–56.

66   "Down with the Dole," *Time* 71 (May 12, 1958): 18; *Congressional Record*, April 23, 30, May 1, 1958, pp. 7151, 7747, 7869–911; *Congressional Quarterly Almanac*, 1958, pp. 154–56.

67   *Washington Post*, May 6, 1958; *Congressional Quarterly Almanac*, 1958, pp. 281–85.

68   *Congressional Record*, May 21, 22, 1958, pp. 9219–32, 9339–68; *Congressional Quarterly Almanac*, 1958, pp. 283–85.

69   *Richmond Times-Dispatch*, Oct. 7, 1958; Raymond Moley, "Smith of Virginia," *Newsweek* 52 (Aug. 25, 1958): 80; *Congressional Quarterly Almanac*, 1958, p. 290.

70   *Richmond News Leader*, June 20, 1958; *Washington Post*, Sept. 7, 1958; *Congressional Quarterly Almanac*, 1958, pp. 289–91; HWS to Lawrence Dumas, Jr., Jan. 2, 1959, Smith Papers; *Congressional Record*, July 15, 17, 30, 1958, pp. 13850, 14140–41, 14161.

71   *Congressional Record*, Aug. 21, 1958, pp. 18917–28; *Congressional Quarterly Almanac*, 1958, p. 289; *Washington Post*, Sept. 7, 1958; *Columbia* [S.C.] *Record*, Aug. 23, 1958; A. Willis Robertson to HWS, Aug. 9, 1958, Robertson Papers.

72   *Washington Post*, Nov. 24, Dec. 8, 19, 1958; James L. Sundquist, *The Decline and Resurgence of Congress* (Washington, D.C., 1981), pp. 184–85; *Richmond Times-Dispatch*, Dec. 14, 1958; "Who Rules the House?" *New Republic* 139 (Dec. 15, 1958): 5.

73   *Congressional Quarterly Almanac*, 1958, pp. 712–36; HWS to Mrs. S. Campbell Legard, March 3, 1959, Smith Papers.

74   *Washington Post*, April 21, 1959; *Congressional Quarterly Almanac*, 1959, pp. 245–56; John W. McCormack to HWS, March 26, 1959, Smith Papers; interviews with Bolling and Elliott.

75   Interview with Elliott; H. G. Dulaney and Edward H. Phillips, eds., *"Speak, Mr. Speaker"* (Bonham, Tex., 1978), p. 428.

76   *Washington Post*, April 21, 1959; *Washington Star*, Dec. 20, 1959; Steinberg, *Rayburn*, pp. 315–18.

77   *Washington Daily News*, May 4, 1959; *Washington Post*, May 15, 1959; *Congressional Quarterly Almanac*, 1959, pp. 245–56, 360–61, 372–73.

78   *Congressional Quarterly Almanac*, 1959, p. 251; *Washington Post*, May 8, 1959; *Richmond Times-Dispatch*, May 18, 1959.

79   *Congressional Quarterly Almanac*, 1959, p. 251; *Congressional Record*, May 20, 21, July 7, Aug. 12, Sept. 10, 14, 1959, pp. 8636–74, 8852, 12788–89, 15609–10, 18983–95, 19690; HWS to Richard L. Nunley, May 20, 1959, HWS to J. Clifford Miller, Jr., May 27, 1959, Smith Papers.

80   Doris B. McLaughlin and Anita W. Schoomaker, *The Landrum-Griffin Act and Union Democracy* (Ann Arbor, Mich., 1979); Janice R. Bellace and Alan D. Berkowitz, *The Landrum-Griffin Act: Twenty Years of Federal Protection of Union Members' Rights* (Philadelphia, 1979); *Washington Post*, Aug. 12, 1959; *Washington Daily News*, Aug. 13, 1959; *Congressional Quarterly Almanac*, 1959, pp. 156–72, 382–83; Bolling, *House Out of Order*, pp. 156–73; William Colmer to James B. Carey, Sept. 1, 1959, Colmer Papers; McAdams, *Power and Politics*, pp. 113–73.

81   *Washington Daily News*, Aug. 13, 1959; McAdams, *Power and Politics*, pp. 171–266; *Wall Street Journal*, Sept. 16, 1959; *Congressional Record*, Aug. 14, 1959, pp. 15882–92.

82   McLaughlin and Schoomaker, *Landrum-Griffin Act*, pp. 178–87.

83   *Washington Post*, Aug. 23, 1959; Davidson, *Congress in Crisis*, pp. 129–42.

84   *Washington Post*, Dec. 26, 1959; *Washington Star*, Dec. 20, 1959; Brady and Bullock, "Coalition Politics," p. 188; Bendiner, *Obstacle Course on Capitol Hill*, pp. 172–73; Bolling, *House Out of Order*, pp. 54–57; Wicker, *JFK and LBJ*, p. 52.

85   Interview with Bolling; Peabody, *Leadership in Congress*, p. 85.

86   *Washington Post*, Jan. 7, 1960; *Washington Star*, Jan. 28, 1960; *Congressional Quarterly Almanac*, 1960, pp. 185–207; HWS speech to the Rules Committee and P. S. Purcell to HWS, Feb. 28, 1960, Smith Papers.

87   *Congressional Quarterly Almanac*, 1960, pp. 190, 199, 434–35; *Washington Post*, Jan. 7, 1960.

88   *Congressional Record,* March 14, 1960, pp. 5452–53.

89   Ibid., March 24, 1960, p. 6512; *New York Times,* March 16, 1960; *Washington Star,* March 20, 1960; HWS to D. R. Matthews, March 28, 1960, HWS to J. D. Edwards, April 11, 1960, Smith Papers.

90   *Congressional Quarterly Almanac,* 1960, pp. 199–200; Byrd press release, April 7, 1960, Smith Papers.

91   *Congressional Quarterly Almanac,* 1960, pp. 232–37; CBS, "Keeper of the Rules," p. 25.

92   *Congressional Quarterly Almanac,* 1960, pp. 232–37.

93   "Democratic Debacle," *Time* 76 (Sept. 5, 1960): 12.

94   Ibid.; *Washington Post,* June 26, 1959; CBS, "Keeper of the Rules," pp. 22, 26; Frank Thompson, Jr., press release, July 2, 1960, Colmer Papers.

Chapter 7   *Chairman of the Rules Committee: The Kennedy and Johnson Years*

1   John A. Blatnik, interview by Joseph E. O'Connor, Feb. 4, 1966, John F. Kennedy Library, Boston; Wicker, *JFK and LBJ,* p. 72; Steinberg, *Rayburn,* pp. 335–38; *New York Times,* Feb. 1, 1961; *Congressional Quarterly Almanac,* 1961, pp. 402–7, 508–9; MacNeil, *Forge of Democracy,* pp. 412–47; Charles O. Jones, "Joseph G. Cannon and Howard W. Smith: An Essay on the Limits of Leadership in the House of Representatives," *Journal of Politics* 30 (Aug. 1968): 617–46; U.S. Congress, House of Representatives, *Committee on Rules,* p. 186; Richard B. Cheney and Lynne V. Cheney, *Kings of the Hill: Power and Personality in the House of Representatives* (New York, 1983), pp. 181–89.

2   William M. Colmer to D. R. Matthews, George W. Andrews, Robert Sikes, and John Bell Williams, all Dec. 5, 1960, Robert Sikes to Colmer, Dec. 7, 1960, Overton Brooks to Colmer, Dec. 9, 1960, Harry F. Byrd to Colmer, Dec. 14, 1960, Colmer Papers.

3   Steinberg, *Rayburn,* pp. 315–18; *Washington Report,* Dec. 16, 1961; Clark, *Congress: The Sapless Branch,* p. 132; interview with Elliott.

4   Interviews with Bolling and Elliott; Wicker, *JFK and LBJ,* pp. 29–39; U.S. Congress, House of Representatives, *Committee on Rules,* p. 168; Peabody, *Leadership in Congress,* p. 46; CBS, "The Keeper of the Rules," pp. 30–31; Bolling, *House Out of Order,* pp. 210–20; Robinson, *House Rules Committee,* pp. 71–80; Cheney and Cheney, *Kings of the Hill,* p. 186; Bendiner, *Obstacle Course on Capitol Hill,* pp. 174–80; Daniel M. Berman, *In Congress Assembled* (New York, 1964), p. 222n.

5   *Congressional Quarterly Almanac,* 1961, pp. 404–5; Bolling, *House Out of Order,* pp. 195–220; interview with Elliott; Lawrence F. O'Brien, *No Final Victories* (Garden City, N.Y., 1974), pp. 104–5.

6   *Congressional Quarterly Almanac,* 1961, pp. 404–5; interviews with Bolling and Elliott; Wicker, *JFK and LBJ,* p. 69; Cheney and Cheney, *Kings*

of the Hill, p. 184; CBS, "Keeper of the Rules," pp. 3, 31; O'Brien, *No Final Victories*, 105–7; "Darkened Victory," *Time* 77 (Feb. 10, 1961): 14.

7   *Congressional Record*, Jan. 31, 1961, pp. 1573–90; interviews with Carruthers and Elliott; *Washington Post*, Feb. 1, 1961; "Darkened Victory," *Time* 77 (Feb. 10, 1961): 11–14; Wicker, *JFK and LBJ*, p. 70.

8   "Darkened Victory," *Time* 77 (Feb. 10, 1961): 11–14; *Washington Post*, Feb. 1, 1961; Wicker, *JFK and LBJ*, pp. 31–32.

9   Interview with Elliott; *New York Times*, Feb. 14, 1961.

10   *Congressional Quarterly Almanac*, 1961, p. 407; *Washington Post*, Feb. 22, 23, 1961; Steinberg, *Rayburn*, p. 340; Donald C. Lord, *John F. Kennedy: The Politics of Confrontation and Conciliation* (New York, 1977), pp. 98–102.

11   Henry H. Wilson, Jr., to Kenneth O'Donnell, May 11, 1961, Wilson to Lawrence O'Brien, June 23, 1961, Kennedy Library; interview with Bryan.

12   Interviews with Elliott and Bolling; Walter Kravitz, "The Influence of the House Rules Committee on Legislation in the 87th Congress," in *Congressional Reform: Problems and Prospects*, ed. Joseph S. Clark (New York, 1965), pp. 127–37; U.S. Congress, House of Representatives, *Committee on Rules*, p. 194.

13   *Congressional Quarterly Almanac*, 1961, pp. 406–7, 1963, p. 370; Robert L. Peabody and Nelson W. Polsby, *New Perspectives on the House of Representatives* (Chicago, 1963), pp. 151–54; Kravitz, "The Influence of the House Rules Committee on Legislation in the 87th Congress," pp. 127–37; MacNeil, *Forge of Democracy*, pp. 447–48; Sundquist, *Decline and Resurgence of Congress*, p. 374; interview with Albert.

14   Interview with Elliott.

15   Berman, *In Congress Assembled*, pp. 347–48; American Enterprise Institute, "Backdoor Spending," pp. 1–5, 12, 15–26, undated but probably late 1967 or early 1968, Smith Papers; *Congressional Quarterly Almanac*, 1961, pp. 159–61.

16   American Enterprise Institute, "Backdoor Spending," pp. 13–18; *Congressional Record*, April 26, June 8, 26, 1961, pp. 6722–23, 9770–72, 11188–89, 11191.

17   Claude Desautels to Lawrence F. O'Brien, Jan. 8, 1962, Kennedy Library; HWS file memorandum, Jan. 11, 1962, in the possession of Smith's secretary, Virginia Mitchell, Fort Lauderdale, Fla.

18   John F. Kennedy to HWS, Jan. 10, 1962, Kennedy to HWS, probably March 6, 1962, Kennedy Library.

19   Claude Desautels to Lawrence F. O'Brien, April 11, 1962, Kennedy Library; Clark, *Congress: The Sapless Branch*, p. 118.

20   Carl D. Perkins to John W. McCormack, July 13, 1962, Perkins to Richard Bolling, July 13, 1962, McCormack to Perkins, July 21, 1962, John

W. McCormack Papers, Mugar Memorial Library, Boston University, Boston; Perkins to Lawrence F. O'Brien, Aug. 6, 1962, Kennedy Library; *Congressional Quarterly Almanac*, 1962, pp. 228–29; *Congressional Record*, March 20, July 30, Aug. 20, 1962, pp. 4598, 14958, 16957.

21   *Washington Post*, Dec. 18, 1962.

22   *Congressional Record*, Jan. 9, 1963, pp. 18–19; *Washington Star*, Jan. 8, 1962.

23   *Congressional Record*, Jan. 9, 1963, pp. 19–22; *Congressional Quarterly Almanac*, 1963, pp. 369–72; Peabody and Polsby, *New Perspectives*, pp. 154–57; HWS to Joe H. Tonahill, Jan. 10, 1963, Tonahill collection; interview with Elliott; *Washington Post*, Dec. 30, 1962; William Colmer to Jessie Maude Johnson, Jan. 10, 1963, Colmer Papers.

24   *Washington Post*, March 22, 1963; *Congressional Record*, April 23, 1963, pp. 6803–45; *Congressional Quarterly Almanac*, 1963, pp. 216–19.

25   *Washington Post*, March 22, 1963; HWS to John F. Kennedy, March 22, 1963, Kennedy Library.

26   John F. Kennedy to HWS, April 4, 1963, Kennedy Library; *Congressional Quarterly Almanac*, 1963, pp. 218–21; *Congressional Record*, April 23, 24, Sept. 24, 1963, pp. 6805, 6899–900, 17900.

27   *Congressional Quarterly Almanac*, 1964, pp. 334–48; Sundquist, *Politics and Policy*, pp. 159–64; Jim Heath, *Decade of Disillusionment: The Kennedy-Johnson Years* (Bloomington, Ind., 1975), pp. 69–73, 109–17, 145, 149–50, 153, 159, 161, 167–68; Carl M. Brauer, *John F. Kennedy and the Second Reconstruction* (New York, 1977), pp. 230–320; Merle Miller, *Lyndon: An Oral Biography* (New York, 1980), pp. 365–72; Lawson, *Black Ballots*, pp. 296–97; Lord, *Politics of Confrontation*, pp. 152–68.

28   *New York Times Magazine*, Jan. 12, 1964, pp. 12, 85; *Congressional Quarterly Almanac*, 1964, p. 343.

29   *New York Times Magazine*, Jan. 12, 1964, p. 85; *Congressional Quarterly Almanac*, 1964, pp. 350–51.

30   Charles and Barbara Whalen, *The Longest Debate: A Legislative History of the 1964 Civil Rights Act* (Cabin John, Md., 1985), pp. 90–99.

31   Ibid., pp. 97–98; *Washington Post*, Jan. 22, 23, 1964.

32   National Broadcasting Corporation, *Meet the Press* (transcript), 8, no. 2 (Jan. 26, 1964): 1–9.

33   *Congressional Quarterly Almanac*, 1964, p. 344; *Washington Post*, Jan. 31, 1964; Whalen, *The Longest Debate*, p. 99.

34   *Congressional Record*, Feb. 1, 3, 1964, pp. 1623–24, 1682–83, 1697, 1704; *Congressional Quarterly Almanac*, 1964, p. 345.

35   *Congressional Record*, Feb. 4, 1964, pp. 1932–33; *Congressional Quarterly Almanac*, 1964, p. 350.

36   Patricia G. Zelman, *Women, Work, and National Policy: The Kennedy-Johnson Years* (Ann Arbor, Mich., 1982), pp. 60–62; U.S. Congress, House of Representatives, *Hearings on H.R. 7152 before the Committee on Rules* (Washington, D.C., 1964); Carl M. Brauer, "Women Activists, Southern Conservatives, and the Prohibition of Sex Discrimination in Title VII of the 1964 Civil Rights Act," *Journal of Southern History* 49 (Feb. 1983): 37–56; interviews with Herlong, Carruthers, Abernethy, and Elliott; *New York Times Magazine*, Jan. 12, 1964, pp. 12, 85. See also Emily George, *Martha W. Griffiths* (Washington, D.C., 1982), pp. 149–52, which credits Griffiths with the amendment's authorship, stating that the Michigan representative shrewdly stepped aside to let the more influential Smith propose it.

37   Zelman, *Women, Work, and National Policy*, pp. 62–64.

38   Caroline Bird, *Born Female: The High Cost of Keeping Women Down* (New York, 1968), pp. 1–14; *Congressional Record*, Feb. 8, 1964, pp. 2577–84; *Minneapolis Tribune*, Jan. 8, 1984.

39   *Congressional Record*, Feb. 8, 1964, pp. 2577–84; *Congressional Quarterly Almanac*, 1964, p. 348.

40   *Congressional Record*, Feb. 8, 1964, pp. 2577–84; *Minneapolis Tribune*, Jan. 8, 1984; Brauer, "Women Activists," p. 51; interview with Elliott; Bird, *Born Female*, p. 9.

41   *Congressional Record*, Feb. 10, 1964, pp. 2708–15; *Congressional Quarterly Almanac*, 1964, p. 352.

42   *Congressional Record*, Feb. 10, 1964, pp. 2790–91, 2804–5.

43   Ibid., p. 2804.

44   Walter Jenkins to Lyndon B. Johnson, April 21, 1964, Lawrence F. O'Brien to Johnson, June 18, 1964, Lyndon B. Johnson Library, Austin, Tex.

45   *Washington Post*, June 23, 25, July 1, 1964; U.S. Congress, House of Representatives, *Committee on Rules*, p. 197; *Congressional Quarterly Almanac*, 1964, pp. 368–69, 377; Ray Madden, B. F. Sisk, and John Young to HWS, June 22, 1964, Colmer Papers.

46   *Congressional Record*, July 2, 1964, pp. 15869–97; *Washington Post*, July 3, 1964.

47   Richard Polenberg, *One Nation Divisible: Class, Race, and Ethnicity in the United States since 1938* (New York, 1980), p. 240; J. Harvie Wilkinson III, *From Brown to Bakke: The Supreme Court and School Integration, 1954–1978* (New York, 1979), pp. 102–8; James Gilbert, *Another Chance: Postwar America, 1945–1968* (New York, 1981), pp. 214–15.

48   Congressional Quarterly, *Representation and Apportionment* (Washington, D.C., 1966), pp. 10–37.

49   Ralph Eisenberg, "Legislative Apportionment: How Representative Is Virginia's Present System?," *University of Virginia News Letter* 37 (April 15, 1961): 29–32; Robert B. McKay, *Reapportionment: The Law and Politics of*

Equal Representation (Hartford, 1965), pp. 112–13, 438–43; *Reapportionment of the State for Representation: Report to the Governor and the General Assembly of Virginia* (Richmond, 1961); Congressional Quarterly, *Congressional Redistricting: Impact of the 1960 Census* (Washington, D.C., 1962), pp. 1685–86.

50 *Congressional Record*, Aug. 19, 1964, pp. 20212–301.

51 Ibid., Aug. 19, 31, 1964, pp. 20212–301, 21070–71; U.S. Congress, House of Representatives, *Committee on Rules*, p. 197.

52 *Richmond Times-Dispatch*, Feb. 9, 1964; *Fredericksburg Free Lance-Star*, April 19, 1964; *Washington Star*, July 19, 1964; *Loudoun Times-Mirror*, July 23, 1964; *Charlottesville Daily Progress*, Sept. 18, 1964.

53 *Orange Review*, Oct. 8, 1964; *Richmond Times-Dispatch*, Oct. 22, 1964; *Fredericksburg Free Lance-Star*, Oct. 11, 24, 1966; *Washington Post*, Oct. 11, 31, 1964; *Manassas Journal-Messenger*, Oct. 22, 1964; *Central Virginian*, Oct. 15, 1964; State Board of Elections, *Statement of the Vote*, 1952 [–1964] *Election*.

54 HWS to Violett Smith Tonahill, Dec. 23, 1964, Tonahill collection; *Congressional Quarterly Almanac*, 1964, p. 1007.

55 *Congressional Record*, March 8, 24, 1965, pp. 4369–70, 5727–28; *Washington Post*, March 23, 1965; *Congressional Quarterly Almanac*, 1965, pp. 275–93.

56 *Congressional Record*, March 24, 1965, pp. 5729–30.

57 Ibid., March 26, 1965, pp. 6129–52; *Congressional Quarterly Almanac*, 1965, pp. 288, 293; *Washington Post*, April 12, 1965.

58 *Congressional Quarterly Almanac*, 1965, p. 538; *Washington Post*, March 16, 1965; Lawson, *Black Ballots*, pp. 278, 308; Sundquist, *Politics and Policy*, pp. 271–75.

59 David J. Garrow, *Protest at Selma: Martin Luther King, Jr., and the Voting Rights Act of 1965* (New Haven, 1978), pp. 31–77; *Congressional Quarterly Almanac*, 1965, pp. 538–40.

60 Garrow, *Protest at Selma*, pp. 78–132.

61 *Congressional Quarterly Almanac*, 1965, pp. 533, 537; Lawson, *Black Ballots*, p. 284.

62 *Congressional Record*, April 13, 1965, pp. 7934–36.

63 Ibid., July 6, 9, 1965, pp. 15641–42, 16285–86; *Congressional Quarterly Almanac*, 1965, pp. 559, 561, 564; *Washington Post*, May 27, July 2, 1965.

64 Garrow, *Protest at Selma*, pp. 179–211; Lawson, *Black Ballots*, p. 331.

65 *Congressional Quarterly Almanac*, 1965, pp. 587–90, 1966, pp. 762–66.

66 Ibid., 1965, pp. 1083–1100.

Chapter 8   *Electoral Upset*

1   John W. Williams to B. C. Garrett, Jr., Aug. 3, 1960, HWS to Edmund T. Dejarnette, Oct. 6, 1960, HWS to Sam Rayburn, Oct. 19, 1960, Blake T. Newton to HWS, Oct. 19, 1960, HWS 1960 campaign circular, HWS to B. C. Garrett, Jr., Oct. 1, 1964, HWS campaign report by T. M. Carruthers, Glenn D. Eberhardt to HWS, Sept. 19, 1964, Smith Papers. For accounts of the Virginia Republican party, see *Richmond Times-Dispatch*, Feb. 9, 1964; Wilkinson, *Harry Byrd and the Changing Face of Virginia Politics*, pp. 199–234; Jim Clay to J. Clifford, Jr., June 1, 1960, Smith Papers; *Rappahannock Record* (Kilmarnock), May 3, 1962; H. Ryland Heflin, interview, Ruby, Va., March 18, 1976.

2   *Washington Star*, Aug. 26, 1960; *Wall Street Journal*, Sept. 30, 1960; *Washington Post*, Oct. 3, 1960, Oct. 31, 1964; Thomas J. Michie to HWS, Oct. 7, 1960, C. K. Rest to HWS, Oct. 22, 1960, Margaret J. Martin to HWS, Oct. 23, 1960, James E. Kern to HWS, Oct. 12, 1960, Joseph L. Savage, Jr., to HWS, Oct. 5, 1960, HWS to Archie Beane, Sept. 21, 1960, copy of the 1960 Spotsylvania County Democratic Committee resolution, Stilson H. Hall to HWS, Oct. 30, 1964, Smith Papers.

3   Interviews with Carruthers and HWS.

4   Monroe Berber, *The Revolution in Civil Rights* (New York, 1968), p. 85; U.S. Department of Commerce, Bureau of the Census, *Congressional District Data Book (Districts of the 88th Congress)* (Washington, D.C., 1963), pp. 512, 519; U.S. Department of Commerce, Bureau of the Census, *United States Census of Population: 1960*, 1, pt. 48, "Characteristics of the Population" (Washington, D.C., 1961), pp. 60–67, 276–83; *Estimates of the Population of the Counties and Cities of Virginia* (Charlottesville, 1966); State Board of Elections, *Estimates of Voter Registration, 1957[-1966]* (Richmond, 1957–66); *Washington Post*, July 13, 31, 1966.

5   Ralph Eisenberg, "Legislative Reapportionment and Congressional Redistricting in Virginia," *Washington and Lee Law Review* 23 (Fall 1966): 295–323; Rocco J. Tresolini and Richard T. Frost, eds., *Cases in American National Government and Politics* (Englewood Cliffs, N.J., 1966), pp. 182–94; *Richmond Times-Dispatch*, May 21, 1961, June 17, 1964, Jan. 19, 1965; *Charlottesville Daily Progress*, Dec. 17, 31, 1962, Feb. 21, 27, 1964, July 22, 1965, Sept. 1, 4, Dec. 1, 1965.

6   Interview with HWS; George C. Rawlings, interviews, Fredericksburg, Va., Oct. 27, Nov. 7, 1975, March 10, 1976, and telephone interview, April 20, 1984; Henry E. Howell, Jr., telephone interview, April 20, 1984; William C. Havard, ed., *The Changing Politics of the South* (Baton Rouge, La., 1972); Malcolm E. Jewell, "The Changing Political Environment of State Government," in *The States and the Metropolis*, ed. Lee S. Greene, Malcolm E. Jewell, and Daniel R. Grant (University, Ala., 1968), pp. 37–49; U.S. Department of Commerce, Bureau of the Census, *Congressional District Data Book (88th Congress)*, pp. 512–21; U.S. Department of Commerce, Bureau of

the Census, *Supplement to Congressional District Data Book, Virginia Districts of the 90th Congress* (Washington, D.C., 1966); *Estimates of the Population of the Counties and Cities of Virginia* (Charlottesville, 1967); Murat W. Williams, "Virginia Politics: Winds of Change," *Virginia Quarterly Review* 42 (Spring 1966): 19; *Washington Post*, July 13, 1966; *Acts of the General Assembly, 1964–1966* (Richmond, 1966), pp. 1–2. After redistricting in 1965, the median income of the Eighth District changed from $4,490 to $5,199, and the median level of education increased from 9 years of school completed to 10.2 years.

7   Rawlings's campaign literature, Smith Papers; interview with Rawlings; Kenneth T. Whitescarver, interview, Fork Union, Va., April 19, 1976; John W. Painter, interview, Fredericksburg, Va., April 1, 1976; interview with Heflin; *Fredericksburg Free Lance-Star*, March 22, July 22, 1963, Jan. 31, Feb. 1, 6, 27, March 9, 13, 1964, March 15, June 19, July 15, 1965.

8   Interview with Rawlings; State Board of Elections, *Statement of the Vote, 1930[-1964] Election*.

9   Ibid.

10   Interviews with Rawlings, Carruthers, HWS, and Abernethy; *Fredericksburg Free Lance-Star*, March 14, 1966; HWS to John Galleher, Feb. 4, 1966, Smith Papers; *Manassas Journal-Messenger*, March 3, 1966.

11   HWS to Julien J. Mason, March 31, 1966, Mason to HWS, March 30, 1966, Stanley A. Owens to HWS, March 26, 1966, Smith Papers; *Richmond Times-Dispatch*, March 27, 1966; *Washington Star*, March 27, 1966.

12   See, for example, 1966 summer editions of the *Ashland Herald-Progress, Central Virginian* (Midland), *King George, Loudoun Times-Mirror, Rappahannock Record, Northern Neck News* (Warsaw), and *Manassas Journal-Messenger*. HWS circular, March 30, 1966, Mrs. Hauford A. Carter to HWS, April 2, 1966, William F. Keys to HWS, April 12, 1966, Norman M. Mills to HWS, April 14, 1966, Smith Papers.

13   Interviews with Muse, Tonahill, and Chilton; W. Ramsdell Chilton to Calvin H. Haley, May 28, 1966, HWS to Hassell B. Leigh, April 18, 1966, Smith Papers.

14   Interview with Muse; *Washington Post*, July 6, 31, 1966; Rawlings's 1966 primary campaign notebooks, Rawlings and Pruitt law office, Fredericksburg, Va.

15   *Fredericksburg Free Lance-Star*, May 10, 1966; *Washington Post*, May 15, 24, 1966; *Charlottesville Daily Progress*, April 30, 1966.

16   *Washington Post*, May 14, 1966; *Washington Star*, May 28, 1966; *Richmond Times-Dispatch*, Oct. 5, 1976; *Fredericksburg Free Lance-Star*, July 10, 1966.

17   HWS to William F. Keys, April 13, 1966, HWS to Norman M. Mills, April 15, 1966, HWS to Fred G. Pollard, April 18, 1966, D. Gardiner Tyler

to HWS, April 25, 1966, HWS to Hassell B. Leigh, April 16, 1966, Smith Papers.

18   *King George*, April 21, 1966; *Washington Post*, May 18, 26, 1966; *Fredericksburg Free Lance-Star*, June 3, 17, 1966; HWS campaign brochure, 1966, Smith Papers; letter to Joe H. Tonahill, Tonahill Collection.

19   *Washington Star*, June 20, 1966; *Loudoun Times-Mirror*, July 7, 1966.

20   *Fredericksburg Free Lance-Star*, July 9, 1966; *Washington Post*, June 21, 1966; *Stafford Ranger*, June 6, 1966.

21   *Fredericksburg Free Lance-Star*, June 27, 1966.

22   Lewis P. Fickett, Jr., interview, Charlestown, S.C., March 29, 1984; interview with Howell.

23   Interview with Fickett.

24   *Washington Post*, Feb. 1, June 26, July 6, 1966; interview with Rawlings; *Fredericksburg Free Lance-Star*, May 10, 1966.

25   *Fredericksburg Free Lance-Star*, June 25, 1966; *Richmond Times-Dispatch*, July 3, 1966; Mills E. Godwin, Jr., to Tom Frost, June 29, 1966, Smith Papers.

26   *Richmond Times-Dispatch*, July 7, 1966; *Stafford Ranger*, July 11, 1966; *Washington Post*, July 27, 1966; Dabney, *Virginia: The New Dominion*, pp. 559–60.

27   *Richmond News Leader*, June 30, 1966.

28   *Richmond Times-Dispatch*, July 13, Aug. 12, 1966; State Board of Elections, *Statement of the Vote, 1966 Primary*.

29   *Richmond Times-Dispatch*, July 15, 1966; *Ashland Herald-Progress*, July 21, 1966.

30   Interview with Carruthers; State Board of Elections, *Statement of the Vote, 1966 Primary*; *Washington Post*, July 31, 1966; *Fauquier Democrat*, Nov. 13, 1975.

31   State Board of Elections, *Statement of Voter Registration, 1960[-1966]*; State Board of Elections, *Statement of the Vote, 1966 Primary*; John W. Williams, interview, Charlottesville, Va., March 17, 1976; interviews with Rawlings and Painter; U.S. Department of Commerce, Bureau of the Census, *County and City Data Book, A Statistical Abstract Supplement* (Washington, D.C., 1967), pp. 382, 392, 554; ibid. (Washington, D.C., 1973), pp. 486–98, 774.

32   Interview with Muse.

33   State Board of Elections, *Statement of the Vote, 1966 Primary*; *Washington Post*, July 31, 1966; *Richmond News Leader*, Oct. 4, 1976; interview with Rawlings.

34   *Fredericksburg Free Lance-Star*, June 6, July 14, 16, 18, 25, 27, Aug. 9, 24, 31, Sept. 15, 21, 24, 27, Oct. 1, 5, 6, 14, 24, 29, Nov. 2, 27, 1966.

35   HWS to C. B. McDaniel, Sept. 12, 1966, Smith Papers; *Fredericksburg Free Lance-Star*, Oct. 25, 1966.

36   *Fredericksburg Free Lance-Star*, Sept. 24, Oct. 7, 27, Nov. 5, 1966; State Board of Elections, *Statement of the Vote, 1966 Election*.

37   *Fredericksburg Free Lance-Star*, Oct. 1, Nov. 9, 27, 1966, Jan. 16, 1968; interview with Rawlings; William L. Scott, telephone interview, March 21, 1978.

Chapter 9   *Retirement*

1   *Richmond Times-Dispatch*, Sept. 25, 1966, Oct. 5, 1976; *Congressional Record*, Oct. 19, 1966, p. 27834.

2   *Congressional Record*, Oct. 20, 1966, pp. 28099–112.

3   Interviews with Chilton and Smith, Jr.; HWS to Violett Smith Tonahill, March 29, 1967, Tonahill collection.

4   HWS to Violett Smith Tonahill, March 29, July 26, 1967, Tonahill collection; interview with Dudley.

5   HWS to Violett Smith Tonahill, July 26, 1967, Tonahill collection; *Washington Post*, July 27, 1967.

6   HWS to Violett and Joe Tonahill, June 20, July 18, 1968, Jan. 14, 1970, Tonahill collection. For copies of the American Enterprise Institute's chapters, see the Smith Papers.

7   HWS to Violett and Joe Tonahill, July 18, Oct. 24, 1968, Tonahill collection.

8   Ibid., Jan. 14, July 23, Dec. 3, 1970, Aug. 18, Sept. 14, 28, 1971; Smith, *Our Paternal Hearth*.

9   HWS to Violett and Joe Tonahill, June 15, 1972, Tonahill collection; HWS to Virginia and Landon Mitchell, Nov. 15, 1972, Mitchell collection, Fort Lauderdale, Fla.; *Richmond News Leader*, Oct. 4, 1976; interview with Elliott.
Smith's will showed that his net worth was at least $1,736,744. Of this amount, he had $184,000 in realty and $1,552,744 in personalty. Since Smith was a shrewd investor and knowledgeable about tax law, it is likely that before his death he reduced his net worth by transferring property to relatives or to business associates in order to avoid inheritance taxes. See Wills, Jan. 10, 1975, pp. 120–26, City Clerk's Office, Alexandria, Va.

10   HWS to Virginia and Landon Mitchell, Nov. 14, 1973, Mitchell collection; HWS to Violett and Joe Tonahill, Aug. 15, 28, 1974, Tonahill collection.

11   Interview with Chilton; *Washington Post*, Oct. 4, 7, 1976; *Washington Star*, Oct. 4, 1976; *Richmond Times-Dispatch*, Oct. 4, 1976; *Richmond News Leader*, Oct. 4, 5, 1976; Carl Albert to Annie C. Smith, Oct. 7, 1976, B. F Sisk to Annie C. Smith, Oct. 7, 1976, Gerald R. Ford to Annie C. Smith, Oct. 7, 1976, Smith Papers.

Bibliography

Manuscript Collections

Almond, J. Lindsay, Jr. Virginia State Library. Richmond.
Battle, John S. Virginia State Library.
Byrd, Harry F. University of Virginia Library. Charlottesville.
——. Virginia State Library.
Colmer, William M. William D. McCain Graduate Library, University of Southern Mississippi. Hattiesburg.
Combs, Everett R. University of Virginia Library.
Darden, Colgate W., Jr. Virginia State Library.
Eisenhower, Dwight D. Dwight D. Eisenhower Library. Abilene, Kans.
Ford, Gerald R., Jr. Gerald R. Ford Library. Ann Arbor, Mich.
Glass, Carter. University of Virginia Library.
Godwin, Mills E., Jr. Virginia State Library.
Johnson, Lyndon B. Lyndon B. Johnson Library. University of Texas. Austin.
Kennedy, John F. John F. Kennedy Library. Boston.
Kilpatrick, James J. University of Virginia Library.
McCormack, John W. Mugar Memorial Library. Boston University.
McNaughton, Frank. Harry S Truman Library. Independence, Mo.
Mitchell, Landon and Virginia. Fort Lauderdale, Florida.
Moore, R. Walton. Franklin D. Roosevelt Library. Hyde Park, N.Y.
Peery, George C. Virginia State Library.
Pollard, John G. Virginia State Library.
President's Papers. University Archives, University of Virginia.
Price, James H. Virginia State Library.
Rawlings, George C., Jr. Law offices of Rawlings and Pruitt. Fredericksburg, Va.
Rayburn, Sam. Sam Rayburn Library. Bonham, Tex.
Ribble, F. D. G. Arthur J. Morris Law Library, University of Virginia. Charlottesville.
Richey, Homer G. Charlottesville, Va.
Robertson, A. Willis. Earl Gregg Swem Library, College of William and Mary. Williamsburg, Va.

Roosevelt, Franklin D. Franklin D. Roosevelt Library.
Smith, Howard W. Federal Bureau of Investigation. Department of Jus-
    tice. Washington, D.C.
————. Labor-Management Documentation Center, Martin P. Cather-
    wood Library, New York State School of Industrial and Labor Re-
    lations, Cornell University. Ithaca, N.Y.
————. University of Virginia Library.
Smith, W. Worth, Jr. University of Virginia Library.
Stanley, Thomas B. Virginia State Library.
Sumners, Hatton W. Dallas Historical Society.
Swanson, Claude A. University of Virginia Library.
Tonahill, Violett Smith. Jasper, Tex.
Trinkle, E. Lee. Virginia State Library.
Truman, Harry S. Harry S Truman Library.
Tuck, William M. Earl Gregg Swem Library, College of William and
    Mary.
————. Virginia State Library.
University of Virginia Board of Visitors Minutes. University of Virginia
    Library.

Government Documents

National

Cases Adjudged in the Supreme Court at October Term, 1936. Vol. 299,
    Washington, D.C.: GPO, 1937.
Congressional Directory, Washington, D.C.: GPO, 1895–1970.
Congressional Quarterly. Congressional Quarterly Almanac. Nos. 1–
    22. Washington, D.C.: GPO, 1945–66.
————. Congressional Redistricting: Census. Washington, D.C.: GPO,
    1962.
————. Representation and Apportionment. Washington, D.C.: GPO,
    1966.
Congressional Record. Washington, D.C.: GPO, 1897–1967.
Simon, Kenneth A., and W. Vance Grant. Digest of Educational Sta-
    tistics. Washington, D.C.: GPO, 1965.
U.S. Commission on Civil Rights. Southern School Desegregation,
    1966–67. N.p., July 1967.
U.S. Congress. House of Representatives. Final Report on the Investi-
    gation of the National Labor Relations Board. Washington, D.C.:
    GPO, 1941.
————. Hearings on H.R. 7152 before the Committee on Rules. Wash-
    ington, D.C.: GPO, 1964.

——. A *History of the Committee on Rules, 1789–1981*. Washington, D.C.: GPO, 1983.

——. *Intermediate Report on the Investigation of the National Labor Relations Board*. Washington, D.C.: GPO, 1940.

U.S. Department of Commerce. Bureau of the Census. *Congressional District Atlas, 90th Congress*. Washington, D.C.: GPO, 1966.

——. *Congressional District Data Book (Districts of the 88th Congress)*. Washington, D.C.: GPO, 1963.

——. *Congressional District Data Book: A Statistical Abstract Supplement*. Washington, D.C.: GPO, 1963, 1973.

——. *County and City Data Book: A Statistical Abstract Supplement*. Washington, D.C.: GPO, 1967, 1973.

——. *Current Population Reports*. Ser. P-20, no. 174, "Voting and Registration in the Election of November, 1966." Washington, D.C.: GPO, 1968.

——. *Fifteenth Census of the United States: 1930*. Vol. 3, pt. 2., "Population." Washington, D.C.: GPO, 1932.

——. *Report on Statistics of Churches in the United States at the Eleventh Census: 1890*. Washington, D.C.: GPO, 1894.

——. *Supplement to Congressional District Data Book, Virginia Districts of the 90th Congress*. Washington, D.C.: GPO, 1966.

——. *United States Census of Population: 1960*. Vol. 1, pt. 48. "Characteristics of the Population." Washington, D.C.: GPO, 1961.

——. *United States Census of Population: 1970*. Vol. 1, pt. 48. "Characteristics of the Population." Washington, D.C.: GPO, 1973.

U.S. Department of Health, Education, and Welfare. Social Security Administration. *Social Security Programs in the United States*. Washington, D.C.: GPO, 1968.

State and Local

Acts of the General Assembly of the Commonwealth of Virginia, 1964–1966. Richmond: Division of Purchase and Printing, 1966.

Alexandria, Va. City Clerk's Office. Wills.

——. City Council. Minutes, 1908–18.

——. Corporation Court. Chancery Books.

————. Criminal Policy Files.

————. Deeds.

————. Minutes.

Annual Report of the Secretary of the Commonwealth to the Governor and General Assembly of Virginia. Richmond: Superintendent of Public Printing, 1920.

Cases Decided in the Supreme Court of Appeals of Virginia. Vol. 159. Richmond: Division of Purchase and Printing, 1933.

Estimates of the Population of the Counties and Cities of Virginia. Charlottesville: University of Virginia Bureau of Population and Economic Research, 1966–67.

Fauquier County, Warrenton, Va. Circuit Court. Marriage Register.

Journal of the House of Delegates of the Commonwealth of Virginia.
Richmond: Division of Purchase and Printing, 1902–4.

Pollard, Robert N., ed. *Pollard's Code Biennial, 1918, Containing All
Statutes of a General and Permanent Nature Passed by the General Assembly of Virginia.* Richmond: Everett Waddey Co., 1918.

*Reapportionment of the State for Representation: Report to the Governor
and the General Assembly of Virginia.* Richmond: Commission
on Redistricting, 1961.

State Board of Education. *Annual Report of the Superintendent of Public Instruction of the Commonwealth of Virginia.* Vol. 48, no. 2.
Richmond: State Board of Education, Oct. 1965.

State Board of Elections. *Estimates of Voter Registration.* Richmond:
State Board of Elections, 1957–66.

——. Official Records of Voter Registration in Counties and Cities of
Virginia. Richmond: State Board of Elections, 1960–70.

——. *Official Statements of the Vote.* Richmond: Department of Purchases and Supply, 1920–70.

——. Reports on Campaign Expenditures. Richmond: State Board of
Elections, 1964–66.

University of Virginia. *Bulletin.* Vol. 1, no. 1. Charlottesville, 1901.

Virginia Constituency: Election District Data—1970. Charlottesville:
Tayloe Murphy Institute and the Institute of Government, 1973.

Virginia Election Laws in Effect as of July 1, 1966. Richmond: Department of Purchases and Supply, 1966.

Books

Adams, Henry H. *Harry Hopkins.* New York, 1977.

Alexander, Charles C. *Holding the Line: The Eisenhower Era, 1952–
1961.* Bloomington, Ind., 1975.

Allan-Olney, Mary. *The New Virginians.* Vol. 2. London, 1880.

Altmeyer, Arthur J. *The Formative Years of Social Security.* Madison,
Wis., 1966.

*Annual Announcement for 1892–93 and Catalogue of Bethel Military
Academy, Fauquier County, Va.* Warrenton, 1892.

Baird, Nancy Chappelear, ed. *Journals of Amanda Virginia Edmonds:
Lass of the Mosby Confederacy, 1859–1867.* Stephens City, Va.,
1984.

Bartley, Numan V. *The Rise of Massive Resistance: Race and Politics in
the South during the 1950s.* Baton Rouge, La., 1969.

Bass, Jack, and Walter DeVries. *The Transformation of Southern Politics: Social Change and Political Consequence since 1945*. New York, 1977.

Belknap, Michal R., ed. *American Political Trials*. Westport, Conn., 1981.

———. *Cold War Political Justice: The Smith Act, the Communist Party and American Civil Liberties*. Westport, Conn., 1977.

Bellace, Janice R., and Alan D. Berkowitz. *The Landrum-Griffin Act: Twenty Years of Federal Protection of Union Members' Rights*. Philadelphia, 1979.

Bendiner, Robert. *Obstacle Course on Capitol Hill*. New York, 1964.

Berber, Monroe. *The Revolution in Civil Rights*. New York, 1968.

Berman, Daniel M. *A Bill Becomes a Law: Congress Enacts Civil Rights Legislation*. New York, 1966.

———. *In Congress Assembled*. New York, 1964.

Berman, William C. *The Politics of Civil Rights in the Truman Administration*. Columbus, Ohio, 1970.

Bernstein, Irving. *Turbulent Years: A History of the American Worker, 1933–1941*. Boston, 1970.

Bird, Caroline. *Born Female: The High Cost of Keeping Women Down*. New York, 1968.

Bolling, Richard. *House Out of Order*. New York, 1965.

———. *Power in the House: A History of the Leadership of the House of Representatives*. New York, 1968.

Booth, Philip. *Social Security in America*. Ann Arbor, Mich., 1973.

Bowman, D. O. *Public Control of Labor Relations*. New York, 1942.

Boyd, W. Andrew. *Boyd's Directory of Alexandria, Va*. Washington, D.C., 1917.

Braisted, William C., and William H. Bell. *The Life Story of Presley Marion Rixey: Surgeon General, U.S. Navy, 1902–1910*. Strasburg, Va., 1930.

Brauer, Carl M. *John F. Kennedy and the Second Reconstruction*. New York, 1977.

Brockett, F. L., and George W. Rock. *A Concise History of the City of Alexandria, Va., from 1669–1883*. Alexandria, 1883.

Bruce, Philip A. *History of the University of Virginia, 1819–1919*. Vol. 4. New York, 1921.

Bryson, W. Hamilton. *Legal Education in Virginia, 1779–1979: A Biographical Approach*. Charlottesville, 1982.

Buck, J. L. Blair. *The Development of Public Schools in Virginia, 1607–1952*. Richmond, 1952.

Burner, David. *Herbert Hoover: A Public Life*. New York, 1979.

Burns, James MacGregor. *Congress on Trial: The Legislative Process and the Administrative State.* New York, 1949.

———. *Roosevelt: The Lion and the Fox.* New York, 1956.

———. *Roosevelt: The Soldier of Freedom.* New York, 1970.

Campbell, Rita Riccardo. *Social Security: Promise and Reality.* Stanford, Calif., 1977.

Carr, Robert K. *The House Committee on Un-American Activities, 1945–1950.* Ithaca, N.Y., 1952.

Chafee, Zechariah, Jr. *Free Speech in the United States.* Cambridge, Mass., 1941.

Champagne, Anthony. *Congressman Sam Rayburn.* New Brunswick, N.J., 1984.

Cheney, Richard B. and Lynne V. *Kings of the Hill: Power and Personality in the House of Representatives.* New York, 1983.

Clark, Jane Perry. *Deportation of Aliens from the United States to Europe.* New York, 1931.

Clark, Joseph S. *Congress: The Sapless Branch.* New York, 1964.

Comstock, Jim, ed. *West Virginia Heritage.* Vol. 7. Richwood, 1972.

Connally, Tom. *My Name Is Tom Connally.* New York, 1954.

Cooley, Thomas M. *The General Principles of Constitutional Law in the United States of America.* Boston, 1891.

Crawford, Kenneth G. *The Pressure Boys: The Inside Story of Lobbying in America.* New York, 1939.

Crawley, William B., Jr. *Bill Tuck: A Political Life in Harry Byrd's Virginia.* Charlottesville, 1978.

Cutler, James E. *Lynch-law: An Introduction into the History of Lynching in the United States.* Montclair, N.J., 1969.

Dabney, Virginius. *Mr. Jefferson's University: A History.* Charlottesville, 1981.

———. *Virginia: The New Dominion.* Garden City, N.Y., 1971.

Dallek, Robert. *Democrat and Diplomat: The Life of William E. Dodd.* New York, 1968.

Davidson, Robert H., et al. *Congress in Crisis: Politics and Congressional Reform.* Belmont, Calif., 1966.

Day, Annie G. *Sketches and Illustrations of Warrenton and Fauquier County, Virginia.* N.p., 1908.

Directory of Alumni of the Law School: The University of Virginia. Charlottesville, 1963.

Di Zerega, A., Jr., et al. *Fauquier County Geography Supplement.* Warrenton, Va., 1927.

Donovan, Robert J. *Conflict and Crisis: The Presidency of Harry S Truman, 1945–1948.* New York, 1977.

Dow, Richard B. *A History of the Second Presbyterian Church: Alexandria, Virginia, 1817–1950.* Richmond, 1952.

Dulaney, H. G., and Edward H. Phillips, eds. *"Speak, Mr. Speaker."* Bonham, Tex., 1978.

Ely, James W., Jr. *The Crisis of Conservative Virginia: The Byrd Organization and the Politics of Massive Resistance.* Knoxville, Tenn., 1976.

Engelbarts, Rudolf. *Women in the United States Congress, 1917–1972: Their Accomplishments with Bibliographies.* Littleton, Colo., 1974.

Farley, James A. *Jim Farley's Story: The Roosevelt Years.* New York, 1948.

Ferrell, Henry C., Jr. *Claude A. Swanson of Virginia: A Political Biography.* Lexington, Ky., 1985.

Freeman, Edward A. *Some Impressions of the United States.* London, 1883.

Freidel, Frank. *FDR: Launching the New Deal.* Boston, 1973.

——. *F.D.R. and the South.* Baton Rouge, La., 1965.

Fried, Richard M. *Men against McCarthy.* New York, 1976.

Frisch, Morton J. *Franklin D. Roosevelt: The Contribution of the New Deal to American Political Thought and Practice.* Boston, 1975.

Galloway, George B. *Congress at the Crossroads.* New York, 1946.

——. *History of the House of Representatives.* New York, 1961.

Garrow, David J. *Protest at Selma: Martin Luther King, Jr., and the Voting Rights Act of 1965.* New Haven, 1978.

Gates, Robbins L. *The Making of Massive Resistance: Virginia's Politics of Public School Desegregation, 1954–1956.* Chapel Hill, N.C., 1964.

Gellerman, William. *Martin Dies.* New York, 1972.

George, Emily. *Martha W. Griffiths.* Washington, D.C., 1982.

Gilbert, James. *Another Chance: Postwar America, 1945–1968.* New York, 1981.

Goodwin, George, Jr. *The Little Legislatures: Committees of Congress.* Amherst, Mass., 1970.

Gottmann, Jean. *Virginia in Our Century.* Charlottesville, 1969.

Green, Mark. *Who Runs Congress?* New York, 1979.

Groome, Harry Connelly. *Fauquier County, Virginia: Historical Notes.* Warrenton, 1914.

Gross, James A. *The Reshaping of the National Labor Relations Board: National Labor Policy in Transition, 1937–1947.* Albany, 1981.

Gunther, Gerald, and Noel T. Dowling. *Cases and Materials on Constitutional Law.* 8th ed. New York, 1970.

Hamby, Alonzo L. *Beyond the New Deal: Harry S. Truman and American Liberalism*. New York, 1973.

Harbaugh, William H. *The Life and Times of Theodore Roosevelt*. New York, 1961.

Hartley, Fred A., Jr. *Our New National Labor Policy: The Taft-Hartley Act and the Next Steps*. New York, 1948.

Havard, William C., ed. *The Changing Politics of the South*. Baton Rouge, La., 1972.

Heath, Jim. *Decade of Disillusionment: The Kennedy-Johnson Years*. Bloomington, Ind., 1975.

Heatwole, Cornelius J. *A History of Education in Virginia*. New York, 1916.

Heinemann, Ronald L. *Depression and New Deal in Virginia: The Enduring Dominion*. Charlottesville, 1983.

Hill, C. William, Jr. *The Political Theory of John Taylor of Caroline*. Cranbury, N.J., 1977.

Hill's Alexandria (Virginia) City Directory. Vols. 36, 40. Richmond, 1938, 1947.

Houston, Charles. *Virginians in Congress*. Richmond, 1966.

Howe, Irving, and Lewis Coser. *The American Communist Party: A Critical History, 1919–1957*. Boston, 1957.

Huthmacher, J. Joseph. *Senator Robert Wagner and the Rise of Urban Liberalism*. New York, 1968.

Ickes, Harold L. *The Secret Diary of Harold L. Ickes: The Inside Struggle, 1936–1939*. New York, 1954.

Josephy, Alvin M., Jr. *On the Hill: A History of the American Congress*. New York, 1979.

Kelly, Alfred H., and Winfred A. Harbison. *The American Constitution: Its Origins and Development*. New York, 1976.

Key, V. O., Jr. *Southern Politics in State and Nation*. New York, 1949.

Kilpatrick, James J. *The Sovereign States: Notes of a Citizen of Virginia*. Chicago, 1957.

Kirby, Jack T. *Westmoreland Davis: Virginia Planter-Politician, 1859–1942*. Charlottesville, 1968.

Kluger, Richard. *Simple Justice: The History of Brown v. Board of Education and Black America's Struggle for Equality*. New York, 1975.

Kousser, J. Morgan. *The Shaping of Southern Politics: Suffrage Restriction and the Establishment of the One-Party South, 1880–1910*. New Haven, 1974.

Lahr, Raymond M., and J. William Theis. *Congress: Power and Purpose in Capitol Hill*. Boston, 1967.

Latham, Earl. *The Communist Controversy in Washington: From the New Deal to McCarthy*. Cambridge, Mass., 1966.

Latimer, James. *Virginia Politics: The Way It Was*. Richmond, 1976.

Lawson, Steven F. *Black Ballots: Voting Rights in the South, 1944–1969*. New York, 1976.

Lee, R. Alton. *Truman and Taft-Hartley*. Lexington, Ky., 1966.

Leuchtenburg, William E. *Franklin D. Roosevelt and the New Deal, 1932–1940*. New York, 1963.

Lile, William Minor. *Legal Education and Admission to the Bar in the Southern States*. Louisville, Ky., 1914.

Lord, Donald C. *John F. Kennedy: The Politics of Confrontation and Conciliation*. New York, 1977.

Lubove, Roy. *The Struggle for Social Security, 1900–1935*. Cambridge, Mass., 1968.

McAdams, Alan K. *Power and Politics in Labor Legislation*. New York, 1964.

McCoy, Donald R., and Richard T. Ruetten. *Quest and Response: Minority Rights and the Truman Administration*. Lawrence, Kans., 1973.

McDaniel, Ralph C. *The Virginia Constitutional Convention of 1901–1902*. Baltimore, 1928.

McGeary, M. Nelson. *The Development of Congressional Investigative Power*. New York, 1973.

McKay, Robert B. *Reapportionment: The Law and Politics of Equal Representation*. Hartford, 1965.

McKinley, Charles, and Robert W. Frase. *Launching Social Security: A Capture-and-Record Account, 1935–1937*. Madison, Wis., 1970.

McLaughlin, Doris B., and Anita W. Schoomaker. *The Landrum-Griffin Act and Union Democracy*. Ann Arbor, Mich., 1979.

MacNeil, Neil. *Forge of Democracy: The House of Representatives*. New York, 1963.

Martin, Joseph W., Jr. *My First Fifty Years in Politics*. New York, 1960.

Meriam, Lewis. *Relief and Social Security*. Washington, D.C., 1946.

Mikva, Abner J., and Patti B. Saris. *The American Congress: The First Branch*. New York, 1983.

Miller, Francis Pickens. *Man From the Valley: Memoirs of a 20th-Century Virginian*. Chapel Hill, N.C., 1971.

Miller, Merle. *Lyndon: An Oral Biography*. New York, 1980.

Milligan, Maurice M. *Inside Story of the Pendergast Machine*. New York, 1948.

Millis, Harry A., and Emily Clark Brown. *From the Wagner Act to Taft-Hartley: A Study of National Labor Policy and Labor Relations*. Chicago, 1950.

Minor, Raleigh C. *Centralization versus Decentralization*. Richmond, 1911.

——. *Notes on the Science of Government and the Relations of the States to the United States*. Charlottesville, Va., 1913.

Moger, Allen W. *Virginia: Bourbonism to Byrd, 1870–1925*. Charlottesville, 1968.

Moon, Henry Lee. *Balance of Power: The Negro Vote*. New York, 1948.

Mooney, Booth. *Roosevelt and Rayburn: A Political Partnership*. Philadelphia, 1971.

Morton, Richard L. *The Negro in Virginia Politics, 1865–1902*. Charlottesville, 1919.

Muse, Benjamin. *Virginia's Massive Resistance* Gloucester, Mass., 1969.

O'Brien, Lawrence F. *No Final Victories*. Garden City, N.Y., 1974.

Page, Thomas Nelson. *The Old Dominion: Her Making and Her Manners*. New York, 1908.

Paterson, Thomas G., et al., *American Foreign Policy: A History since 1900*. Lexington, Mass., 1983.

Patterson, James T. *Congressional Conservatism and the New Deal: The Growth of the Conservative Coalition in Congress, 1933–1939*. Lexington, Ky., 1967.

——. *Mr. Republican: A Biography of Robert A. Taft*. Boston, 1972.

Peabody, Robert L. *Leadership in Congress: Stability, Succession, and Change*. Boston, 1976.

——, and Nelson W. Polsby. *New Perspectives on the House of Representatives*. Chicago, 1963.

Pearson, C. C., and J. Edwin Hendricks. *Liquor and Anti-Liquor in Virginia, 1619–1919*. Durham, N.C., 1967.

Pearson, Drew, and Jack Anderson. *The Case against Congress: A Compelling Indictment of Corruption on Capitol Hill*. New York, 1968.

Perkins, Frances. *The Roosevelt I Knew*. New York, 1946.

Perrett, Geoffrey. *Days of Sadness, Years of Triumph: The American People, 1939–1945*. New York, 1973.

Peterson, Merrill D. *The Jeffersonian Image in the American Mind*. New York, 1962.

Polenberg, Richard. *One Nation Divisible: Class, Race, and Ethnicity in the United States since 1938*. New York, 1980.

——. *War and Society: The United States, 1941–1945*. Philadelphia, 1972.

Pollard, Edward A. *The Virginia Tourist: Sketches of the Springs and Mountains of Virginia*. Philadelphia, 1870.

Porter, David L. *Congress and the Waning of the New Deal*. Port Washington, N.Y., 1980.

Price, Lucy Montgomery Smith. *The Sydney-Smith and Clagett-Price Genealogy*. Strasburg, Va., 1927.

Pritchett, C. Herman. *Civil Liberties and the Vinson Court*. Chicago, 1954.

Proceedings of the Fifty-ninth Annual Convention of the American Federation of Labor. Washington, D.C., 1939.

Reitman, Alan, ed. *The Pulse of Freedom: American Liberties, 1920–1970*. New York, 1975.

Rhodes, John J. *The Futile System: How to Unchain Congress and Make the System Work Again*. Garden City, N.Y., 1976.

Richmond's Directory of Alexandria, Va., 1900. Washington, D.C., 1900.

Ripley, Randall B. *Majority Party Leadership in Congress*. Boston, 1969.

——. *Party Leaders in the House of Representatives*. Washington, D.C., 1967.

Ritchie, John. *The First Hundred Years: A Short History of the School of Law of the University of Virginia for the Period 1826–1926*. Charlottesville, 1978.

Robert, Joseph. *The Tobacco Kingdom: Plantation, Market, and Factory in Virginia and North Carolina, 1800–1860*. Durham, N.C., 1938.

Robinson, James A. *The House Rules Committee*. Indianapolis, 1963.

Roosevelt, Franklin D. *The Public Papers and Addresses of Franklin D. Roosevelt*. Vol. 7. Comp. Samuel I. Rosenman. N.Y., 1941.

Rothbard, Murray N. *America's Great Depression*. Los Angeles, 1972.

Ryland, Garnett. *The Baptists of Virginia, 1699–1926*. Richmond, 1955.

Sabato, Larry. *The Democratic Party Primary in Virginia: Tantamount to Election No Longer*. Charlottesville, 1977.

Schaffer, Alan. *Vito Marcantonio: Radical in Congress*. New York, 1966.

Schlesinger, Arthur M., Jr. *The Coming of the New Deal*. Boston, 1958.

——. *The Politics of Upheaval*. Boston, 1960.

Shalhope, Robert E. *John Taylor of Caroline: Pastoral Republican*. Columbia, S.C., 1980.

Shannon, David A. *The Decline of American Communism: A History of the Communist Party of the United States since 1945*. New York, 1959.

Shelley, Mack C., II. *The Permanent Majority: The Conservative Coalition in the United States Congress*. University, Ala., 1983.

Sitkoff, Harvard. *The Struggle for Black Equality, 1954–1980.* New York, 1981.

Smith, Bob. *They Closed Their Schools: Prince Edward County, Virginia, 1951–1964.* Chapel Hill, N.C., 1965.

Smith, Howard W. *Our Paternal Hearth.* Privately printed, 1976.

——. *A Supplemental List of the Descendants of Henry Marrs Lewis and Presley Lycurgus Smith to Include Those Born Subsequent to the Publication in 1927 of the Book by Lucy Montgomery Smith Price.* Privately printed, 1970.

Smith, Presley Alexander Lycurgeos, Jr. *Boyhood Memories of Fauquier.* Richmond, 1926.

Smoot, Betty Carter. *Days in an Old Town.* Washington, D.C., 1934.

Sorensen, Theodore C. *Kennedy.* New York, 1965.

Starobin, Joseph R. *American Communism in Crisis, 1943–1957.* Cambridge, Mass., 1972.

Steinberg, Alfred. *Sam Rayburn: A Biography.* New York, 1975.

Stokes, Thomas L. *Chip off My Shoulder.* Princeton, N.J., 1940.

Stover, John F. *The Railroads of the South, 1865–1900.* Chapel Hill, N.C., 1959.

Sundquist, James L. *The Decline and Resurgence of Congress.* Washington, D.C., 1981.

——. *Politics and Policy: The Eisenhower, Kennedy, and Johnson Years.* Washington, D.C., 1968.

Tariello, Frank, Jr. *The Reconstruction of American Political Ideology, 1865–1917.* Charlottesville, Va., 1982.

Thomas, Norman C., and Karl A. Lamb. *Congress: Politics and Practice.* New York, 1964.

Tresolini, Rocco J., and Richard T. Frost, eds. *Cases in American National Government and Politics.* Englewood Cliffs, N.J., 1966.

Tyler, John G., ed. *Men of Mark in Virginia.* Vol. 2. Washington, D.C., 1907.

University of Virginia. *Corks and Curls.* Yearbook. Charlottesville, 1900–1903.

We, the People: The Story of the United States Capitol. Washington, D.C., 1965.

Whalen, Charles and Barbara. *The Longest Debate: A Legislative History of the 1964 Civil Rights Act.* Cabin John, Md., 1985.

Wharton, Leslie. *Polity and the Public Good: Conflicting Theories of Republican Government in the New Nation.* Ann Arbor, Mich., 1980.

Whitney, Fred. *Wartime Experiences of the National Labor Relations Board.* Urbana, Ill., 1949.

Who's Who in America, 1974 & 1975. 38th ed. Chicago, 1975.

Wicker, Tom. *JFK and LBJ: The Influence of Personality upon Politics*. New York, 1968.

Wilkinson, J. Harvie, III. *From Brown to Bakke: The Supreme Court and School Integration, 1954–1978*. New York, 1979.

——. *Harry Byrd and the Changing Face of Virginia Politics, 1945–1966*. Charlottesville, 1968.

Williams, John A. *West Virginia: A Bicentennial History*. New York, 1976.

Williamson, Samuel T. *Frank Gannett: A Biography*. New York, 1940.

Woodward, C. Vann. *The Strange Career of Jim Crow*. 3d rev. ed. New York, 1974.

Writers' Program of the Works Projects Administration in the State of Virginia. *Alexandria*. Alexandria, 1939.

Wynes, Charles E. *Race Relations in Virginia, 1870–1902*. Charlottesville, 1961.

Young, Roland. *Congressional Politics and the Second World War*. New York, 1956.

Zelman, Patricia G. *Women, Work, and National Policy: The Kennedy-Johnson Years*. Ann Arbor, Mich., 1982.

Articles

Aaron, Benjamin. "Amending the Taft-Hartley Act: A Decade of Frustration." *Industrial and Labor Relations Review* 11 (April 1958): 327–38.

"Accusing the Labor Board." *United States News* 8 (April 5, 1940): 33.

Altman, O. R. "First Session of the Seventy-fifth Congress." *American Political Science Review* 31 (Dec. 1937): 1071–93.

Amidon, Beulah. "Aliens in America." *Survey Graphic* 30 (Feb. 1941): 58–61.

——. "Can We Afford Martyrs?" *Survey Graphic* 29 (Sept. 1940): 457–58.

"Angry Congress Deals Labor Biggest Setback in 10 Years." *Newsweek* 22 (July 5, 1943): 64, 66, 69.

"The Antagonism of State and National Authorities." *Virginia Law Register* 15 (November 1909): 550–51.

Bailyn, Bernard. "Politics and Social Structure in Virginia." In *Seventeenth-Century America: Essays in Colonial America*, pp. 90–115. Ed. James M. Smith. Chapel Hill, N.C., 1959.

Barber, Kathleen L. "The Legal Status of the American Communist Party: 1965." *Journal of Public Law* 15 (1966): 94–121.

Bickel, Alexander M. "Civil Rights: A New Era Opens." In *John Kennedy and the New Frontier*, pp. 138–64. Ed. Aida DiPace Donald. New York, 1966.

Bolling, Richard. "A Congressman's View of the Problem." *New Republic* 151 (Nov. 21, 1964): 13–14.

Boudin, Louis B. "'Seditious Doctrines' and the 'Clear and Present Danger' Rule." *Virginia Law Review* 38 (1952): 143–86, 315–56.

Brady, David W., and Charles S. Bullock III. "Coalition Politics in the House of Representatives." In *Congress Reconsidered*, pp. 186–203. Ed. Lawrence C. Dodd and Bruce I. Oppenheimer. Washington, D.C., 1981.

Brauer, Carl M. "Women Activists, Southern Conservatives, and the Prohibition of Sex Discrimination in Title VII of the 1964 Civil Rights Act." *Journal of Southern History* 49 (Feb. 1983): 37–56.

Brown, Emily Clark. "The Employer Unit for Collective Bargaining in National Labor Relations Board Decisions." *Journal of Political Economy* 50 (June 1942): 321–56.

Bryson, W. Hamilton. "The History of Legal Education in Virginia." *University of Richmond Law Review* 14 (Fall 1979): 155–212.

"Changed Climate." *Time* 88 (September 16, 1966): 30–31.

Chasan, Will. "Keep Them Out! Our Worst Congressmen." *Nation* 155 (October 31, 1942): 438–41.

Cohen, Julius, and Lillian Cohen. "The National Labor Relations Board in Retrospect." *Industrial and Labor Relations Review* 1 (July 1948): 648–56.

"Collapse in the Capitol." *Time* 34 (July 31, 1939): 8–10.

Columbia Broadcasting System. *CBS Reports*. "The Keeper of the Rules: Congressman Smith and the New Frontier." Jan. 19, 1961.

"Congress and the Cost of Living." *New Republic* 109 (Aug. 2, 1943): 167–68.

"The Court, Congress, Chaos." *Newsweek* 50 (July 1, 1957): 19–20.

"Court Upholds Conviction of Communist Leaders." *Christian Century* 68 (June 20, 1951): 733.

Crawford, Kenneth. "Open Season on Reds." *Nation* 148 (May 6, 1939): 519–20.

"Darkened Victory." *Time* (Feb. 10, 1961): 11–14.

Davis, Virginia Waller. "Howard W. Smith of Virginia." *Commonwealth* 22 (Aug. 1955): 11–14, 17.

———. "Star Performer on 'The Hill.'" *Virginia Record* 79 (May 1957): 8–14, 49, 51, 53.

"Deal to Change Labor Law." *United States News* 8 (April 12, 1940): 35.

"Democratic Debacle." *Time* 76 (Sept. 5, 1960): 12.

Dierenfield, Bruce J. "Conservative Outrage: The Defeat in 1966 of Representative Howard W. Smith of Virginia." *Virginia Magazine of History and Biography* 80 (April 1981): 181–205.

——. "Growing Up at Cedar Hill: The Boyhood Years of Judge Howard W. Smith." *Northern Virginia Heritage* 4 (Feb. 1982): 11–16.

——. "A New Deal Backlash: The Attempted Purge of Representative Howard W. Smith." *Magazine of Albemarle County History* 37–38 (1979–80): 187–229.

Donner, Frank J. "The Smith Act—Baltimore Version." *Nation* 175 (Nov. 8, 1952): 426–28.

Doptis, Jean S. "Presley Marion Rixey." *Arlington Historical Magazine* 6 (Oct. 1977): 27–38.

"Down with the Dole." *Time* 71 (May 12, 1958): 18–19.

"Editorial." *Virginia Law Register* 4 (Oct. 1898): 390–91.

Eisenberg, Ralph. "Legislative Apportionment: How Representative Is Virginia's Present System?" *University of Virginia News Letter* 37 (April 15, 1961): 29–32.

——. "Legislative Reapportionment and Congressional Redistricting in Virginia." *Washington and Lee Law Review* 23 (Fall 1966): 294–323.

——. "The 1964 Presidential Election in Virginia: A Political Omen?" *University of Virginia News Letter* 41 (April 15, 1965): 29–32.

——. "1966 Politics in Virginia: The Democratic Senatorial Primary." *University of Virginia News Letter* 43 (Jan. 15, 1967): 17–20.

——. "1966 Politics in Virginia: The Elections for United States Representatives." *University of Virginia News Letter* 43 (June 15, 1967): 37–40.

——. "1966 Politics in Virginia: The Elections for United States Senators." *University of Virginia News Letter* 43 (May 15, 1967): 33–36.

——. "Virginia Votes for President: Patterns and Prospects." *University of Virginia News Letter* 41 (Sept. 15, 1964): 1–4.

"An Elder Statesman Looks at U.S. Today." *U.S. News & World Report* 61 (Oct. 31, 1966): 50–54.

"The Enemy within Our Gates." *National Republic* 28 (Aug. 1940): 9–10, 24.

"Faint Prelude to a Labor Policy." *Saturday Evening Post* 216 (July 31, 1943): 96.

Ferrell, Henry C., Jr. "Claude Augustus Swanson: 'Fully Concur and Cordially Co-operate,'" In *Governors of Virginia, 1860–1978*, pp. 171–81. Ed. Edward Younger and James T. Moore. Charlottesville, 1982.

"Fix NLRB, Not Law?" *Business Week*, no. 541 (Jan. 13, 1940): 39–40.

"Friendless NLRB." *Newsweek* 14 (Oct. 23, 1939): 50–52.

Fuller, Helen. "Reform, Howard Smith Style." *New Republic* 111 (Dec. 11, 1944): 791–93.

Harlow, Ralph V. "Why the Anti-Labor Drive?" *Current History*, new ser., 2 (May 1942): 198–204.

Harris, Herbert. "Politics and the C.I.O." *Nation* 149 (Nov. 18, 1939): 545–46.

"Herzog Brings Stabilizing Influence to NLRB." *Business Week*, no. 824 (June 16, 1945): 94.

Hook, Sidney. "Does the Smith Act Threaten Our Liberties?" *Commentary* 15 (Jan. 1953): 63–73.

"Hottest Potato." *Newsweek* 68 (Aug. 8, 1966): 20–21.

Houston, Charles. "Smith and Robertson." *Commonwealth* 33 (Oct. 1966): 27–31.

Hunter, Robert F. "Virginia and the New Deal." In *The New Deal: The State and Local Levels*, pp. 103–36. Ed. John Braeman et al. Columbus, Ohio, 1975.

Jewell, Malcolm E. "The Changing Political Environment of State Government." In *The States and the Metropolis*, pp. 36–62. Ed. Lee S. Green et al. University, Ala., 1968.

Johnson, Victor H. "A Trade Unionist on F.D.R." *New Republic* 109 (July 19, 1943): 74–75.

Jones, Charles O. "Joseph G. Cannon and Howard W. Smith: An Essay on the Limits of Leadership in the House of Representatives." *Journal of Politics* 30 (Aug. 1968): 617–46.

Kesselman, Louis C. "The Fair Employment Practice Commission Movement in Perspective." *Journal of Negro History* 31 (Jan. 1946): 30–46.

Kirby, Jack T. "Westmoreland Davis: Progressive Insurgent." In *The Governors of Virginia, 1860–1978*, pp. 209–19. Ed. Edward Younger and James T. Moore. Charlottesville, 1982.

Koeniger, A. Cash. "The New Deal and the States: Roosevelt versus the Byrd Organization in Virginia." *Journal of American History* 68 (March 1982): 876–96.

Kravitz, Walter. "The Influence of the House Rules Committee on Legislation in the 87th Congress." In *Congressional Reform: Problems and Prospects*, pp. 127–37. Ed. Joseph S. Clark. New York, 1965.

"Labor Board Belabored." *Time* 35 (April 1, 1940): 14.

"Labor Inquiry." *Newsweek* 14 (Aug. 14, 1939): 40.

"Labor's Safeguardians." *Time* 34 (Dec. 25, 1939): 8.

"Legal Education." *Virginia Law Register* 14 (July 1908): 219–20.

"Legal Ethics." *Virginia Law Register* 11 (Aug. 1905): 336–39.

MacNeil, Neil. "The House Confronts Mr. Kennedy." *Fortune* 65 (Jan. 1962): 70–73, 168, 171–72, 174.

Manchester, William. "The Byrd Machine." *Harper's Magazine* 205 (Nov. 1952): 80–87.

Manley, John F. "The Conservative Coalition in Congress." *American Behavioral Scientist* 17 (Nov./Dec. 1973): 223–47.

Marcantonio, Vito. "Dusty Death." *New Republic* 86 (March 4, 1936): 105–6.

Maslow, Will. "FEPC—A Case History in Parliamentary Maneuver." *University of Chicago Law Review* 13 (June 1946): 407–44.

Mendelson, Wallace. "Clandestine Speech and the First Amendment—A Reappraisal of the Dennis Case." *Michigan Law Review* 51 (Feb. 1953): 553–59.

Minor, Raleigh C. "The Graduating Examination in the Law School." *Virginia Law Register* 7 (Nov. 1901): 468–75.

"Miscellaneous Notes." *Virginia Law Register* 3 (Jan. 1898): 670–71.

Mitchell, Jonathan. "Dr. Millis: Scientist of Labor." *New Republic* 104 (Jan. 6, 1941): 16–17.

Moger, Allen W. "Industrial and Urban Progress in Virginia from 1880 to 1900." *Virginia Magazine of History and Biography* 66 (1958): 307–36.

Moley, Raymond. "Smith of Virginia." *Newsweek* 52 (Aug. 25, 1958): 80.

Mollan, Robert. "Smith Act Prosecutions: The Effect of the Dennis and Yates Decisions." *University of Pittsburgh Law Review* 26 (1965): 705–48.

Murdock, Abe. "NLRB—Should the Act Be Amended?" *Virginia Law Review* 27 (March 1941): 633–63.

National Broadcasting Company. *Meet the Press.* 8, no. 2 (Jan. 26, 1964): 1–9.

"The New Personnel and Policies of the National Labor Relations Board." *Harvard Law Review* 55 (Nov. 1941): 269–79.

"New Style NLRB." *Business Week,* no. 586 (Nov. 23, 1940): 55–56.

"NLRB Bats for the Wagner Act." *Business Week,* no. 521 (Aug. 26, 1939): 45–46.

"NLRB's Purge." *Business Week,* no. 605 (April 5, 1941): 53.

Oberdorfer, Don. "'Judge' Smith Moves with Deliberate Drag." *New York Times Magazine,* Jan. 12, 1964, pp. 12, 85, 90–91.

Phelps, James R. "Judicial Technique and the Communist Party: The Internal Security and Smith Acts Construed." *University of Cincinnati Law Review* 31 (1962): 152–72.

Pollack, J. H. "America Registers Her Aliens." *American Scholar* 10 (April 1941): 196–208.

"A Practical Side of Industrial Relations." *Washington Review* 7 (May 6, 1940): 18–19.

Price, Hugh D. "Race, Religion, and the Rules Committee: The Kennedy Aid-to-Education Bills." In *The Uses of Power*, pp. 1–71. Ed. Alan F. Westin. New York, 1962.

"Reformed NLRB." *Business Week*, no. 598 (Feb. 15, 1941): 52.

Reilly, Gerard. "The Legislative History of the Taft-Hartley Act." *George Washington Law Review* 29 (1960): 285–300.

"Reilly for Smith." *Business Week*, no. 630 (Sept. 27, 1941): 67–68.

"Report on NLRB." *Newsweek* 17 (Jan. 6, 1941): 39.

"Rest in Peace." *Time* 48 (Nov. 11, 1946): 28.

"Roast Chicken." *Time* 30 (Aug. 23, 1937): 11–12.

Robinson, James A. "The Role of the Rules Committee in Arranging the Program of the U.S. House of Representatives." *Western Political Quarterly* 12 (Sept. 1959): 653–69.

Rostow, Eugene V. "The Democratic Character of Judicial Review." *Harvard Law Review* 66 (Dec. 1952): 193–224.

Schlesinger, Emil. "Repressive Labor Legislation: An Analysis of the Smith Bill." *American Bar Association Journal* 28 (Jan. 1942): 7–19.

"Second Thoughts on the Communist Decision." *Christian Century* 68 (July 11, 1951): 812.

"Senators Ponder Smith Bill." *Newsweek* 18 (Dec. 15, 1941): 52, 57.

Shalloo, J. P. "United States Immigration Policy, 1882–1948." In *Essays in History and International Relations: In Honor of George Hubbard Blakeslee*, pp. 126–52. Ed. Dwight E. Lee and George E. McReynolds. Worcester, Mass., 1949.

Shister, Joseph. "The Impact of the Taft-Hartley Act on Union Strength and Collective Bargaining." *Industrial and Labor Relations Review* 11 (April 1958): 339–51.

"Silicosis." *Time* 27 (Feb. 3, 1936): 54.

"Silicosis Village." *Nation* 142 (Feb. 5, 1936): 162.

Slichter, Sumner. "Revision of the Taft-Hartley Act." *Quarterly Journal of Economics* 63 (Feb. 1949): 1–31.

——. "The Taft-Hartley Act." *Quarterly Journal of Economics* 67 (May 1953): 149–80.

Smith, Howard W. "Ensure Business a Fair Trial." *Christian Science Monitor (Weekly Magazine)*, April 27, 1940, pp. 5, 14.

——. "In Defense of the House Rules Committee." In *Congressional Reform: Problems and Prospects*, pp. 138–50. Ed. Joseph S. Clark. New York, 1965.

——. "NLRA—Abuses in Administrative Procedure." *Virginia Law Review* 27 (March 1941): 615–32.

——. "Pending Labor Act Amendments." *Investor America* 6 (May 1940): 8–19.

——. "What Laws Should Be Passed to Prevent Strikes in Defense Industries?" *American Bar Association Journal* 28 (Jan. 1942): 4–7.

"Smith of Virginia." *Newsweek* 19 (March 30, 1942): 32.

"Something to Veto: Connally-Smith Bill." *Nation* 156 (June 19, 1943): 851–52.

"Stale Lies and a New Trick." *Nation* 152 (Jan. 11, 1941): 33–34.

Stevens, Arthur G., Jr., Arthur H. Miller, and Thomas E. Mann. "Mobilization of Liberal Strength in the House, 1955–1970: The Democratic Study Group." *American Political Science Review* 68 (June 1974): 667–81.

Stocker, Edward S. "Federal Legislation: Alien Registration." *Georgetown Law Journal* 29 (1940): 187–93.

Stone, Russ. "Blitzkrieg against the Labor Board." *New Republic* 102 (Jan. 22, 1940): 106–7.

"Strike Curbs: Highlights of the War Labor Disputes Act." *Newsweek* 21 (June 21, 1943): 70, 72.

Summers, Clyde W. "A Summary Evaluation of the Taft-Hartley Act." *Industrial and Labor Relations Review* 11 (April 1958): 405–12.

"Supreme Court Challenges Usurpation by Congress." *Christian Century* 74 (July 10, 1957): 836.

"Tale of Plots and Pressure Unreeled in NLRB Inquiry." *Newsweek* 14 (Dec. 25, 1939): 40–42.

Thornton, J. Mills, III. "Challenge and Response in the Montgomery Bus Boycott of 1955–1956." *Alabama Review* 33 (July 1980): 163–235.

Tyler, Alicia. "Dust to Dust." *Washington Monthly* 6 (Jan. 1975): 49–58.

"The University Law School." *Virginia Law Register* 17 (Oct. 1911): 479–80.

"Up from the Underground." *Time* 86 (Nov. 26, 1965): 26.

"Uprising." *Time* 42 (July 5, 1943): 17–18.

"Wagner on the Wagner Act." *Time* 35 (March 25, 1940): 21–22.

"War Labor Disputes Act, or Smith-Connally Act." *Monthly Labor Review* 57 (Aug. 1943): 305–7.

Warne, Colston E. "Pulling the OPA's Teeth." *Current History* 6 (May 1944): 410–16.

"Washington Turnabout." *Time* 41 (Feb. 22, 1943): 15–16.

"The Week." *New Republic* 124 (June 18, 1951): 7.

"The Week." *New Republic* 125 (July 2, 1951): 7.

Whalen, Charles W., Jr. "An Unwitting Champion in the Movement for Women's Rights." *Minneapolis Star and Tribune*, Jan. 8, 1984, p. 17A.

"What Labor Law? House Passage of Smith Bill Is Only First Step." *Business Week*, no. 640 (Dec. 6, 1941): 16–17.

"White Academies in the South—Booming despite Obstacles." *U.S. News and World Report* 70 (April 19, 1971): 75–76.

"Who Rules the House?" *New Republic* 139 (Dec. 15, 1958): 5.

Williams, Murat W. "Virginia Politics: Winds of Change." *Virginia Quarterly Review* 42 (Spring 1966): 177–88.

Willis, L. Stanley. "E. Lee Trinkle: Prelude to Byrd." In *The Governors of Virginia, 1860–1978*, pp. 221–32. Ed. Edward Younger and James T. Moore. Charlottesville, 1982.

Wirin, A. L., and Sam Rosenwein. "The Smith Act Score." *Nation* 180 (Feb. 26, 1955): 177–80.

——. "The Smith Act Prosecutions." *Nation* 177 (Dec. 12, 1953): 485–90.

Woodhouse, Edward J. "Raleigh Colston Minor: Scholar, Teacher, Jurist, Leader of American International Thinking." *Virginia Law Review* 12 (Feb. 1926): 1–24.

Dissertations, Theses, and Unpublished Papers

Bear, James A., Jr., "Thomas Staples Martin: A Study in Virginia Politics, 1883–1896." M.A. thesis, University of Virginia, 1952.

Bowman, Raymond P. G. "Secondary Education in Virginia, 1870–1886." Ph.D. dissertation, University of Virginia, 1938.

Ferrell, Henry C., Jr. "Claude A. Swanson of Virginia." Ph.D. dissertation, University of Virginia, 1964.

Fickett, Lewis P., Jr. "Virginia: A 'Political Museum Piece' Revisited." Paper presented at The Citadel's Symposium on Southern Politics, March 1984.

Fitzsimmons, Holly Beth. "The Law and the Reason Thereof: John B. Minor and Legal Education at the University of Virginia, 1845–1895." M.A. thesis, University of Virginia, 1976.

Fry, Joseph A. "George Campbell Peery: Conservative Son of Old Virginia." M.A. thesis, University of Virginia, 1970.

Hall, Alvin L. "James H. Price and Virginia Politics, 1878 to 1943." Ph.D. dissertation, University of Virginia, 1970.

Heinemann, Ronald L. "The Great Depression in Virginia, 1929–1934." M.A. thesis, University of Virginia, 1967.

Henriques, Peter R. "John S. Battle and Virginia Politics, 1948–1953." Ph.D. dissertation, University of Virginia, 1971.

Hershman, James H., Jr. "The Opponents of Virginia's Massive Resistance." Ph.D. dissertation, University of Virginia, 1978.

Horn, Herman L. "The Growth and Development of the Democratic

Party in Virginia since 1900." Ph.D. dissertation, Duke University, 1949.

Link, William A. "Public Schooling and Social Change in Rural Virginia, 1870–1920." Ph.D. dissertation, University of Virginia, 1981.

Murphy, Kathleen A. "Sarah Patton Boyle and the Crusade against Virginia's Massive Resistance." M.A. thesis, University of Virginia, 1983.

Ogden, August R. "The Dies Committee." Ph.D. dissertation, Catholic University, 1943.

Van Hollen, Christopher. "The House Committee on Rules (1933–1951): Agent of Party and Agent of Opposition." Ph.D. dissertation, Johns Hopkins University, 1951.

Newspapers
Alexandria Gazette
Alexandria Daily News
Alexandria Journal-Tribune
Arlington Chronicle
Arlington Courier
Arlington Sun
Ashland Herald-Progress
Atlanta Constitution
Baltimore Daily Record
Baltimore Sun
Buffalo News
Central Virginian (Louisa)
Charlotte Observer
Charlottesville Daily Progress
Chicago Sun-Times
Chicago Tribune
Christian Science Monitor
College Topics, University of Virginia
Columbia [S.C.] *Record*
Commonwealth-Monitor (Rosslyn)
Daily Worker (New York)
Detroit Free Press
Fairfax Herald
Falls Church Free Press
Fauquier Democrat (Warrenton)
Fredericksburg Free Lance-Star
Goochland Gazette
King George

Labor (New York)
Los Angeles Times
Loudoun Times-Mirror (Leesburg)
Lynchburg News
Manassas Journal-Messenger
Midland Virginian (Palmyra)
Newport News Daily Press
New York Evening Post
New York Herald Tribune
New York Times
Norfolk Ledger-Dispatch
Northern Neck News (Warsaw)
Orange County News (Gordonsville)
Orange Review
Rappahannock Record (Kilmarnock)
Rappahannock Times (Tappahannock)
Richmond Afro-American
Richmond Exchange Reporter
Richmond News Leader
Richmond Times-Dispatch
Richmond Whig
Roanoke Times
St. Louis Post-Dispatch
Stafford Ranger
Staunton News-Leader
True Index (Warrenton)
Virginia Star/Culpeper Star-Exponent
Wall Street Journal
Warrenton Virginian
Washington Bulletin
Washington Daily News
Washington Herald
Washington Post
Washington Report
Washington Star
Washington Times

Personal Interviews

Abbitt, Watkins M. Appomattox, Va. Oct. 31, 1980.
Abernethy, Thomas G. Jackson, Miss. Jan. 11, 1984.
Albert, Carl. Telephone interview, Aug. 3, 1983.
Bolling, Richard D. Washington, D.C. May 31, 1983.
Boothe, Armistead L. Alexandria, Va. Feb. 28, 1976.

Bryan, Albert V., Sr. Alexandria, Va. Nov. 24, 1978.
Byrd, Harry F., Jr. Washington, D.C. March 8, 1976.
Campbell, Leslie D., Jr. Ashland, Va. March 26, 1976.
Carruthers, T. M. Charlottesville, Va. Sept. 8, 18, Dec. 8, 1982.
Chilton, Rt. Rev. Samuel B. Alexandria, Va. Nov. 11, 1978.
Dudley, Luther H. Alexandria, Va. Nov. 11, 1978.
Dyer, Mrs. James M. Rixeyville, Va. April 26, 1979.
Elliott, Carl, Sr. Jasper, Ala. Jan. 12, 1984.
Fickett, Lewis P., Jr. Charleston, S.C. March 29, 1984.
Gossett, Ed. Telephone interview, June 18, 1984.
Gouldman, Francis B. Spotsylvania, Va. March 16, 1976.
Halleck, Charles A. Rensselaer, Ind. June 15, 1983.
Heflin, H. Ryland. Ruby, Va. March 18, 1976.
Herlong, A. Sydney, Jr. Telephone interview, Sept. 11, 1983.
Howell, Henry E., Jr. Telephone interview, April 20, 1984.
Kirk, Hanno W. Denton, Tex. Sept. 22, 1983.
Lewis, Gordon. The Plains, Va. April 26,1979.
Mitchell, Virginia and Landon. Fort Lauderdale, Fla. Jan. 13, 1979.
Mudd, Roger. Telephone interview, April 18, 1984.
Muse, Paul. Dumfries, Va. Nov. 21, 1975.
Olson, David M. Charleston, S.C. March 30, 1984.
Painter, John W. Fredericksburg, Va. April 1, 1976.
Poage, W. R. Waco, Tex. Oct. 14, 1983, and telephone interview Oct.
    1, 1984.
Rapp, Kenneth W. Telephone interview, Nov. 21, 1985.
Rawlings, George C., Jr. Fredericksburg, Va. Oct. 27, Nov. 7, 1975,
    March 10, 1976, and telephone interview, April 20, 1984.
Scott, William L. Telephone interview, March 21, 1978.
Smith, Howard W. Alexandria, Va. Oct. 10, 1975.
Smith, Howard W., Jr. Alexandria, Va. Oct. 20, 1978.
Stearman, Lewis A. Telephone interview. Nov. 26, 1985.
Tonahill, Violett Smith. Jasper, Tex. Dec. 30, 1978.
Tuck, William M. South Boston, Va. Feb. 10, 1979.
Whitescarver, Kenneth T. Fork Union, Va. April 19, 1976.
Williams, John W. Charlottesville, Va. March 17, 1976.

Index

DATE DUE

GAYLORD   PRINTED IN U.S.A.